BLUE GUITAR HIGHWAY

BLUE GUITAR HIGHWAY

PAUL METSA

FOREWORD BY DAVID CARR

 University of Minnesota Press
Minneapolis
London

Published by the University of Minnesota Press
111 Third Avenue South, Suite 290
Minneapolis, MN 55401-2520
http://www.upress.umn.edu

Library of Congress Cataloging-in-Publication Data

Metsa, Paul.
  Blue guitar highway / Paul Metsa ; foreword by David Carr.
    p. cm.
  ISBN 978-0-8166-7642-2 (hc)
  ISBN 978-0-8166-7643-9 (pb)
  1. Metsa, Paul. 2. Singers—Minnesota—Biography. I. Title.
  ML420.M4243A3   2011
  782.42164092—dc23
[B]
                                        2011031216

Printed in the United States of America on acid-free paper

The University of Minnesota is an equal-opportunity educator and employer.

30 29 28 27 26 25 24 23   10 9 8 7 6 5 4 3 2 1

This book is dedicated to my father, Elder Emil Metsa,
the strongest and most honest man I know,
and to the memory of my beautiful mother, Bess Margaret Paul.
You gave me *sisu*, she gave me song.

All my love,
Paul Elder Metsa

Stars Over the Prairie

Back in the days when I was buckshot in short pants
Spinning bottles with Tiger Jack
I remember Grandpa's European prayers
Down in the bunkhouse
To this day I use those prayers to try to bring him back

Hand in hand with my brother and sisters,
Chinese jump rope heart to heart
They ain't hiding
But they're just out of earshot
Hope to the heavens their worlds don't fall apart

Chorus:
(And) I wish I could see stars over the prairie
Stars over the prairie tonight
And I wish I could see
Stars over the prairie
Stars over the prairie tonight

Under the gazebo where I stole my first kisses
In the fallen angel Cadillac with chrome
Where me and my buddies like a good gypsy army
Fighting each other's causes like they were our own

In the greased gravel alleys where I ducked sucker punches
In the shadow of my old man
Before I blacked out I wondered how Duke might have done it
Before I found out I took off with the band
Never did go back

Repeat Chorus

There was a Tokyo Rose and a Florida songbird
Loved them both but I could not pick between
They're gone on the downbeat and found true love on the flipflop
Now all I've got is old love letters and magazines

So I sit in this city and I look out the window
Where the neon moons shine when day is done
and I see all the people let it slip through their fingers
You can be with them, but they cannot be with anyone

Repeat Chorus

Words and music by Paul Metsa, 1984

CONTENTS

A TOUGH GIG, BUT IT BEATS WORKING

DAVID CARR

Underneath the music business we see on television, at the Grammy's, on the radio, and in the big arenas, there is a vast long tail of two-bit gigs, recordings that never left the garage, and a thousand nights of songs hurled against an indifferent crowd. In that context, musicians—many as talented or more so than the ones who rule the airwaves—become human accessories. Under certain common circumstances, visible in any juke joint or tavern down the block, the music from the guy playing in the corner becomes no more than a kind of coaster you set a beer on.

If you look up from your conversation and actually see the guy in the corner, I mean, really *see* him, you might wonder why in the world he does it. Schlepping the equipment into a room that smells like seven-day-old tap beer, or worse, and then tuning up while people cast sidelong glances, hoping he won't play so loud that they can't have a decent conversation. During those first few songs, when the crowd is probably drunk and the musician is not yet, a kind of battle ensues. The loud-mouths in front who shout "Freebird," sometimes freighted with irony and sometimes in dead earnest. The bar floozy who wobbles in close, clapping out of time and singing along with a tune only she knows. The hipsters in the back, arms crossed and smirking at a working musician because his sound isn't reflecting some MP3 that is getting its thirty seconds of heat in their circles.

On some nights, there will be real actual fans, or at least people open to the artist in front of them, and a mutual spark will occur. Partway into a good song, even the louder ones will begin to shut their pie holes and listen, and the room, indifferent for much of the evening, will actually give it up when the song ends, whistling and clapping. Even then, though, the magic may not last and the crowd will subside back into itself, leaving the guy in the corner alone with his songs and his guitar.

A silent tick of the clock will come and the people with jobs, kids, cars that work, and houses they own will tap the bar table in front of them and say, "I'm out." By the end of the night, the musician might be left with a few stragglers who have none of those things and end his performance to intermittent slow claps. A few mercy drinks from the bartender, and then it's time to coil up the cords, put the guitar in a battered case, and haul the amp.

So pity the poor working musician, whose nightly task yields enough bucks to make it to the next gig. There is no health insurance, no calling in sick, no vacation days. There is only—and this is for the lucky ones—a promise of many more nights of the same.

Except.

Except when those people go home from the bar, maybe one or two of them whistling or humming a song they heard, many will then stare down their own lives. Making or selling crap no one really wants, working for people whose job it is to keep them in harness, and raising kids who keen for more no matter what they are given. When the 7 A.M. alarm goes off, they wake up in a house that owns them, get in a car owned by a bank, and go to a job whose owners could send their job offshore with the flick of a pen. Whether they know it or not, or admit it or not, they probably work for some rich jackass they never met who was born on third base.

Meanwhile, what of the guy in the corner, the one whose guitar bears the scars of more than five thousand gigs? What if, instead of going to their jobs, they stopped by his cozy house in Northeast Minneapolis for a coffee? There he is with his dog (and, if the gods allow, a cute waitress who served both you and him drinks the night before), and the coffee pot is on. He is waking up slowly, noodling a few songs, retuning his songwriting guitar. He spends some time on the computer lining up his next few gigs and then gets on the phone to work out a little recording he has planned. His day, his life belong to him, and when evening comes he will strap on the guitar, check the mike, and the battle will begin anew.

Now, who is the fool, who is wasting his life?

Civilians, if they are lucky, will get to the end of the road and will have managed their way through the job, the mortgage, the college bills, and the credit cards to a crabbed retirement in a town they have grown to hate. The luckier ones will immerse themselves in playing golf, or watching sports, or yelling invective at the politicians on the television screen.

Meanwhile, the musician will warm himself by the bonfire of all he has done, all he has seen, all the glories that have floated into his ear, propelled by the thump of a kick drum and a plucked guitar.

What if that guy in the corner had handed a tape to Bob Dylan, slipped Jerry Garcia some mushrooms, taught Bruce Springsteen a riff, and played in front of twenty thousand people at a Texas stadium on national television? What if he had made and remade bands that created magic, knocked the roof off bars, and jammed with some of the biggest names the business had ever conjured? What if that guy had written songs that anyone would be proud to play, songs full of real people and real meaning? And consider that he might have accomplished many of his childhood dreams. Gigging in New York and Los Angeles, a sold-out headline show with a ten-piece band at the now-destroyed original Guthrie Theater, and playing in a tribute to Woody Guthrie at the Rock and Roll Hall of Fame with rock and folk royalty.

A life where the best part is shooting bogey golf with an indifferent group of friends on a public course in a third-ring suburb doesn't sound quite so great now.

What if that guy had made his way in Minneapolis, one of the coolest music towns on the planet, and recorded, jammed, and showed up for the best of his cohort? Don't even start about the number of benefits, special shows, and gorgeous outdoor gigs. And let's not get into the girls and women along the way, because you might begin to weep.

What if that guy, the one few were paying attention to the night before, is actually someone who has trouble buying a drink in any bar because there is always someone who saw that one show at the Union Bar with a rocking band or caught an inspired acoustic show at the Dakota? What if our lone loser in the corner is actually a hero, a man who cast off the mundane blandishments of everyday life and went for it, pushing his music and his career as far as they would go?

It would be easy to envy him if he got all the cash and prizes, if the fickle gaze of the music business landed on him for more than a second and the tape he played for John Hammond got him signed to a big label. But even though he shot for the moon and missed—and Paul Metsa will tell you that one of the upsides of obscurity is that you never go out of style—he still ended up a star.

Anybody who knows Paul Metsa will tell you that, for a folk singer, he always had the rock star thing down. He had the leather coat, the sunglasses, the skinny jeans, and the stunt hair from jump. Paul mastered the art of the entrance, whether it was for a big gig or the morning walk of shame into a bar, from the very beginning.

Let me say it plain. I knew a few rockers in my days in Minneapolis as a young working reporter and have met many famous ones since, and I always loved running with Paul Metsa. Literate to a fault, the owner of a dark, heh-heh repertoire of observational humor, and remarkably open to the next caper, Paul always carried a barrel of monkeys in his back pocket.

I have seen Paul at the height of his powers. I was there the night he played the Guthrie, taking his wireless guitar up to the top tier of that secularly sacred space and wailing as all heads turned. I have seen him get a notion playing solo at Nye's Polonaise when something sort of kicked in and he leaned into song in a way that made it jump, morph, and elide. I've seen him work a stage patter that would make Loudon Wainwright or John Prine seem quaint and watched him close a sudden date with a pretty fan in under five minutes. As our mutual friend Fast Eddie would say, that boy can talk more shit than a landlord on rent day. Who else could come up with a thirty-year retrospective on time served in the Minneapolis music scene (Skyway to Hell) and sell out the Parkway Theater?

And then there're the songs. Not to start a brawl, or disrespect Paul, but my favorite Metsa song of all time is also my favorite Christmas song, a supposed throwaway for a promo album for a shopping center. You can keep your "White Christmas": every year when the season arrives, "Christmas at Molly's" hops on my playlist and stays there. "Pass the malt . . . and the . . . mistletoe. . . . It's almost Christmas Day." It's Paul at his best as a writer and performer, a voice dipped in the Iron Range singing out long and strong in a simple, unadorned arrangement, pushing out words that ring truer and deeper as they go. I defy anyone to listen and decide they still hate Santa Claus and Christmas.

There are many, many others. The poetics of "Stars Over the Prairie," the overt political jeremiad of "Ferris Wheels on the Farm," the historical mysteries of "Jack Ruby." His roots as the grandson of a barkeep in a brutally cold working town come through both bare-knuckled and sweet in "Virginia" (Check that guitar, son), "St. Louis County Fair," and "59 Coal Mines."

One of Paul's charms is that he was not only a student of music but also a true fan. Yes, he was a bit of a purist about the blues, and he could be a pain in the ass during a set from a foofy folk singer, but in the main he loved music the same whether he was at the mike or clapping on the woman or man who was doing the same. I have hooted along with him when Doug Maynard wailed, Paul Westerberg screamed, and Prudence Johnson killed it. He was anything but a snob around music, an omnivore who had his own style but was capable of admiring the work and approach of others, in part because he knew what they made look so easy was actually brutally hard.

It would be a lie of omission to say that, like so many other artists and musicians, Paul didn't make it a bit harder than it had to be. I would marvel along with the crowd when he hit the stage at the Cabooze and killed it, but I was the only one who knew we had been on a three-day run with only catnaps.

We were not angels, far from it. I can remember one morning when we pulled ourselves out of Tony the Hat's basement, a lair in South Minneapolis where the coke rap was thick and many unrealized plans and dreams were worked to a nub. We went to the CC bar in South Minneapolis. The morning light was brutal and we ducked in, glad to be back in the womb of darkness. Some woman had brought her young child for breakfast on a bar stool, and he took a look at the three of us and said, "Those are bad men, Mommy."

No, we were not bad guys, just a little moronic. Tony was a bit of a gangster but had a heart with the capacity and ferociousness of a lion. Paul and I were dilettantes who tipped over into some chronic habits, me much more so than Paul. But I will say this: if you stay up too long, drink too much, and ingest too many dry goods, you are bound to tire of the company around you. I never got tired of Paul. He brought gallows humor to the game at hand, laughing as we wobbled our way to the end of the run. He saw us for the fools we were at the time and never pretended otherwise.

And there were many times in between. I regret none of the bad pool playing and brown liquor we put away in the backroom of McCready's before it burned down. Party hopping with Paul after the bars closed was and probably still is (I live in New Jersey now) a stone gas. Musicians, so full of articulation and vividness on stage, frequently shrink when they step off the riser. When Paul wrapped up a gig, he got more interesting, not less, because he was a person who read the paper, talked about ideas, and engaged in the civic matters at hand. He was both a Ranger and a student of the world who had been places and done things, so he backed up for no one in an argument.

For a supposed slacker, Paul never let it rest, whether he was booking acts at Famous Dave's or working his next gig. I say no to outside writing stuff because I have a day job as a reporter that keeps me plenty busy—as much as I love Paul, I was not eager to take on writing a foreword to a book. But Paul didn't drop me an e-mail and cross his fingers: he called, did the ask in an honest and direct way. It's hard to say no to Paul. That's why, four decades into putting his hands on a guitar, he still eats by plucking at it. Every break he got was the result of relentless industry and, yes, self-promotion, which every working musician needs to get his arms around.

The book you are about to read is an epic van ride through music history that is no less vivid for the fact that it didn't end up in rock stardom. The story, as you will see, has a bit of Prince Hal to it—the charming, good times guy who found himself under a bar table, picked himself up, dusted off, then took over the world. Except the "took over the world" part.

Paul, ever the rock star, has yet to achieve rock stardom. He has the records—*Whistling Past the Graveyard, Mississippi Farewell, Lincoln's Bedroom,* and a bunch of others—but, knowing Paul, there is not tons of loot stashed away from all those gigs he has done. So the hustle continues. The book. The digital record label he christened where you can buy his duet album with Sonny Earl, *No Money Down.* The Web site that hosts the words and music to "Second Avenue Sunset." He runs like he is being chased, which he is, in a way. A day job in the hands of Paul Metsa would be a scary, awkward thing.

And make no mistake: if the money is right, or even just the mood, he will come and plug in. Paul is, and always will be, a working musician. And if a couple of know-nothing punks wander into his gig and wonder who the hell the guy in the corner thinks he is, they have no idea what they are talking about. This cat under the stars has lived countless lives, some of them borrowed, some of them spent, and has seen things their cramped, quotidian lives will never know.

Music, anyone will tell you, is something that will nourish your soul, while the business part will suck it out with equal force. Paul explains as much in "Whistling Past the Graveyard": "The same faith that will save you may also break your back." Within the four corners of the book you are about to read and the life it etches, that seems like a fair trade. That guy in the corner? This world has exacted its price, but it's equally true that he has it by the balls.

GUITAR FOOLS

This is a musician's tale, probably best told from the rail at the end of the bar while the band is still playing and before last call. As a seeker and survivor, observer and participant, chronicler and historian, I offer stories that are gleaned from a life lived in the skull orchards and blood buckets of this fine country and occasionally on stages that were raging with glory blessed by the gods and masters who have guided my journey, navigating switchbacks, detours, dead ends, and glimpses of the promised land on the blue guitar highway.

There is a drop of blood—mine and others'—behind every note I play and every word I write. Some have passed on to wherever it is good people go. To those still standing but too shy to share, I have taken the liberty to tell some of their stories as well.

Bob Stinson was the lead guitarist for the Replacements, one of the greatest rock and roll bands to come out of Minneapolis, a town that has always brimmed with them. While he had a reputation as a wild man at midnight, during the light of day when we got to know each other in the record shops and guitar stores in Mill City, he was like any bright-eyed, clean-cut kid in America and as innocent. Though we played different kinds of music at night, during the day we were just two guys in parallel lanes on the musician's journey, sharing the musician's task.

I bumped into Bob one morning going through record bins at Garage D'Or. He had short golden-blond hair and was wearing red tennis shoes and a tattered white jacket. He asked me what I was up to. I told him I had just returned from Nashville where I set out to record a folk record but thought I had made a great rock and roll record instead. He turned away from me, gazed east over the intersection of Twenty-sixth and Nicollet while the sun was breaking through the window, folded his arms together, and with a crooked and beatific smile like someone who knew more than the rest of us replied, "Just goes to show you, Elvis was right all along." It was the last time I would see him alive. And in that spirit, I welcome you to my story.

A BOY AND HIS GUITAR

I have played thousands of gigs, on hundreds of stages, from four empty beer cases in the corner of a saloon with a hanging light bulb to Texas Stadium engulfed in a hundred thousand watts of light and sound, where the encore included forty performers and the Dallas Cowboy cheerleaders. On a certain karmic level, they are all equally important, though some are obviously more fun than others, sort of like the difference between dates with your new girlfriend and holidays with the in-laws. Some are a whirlwind of excitement, in the eye-of-a-hurricane sort of way, and some are just punching the clock. Some are so life affirming and spiritually rewarding and go by so quickly you hardly remember them. Others are so bad they are stuck in your mind forever like a bad jailhouse tattoo. And so it is, ten years as a fledgling amateur and more than thirty years as a professional musician. With my guitar as my lunch pail, off to work I go.

I started playing at family gatherings in my parents' living room during holiday parties, presented by my first promoter, my mother. From there, church basements, garages, boy scout meetings, junior high talent shows and assemblies, VFWs, street dances, city parks, battles of the bands, armories, classrooms, bonfires, keg parties, bars and nightclubs, parking lots, store openings, biker parties, beaches after dark (one in tuxedoes), campgrounds, trailer parks, hospitals and old folks' homes, bingo parlors, casinos, fishing openers, wayside rests, house parties, sheds and pole barns, farm fields, political rallies, funerals, wakes and memorial services, strikes, festivals, radio shows, television shows, acid shakedowns, strip clubs before the strippers came on (and one at a strip club that suddenly gave up the dancing girls and introduced folk music without letting their customers know), small towns, country dance halls, big cities (uptown and downtown), on semi-trailer trucks on blocked-off streets, in the alley next to the garbage cans, theaters, concert halls, performing arts centers, movie houses, backyard barbeques, rent parties, hotel rooms, convention halls, houseboats, airplane hangers, and the back of a pickup truck on a hay bail at a used car lot, to name but a few.

This is the story of a boy and his guitar. The boy was born during a Halloween snowstorm in 1955, the year America went from black-and-white to color, the same year Einstein died, Elvis had his first hit, James Dean (America's first real teenager) took his last breath in a Spider convertible at 124 miles an hour, and the bebop messiah Charlie Parker played his last thirty-second note and passed away in a New York apartment after watching the Tommy Dorsey show. Chuck Berry had just changed the name of an old country song from "Ida Red" to "Maybelline," Woody Guthrie was in his third year at the Brooklyn State Hospital, Pete Seeger stared down Senator Joe McCarthy and the House Committee on Un-American Activities, Rosa Parks refused to sit in the back of an Alabama bus, and Allen Ginsberg read "Howl" for the first time at the Six Gallery in San Francisco. The American Federation of Labor wed the Congress of Industrial Organizations forming the holy union of the AFL-CIO. Elvis Presley, king of the *Louisiana Hayride* and riding the mystery train, hears "Heartbreak Hotel" for the first time, and an Arkansas dirt farmer enters Sun Studios in Memphis and records his first record under his given name of Johnny Cash. Little Richard, son of a Seventh Day Adventist preacher, records a wop-bop-a-loo tune called "Tutti-Frutti." Americans everywhere would soon be able to watch most of history unfold before them, under Eisenhower skies of optimism, in their living rooms on brand-new color televisions. America was in the midst of another cultural efflorescence. In a century that began with the birth of Louis Armstrong in New Orleans in 1900 and ended with the death of Frank Sinatra in 1998, 1955 was a turning point from which America never looked back.

Given his druthers, he wouldn't or maybe couldn't have had it any other way. He was born in Virginia, the Queen City of the Iron Range in northern Minnesota, a stone's throw away from a kid fifteen years older in the neighboring town of Hibbing. The older kid spent his formative years listening to rock and roll from faraway places and watching Marlon Brando terrorize similar small towns on the big screen on a Harley Davidson. That kid's name at the time was Bobby Zimmerman. Both boys were baptized in the grand shadow of Elvis Presley and, with the guitar as their guide, ventured out onto the highways of a changing America. The older kid changed his name to Bob Dylan and became a big star. The other one kept his name and didn't. This is his story.

It is an American story and will be told as one. Bright lights and big cities, ghosts from the farm, the never-ending jukebox, Scandinavian grandma's lullabies, the promise of Camelot, Elvis on the big screen, and the Beatles on the small one. Hank Williams's smoke-tavern backbeat, Stevie Wonder's harmonica, the loud pluck of electric twelve-string guitars, Mama's in the basement mixing up the medicine while Dad sells insurance upstairs. *Sgt. Pepper's Lonely Hearts Club Band*, a Christmas present in 1967, *Mad Magazine*, secret agent television, Tom Jones and some woman named Delilah, Peter Sellers on the left hand and Richard Pryor on the right. Martin Luther King before April in Memphis, Sirhan Sirhan, Richard Speck, Vietnam, Woodstock and then Altamont, a man on the moon, Charlie Manson, Surf City to Sin City, and the kid ain't even out of Junior High. A virgin no longer after a bottle of Boone's Farm Strawberry Hill after his last day of ninth grade. Marijuana, with its bigger and wilder brothers mescaline and LSD, the boy once pure as the driven snow, now drifted. Nixon still in office, majorettes, strippers, the Holy Ghost, a '59 baby blue Cadillac and an electric guitar, Spiro Agnew and Barry Goldwater, Damn Everything but the Circus and teenage immortality, Lenny Bruce, Ravi Shankar, thirteen-year-old spiritual perfect masters. Southern Comfort and cold snow banks, the velvet flesh of country girlfriends, and reading Kerouac's *On the Road* but not yet being able to be on it. That would come soon enough. A lifetime with the guitar. Dropping in but mostly out of college and spending the past thirty-some years of his life in gin joints of this blessed and imperfect country, chasing the ghost of Elvis, ass kicked but soul somewhat intact.

Everything in America is probable if not possible, and there is beauty in the struggle. And that is part of the story—the whole truth and nothing but the truth. God helps, and so does the occasional shot of whiskey. And so it will be told, in prose, street poetry, songs like postcards from a fading America, stolen verses from bathroom walls, culled from erotic letters to old girlfriends, midnight letters to the editors, essays from the damned and for the departed, smoke signals to and from the great beyond. A particular version and vision of America, a story that goes from black-and-white to color. He got to meet most of his heroes, got a letter from the White House, spent a few days in the Big House, and got to spend time with everyone from Pete Seeger to Dave "Snaker" Ray, J. J. Cale to Joey Ramone, John Hartford to Hubert Sumlin, from Bruce Springsteen to Bettye LaVette. Played guitar for Ken Kesey, smoked left-handed cigarettes with Willie Nelson (but who hasn't?), watched the sun come up with silver saints and hell-bound sinners, moved to the big city and heard Andres Segovia, Bill Monroe, and Dexter Gordon before he had the chance to unpack his bags, got cat-whisker-close to a big-time record deal courtesy of the legendary John Hammond Sr., debuted the song "Jack Ruby" to twenty thousand Texans just five miles from Dealey Plaza. Too young to meet Woody Guthrie but got invited to play his tribute at the Rock and Roll Hall of Fame, put out a dozen or so releases on his own label all of which have gone linoleum, has given away more records than he has sold, and has played more than five thousand gigs, many of which he remembers. And tonight he'll take his guitar and do another gig and will play for some who will listen and some who won't. But that is not the point. The point is he is fifty-five years old, too old to either lie about his age or join the FBI, and is still making a living with his guitar. And like he says, "The beauty of obscurity is you never go out of style."

BUCKSHOT IN SHORT PANTS

At the age of seven, in the idyllic summer of 1962 when I got my first guitar, I was too young to know that the little plywood beauty, with the cowboy and horse stenciled in yellow and red on the front, was really a woman.

She looked just like a pretty girl in the guitar store window when I first saw her and she beckoned me to take her home. We started out just holding hands. Over the next forty-five years she blossomed, turning season after season, in ever-changing wardrobes, each more randy and dandy than the next. First a whisper, then first kiss, soon a tease, as I held her Love-Me-Tender-tight, then All-Shook-Up in a dance floor swing with a shorter skirt, a moaning lover, a whiskey-throated Annie Oakley wild woman, an electric goddess of the moon, crazy in love, and devoted to me in sickness and in health, a quotidian angel who watched me sleep and waited for me to wake.

Had I known then what I know now, I would not have done it any differently than on that day in July when the rest of my young grade school buddies were playing baseball in the sandlots, swimming in the silver lakes, riding bikes and playing kick the can till the sun went down, and the older boys were fishing off the same railroad trestle where my dad, "Duke" Metsa, and his Finntown buddies once hooked sunken tires.

We lived in a little tan bungalow on the south side of Virginia, Minnesota, across from an overgrown field on Thirteenth Street that my brother and I lit on fire the previous summer while sneaking our mom's Old Golds.

I remember like it was yesterday draping the burlap string of the six-string beauty over my small shoulders, saying good-bye in the kitchen to Nancy Fairbanks, our Ojibwe babysitter, and heading out the aluminum screen door to the backyard where my dad was waiting in our blue '59 Chevy sedan.

I climbed into the backseat with my new girlfriend, and off we went to my first guitar lesson, tires crunching gravel beneath the Bel Air wings, down the alley and then uptown, years before I came to embrace and not fear the beauty of dusk.

We were headed to Beddow's Music on Chestnut Street, the five-block main drag of Virginia, my hometown, the same street along which Duke, Flitch, Tapper, Scamper, Scuff, Kleba, Ziggy, Sta, Yedjo, and Poga used to roll their waterlogged tires to get to Sam Kaufman and his junkyard on First Street South, who'd pay them a penny apiece to reclaim rubber for the war effort.

My grandfather owned a tavern called the Roosevelt Bar, named after FDR, on Chestnut Street, just west of Second Avenue. Two blocks east on the edge of town, literally, is the Rouchleau Pit, a deep, open mine with stair-stepped walls that had yielded everything she had to supply steel for the war and now lays silent, a rust-colored canyon in repose.

While Grandpa ran the tavern, Grandma ran the twenty-one-room boarding house upstairs from their one-bedroom apartment, cooking meals, scrubbing floors, washing sheets, cutting hair, and tending to the needs of the boarders that lived there. On Sundays after church we would go and visit, entering through the door marked 201½ and climbing the long, steep flight of stairs with the aromas of fried chicken or pork chops leading the way.

If I was lucky, I got to help Grandpa clean the tavern. As his first grandson, I was his favorite sidekick, a buckshot in short pants with a blond butch haircut and a Brylcreem Brunswick twist to boot (put your left hand on your hairline and with your right hand, comb over once to the back, creating a small fence in front, guarding the rest of your hair combed down and smoother than a well-groomed putting green). This chore came replete with all the soda pop I could drink, all the orange-colored cheese popcorn I could eat, and all the change I could find beneath the bar stools and booths (some legit, some planted by Grandpa). He plugged the Wurlitzer jukebox with nickels and dimes, sound tracks for just the two of us—the booming voice of Johnny Cash surrounding us like a blanket, repeated plays of his favorite "The Prisoner's Song," Grandpa singing along with Patti Page on the "Tennessee Waltz," and an occasional melancholy Finnish waltz in a minor key—songs that wafted through the empty bar with the mingled scents of spilled beer, Pine-Sol, and a drop or two of blood and spit, out the open door, onto a quiet Chestnut Street. It was our time, cleaning up the dust and debris from a week of Iron Range rounders, miners, lumberjacks, and the random doctor, lawyer, or businessman who ducked into this working man's bar on his way to any of the other twenty-two bars that lined this strip. Washing lipstick smudges from beer glasses, Grandpa would toss me a clean white towel to help him dry. I was so proud. Me and him.

Little did I know that my girlfriend guitar and I would spend a lifetime playing songs like that within walls like those. No wonder. They were the prayers that helped me bring him back.

Summers in northern Minnesota for a young boy were the stuff of dreams. When I wasn't swimming in truly sky blue waters or fishing with Grandpa, I'd be playing peewee baseball, then little league, and at night making campfires with my friends and family at our cabin on Lake Vermilion. One exquisitely warm July evening, before the loons came out and serenaded each other with their haunting tremolos echoing across the lake, and the stars suddenly appearing by the dozens, then hundreds, in a silver and golden wash across the sky, we had started a cookout, featuring snapping turtle soup cooked over a campfire at our friends the Tuuris who summered down the road from us at the lake. My sister Kathy had invited a friend of hers from high school named Dennis Monroe to join us, and he brought his guitar. She had told him I was learning to play the guitar, and that maybe I could take a few lessons from him and really learn how to play.

He was devilishly handsome, with thick brown hair and a smile as bright as a Reddy Kilowatt neon sign and a laugh that started deep in the gut. I was attracted to anyone who played guitar, like a bug to a light. Now, right in front of me, was a real folksinger around a Carter Family–like campfire, and he would play songs by that first family of folk, popular folk songs, and others as the embers lit him up in a boreal radiance. I was hypnotized. He sang as well as he played, song after song, and his voice and guitar began coalescing into this dark honey and heavenly mist. He ended the twilight serenade with "I Still Miss Someone" by Johnny Cash, and I was knocked on my skinny little ass. I can still close my eyes and remember like it was yesterday. It is still hard to believe he was only eighteen years old. I had found my Pied Piper.

Summer ended, my family was back in Virginia, and I set up weekly lessons with Dennis. He came over every Tuesday night after school and often stayed for supper. He liked to wear button-down shirts under sweaters, corduroy pants, and Indian moccasins. My folks were going through a very rough patch after fifteen years of marriage (and would separate the following summer for several months), and Dennis's presence, besides giving me the gift of music, also brought a joy to our household that would break through the unspoken tension we were all dealing with. We adored him.

He started me slowly and properly and taught me an instrumental version of "Wildwood Flower," one of the first commandments of any blossoming young folk singer, first recorded and popularized by the Carter Family, Mother Maybelle on guitar. Like all great teachers, he had a gentle persuasion that inspired me to please him. He taught me fundamentals of producing a good tone, proper hand position, flat-picking, and fingerpicking.

He taught me the old murder ballad "John Hardy" from his copy of the New Lost City Ramblers songbook. It was a beautiful little tune, one that communicated to me the ground rules for how to tell a story in song, and the power that lies within what are seemingly simple folk songs: both catechism and canon for me in the years to come.

I met Chuck Christianson in the third grade at James Madison grade school, on the south side of Virginia, in 1964, the summer our family moved to a new neighborhood and new school. He was the son of a principal and looked like one. He wore glasses that looked like they were made from a piece out of a woody station wagon, uncool even at that time. He also brought a briefcase to school—in the third grade. I got a big charge out of him, though seemingly very bookish and quiet, and his ventriloquism act, and the wooden dummy who looked a bit like him, when he would feature it in show-and-tell, both of their lips moving together in time. Our teacher's name was Miss Rengo, which those of us who became transfixed after the Beatles performance on Ed Sullivan the previous winter found especially appealing. We didn't become friends until fifth grade in 1966, when I found out he too played guitar. Young guitar fools that we were, we quickly became thick as thieves, and I immediately introduced him to Dennis.

Dennis taught us separately and occasionally in tandem. We were like inkblots, absorbing everything he had to offer. We'd practice together and spurred each other on competitively, little brothers in arms. Chuck was a quick study and also had one of the best natural voices I have ever heard. His mother sang in dance bands in high school and was now a housewife who liked to cover her furniture in plastic, had a runner from the front door to the back, and liked to set her table the night before a dinner party.

We spent most of the winter learning tunes from Dennis, off the radio and from sheet music and songbooks. We learned to harmonize, Chuck's higher tenor riding above mine a couple of years before our voices changed. By spring of 1967, we had a couple of dozen songs, attitude and confidence that belied our age, and shared a sense of humor and adventure. We christened ourselves Paul and Christian, had some business cards made, and were ready to take on the world.

Our first paying gig was at the Lion's Club annual Christmas talent show. We were one of a dozen acts that included young dancers, other folkies, a poetry reading, a guy in a bee costume who pantomimed to a record, and Gary Maki, a future rocker who played his accordion upside down on a table to make it look like an electric keyboard. We passed the hat and made $25—$12.50 apiece. Big money! Hell, we would have had to mow fifty lawns to make that much. At that time, you could see a movie matinee and get popcorn and soda pop, all for a dollar. We were rolling in dough.

We weren't above cutting corners in our rise to the top. While backstage at the Mountain Iron High School Talent Show, when all the other performers went to the auditorium to get instructions before the show, we stayed behind and proceeded to detune all the guitars, about a dozen or so, that were left in the room. The operation was a success. We came in second place, behind the Mountain Iron PTA Mother's Tupperware Jug Band and won a $25 cash prize. We were on our way!

After learning all kinds of songs, we decided to try our hand at writing some originals. We wrote a couple of our first songs together. The very first was a lyric of mine called "How Many Times Must I Cry," a lament written about what looked like my parents' upcoming divorce. Chuck wedded that to the melody of "Slow Boat to China," a song his mother taught him. We played it in public but never for my parents. Our second tune, whose title I forget, was a lyric I wrote about the Six-Day War in Israel in 1967, sung to the melody of Buffy Sainte-Marie's "Universal Soldier." Part of it was spoken word, which took the audience at the talent show at the Gilbert High School a bit by surprise, as did the fact that we had ditched our ties and now wore beads over our turtlenecks and suit coats. It was my first original political song.

Rock and roll bands were everywhere. *American Bandstand* was required Saturday afternoon watching for any self-respecting teenager, the Monkees had their own television show, and national rock bands, besides being all over the radio, were showing up in prime time on all three of the major networks. The Iron Range had a very voracious scene, even before the Beatles were rocking American living rooms across the land. The Electras, a band out of Ely, had a regional hit with "Dirty Old Man," and several songs from Minneapolis bands, including the Castaways' "Liar, Liar" and the Trashmen's "Surfin' Bird" made the national charts. These bands and others were playing the National Guard Armories and dances at high schools around the range. Teenage rebellion at your local roller rink for a dollar at the door.

While Chuck and I were young, Pete Seegers in waiting, our teacher Dennis also sang lead in a band called the Small Society. They had won a WEBC radio–sponsored Battle of the Bands at the Duluth Armory and the chance to record for free their single, "Live for a Real Good Sound," which the radio station played often. They were gods to us.

One day that winter, Glen Isaacson, a neighbor kid, brought his red Airline electric guitar over to my house and taught me the chords to Gloria: E-D-A, E-D-A, E-D-A, over and over again: "She comes around here, round about midnight!" It was a revelation. This song, and these three chords, a kind of rock and roll DNA, started more bands than Elvis Presley's swivel hips. I went to my bedroom and played those three chords until I fell asleep, the only three chords you need to know to start a band. Rock and roll was right around the corner.

Chuck and I went out and got DeArmond pickups to put in our twelve-string acoustic guitars. We recruited my friend Gary Pagliaccetti as our drummer. He was learning how to play on his sister's blue Ludwig drum set in his basement in Parkville, four miles from Virginia. My buddy Mike Weiss couldn't sing but was really cute and could bang on a tambourine, so he became our lead singer. I came up with the name the Positive Reaction, and we started to rehearse in our basement. Just a while later, we got our first gig and were booked to play my first girlfriend Carol Flaim's thirteenth birthday party at the Gun Club, where sportsmen shot skeet overlooking Silver Lake. Gary set up his snare drum on a cigarette ashtray canister, and we rocked the young girls and boys as well. Man, this sure beat playing hockey at Mill 40, an outdoor rink on the south side, in the dead of winter.

We added my neighbor and future brother-in-law Paul Richards on a Woolworth's Magnus organ to fill out our sound. Occasionally, we'd rehearse in Paul's basement. We had devised a "light show," taking an old milk carton, with holes cut in the side, and one of us holding a light bulb on a wire inside, turning the lights out in the basement and placing it on a small record player. We'd turn it on and watch the shadows revolve around the room while the others played. It wasn't exactly the Fillmore East, but it delighted us to no end.

Our first public gig was at Cook Timber Days, in June 1968. By now, my mother had made us matching green plaid Nehru jackets that we would wear over white turtlenecks. We took the stage that afternoon looking sharp. We didn't have a bass player, but with two twelve-string amplified guitars, we didn't need one (predating the White Stripes by almost forty years). I was wearing sunglasses in a nod to John Lennon and Roger McQuinn. We played mostly Byrds songs. We barreled through a quick twenty minutes of our newly found rock and roll glory and, true to our name, got a very positive reaction. I think we even signed a couple of autographs on the way back to mom's car. We felt like the Beatles.

The Positive Reaction started to wind down as we all entered junior high. Paul and Christian picked up the slack and kept playing gigs at whatever school assembly, talent show, or bowling banquet that would have us. When I was in ninth grade, I started taking guitar lessons from a high school English teacher at Roosevelt High School name Tom Moeller. Tom was a brilliant man, an excellent teacher, and a huge Buddy Holly fan.

Tom was playing guitar with Tony Perpich and the Perpatones, a first-rate polka band that played almost every weekend. The Perpatones played all over the Iron Range, and their repertoire consisted of a mix of old-school polkas, country-western, standards, and the occasional rock tune. Tom invited me to play bass guitar with them. I bought a bass and learned how to play it. A few days after learning most of the songbook, I found myself in the back of Tony's van on our way to Ely, Minnesota, to play a VFW dance on a winter night so cold it made you realize why bears sleep all winter.

I always enjoyed when my folks would get ready to go out for a night on the town. Dad would come home and make his never-before-5-P.M. cocktail and mix one for mom as well, both Manhattans. She would be getting dolled up, figuring out what dress she was going to wear, put on matching earrings and necklace, and became a heady mix of hairspray and perfume. Their friends would come over, have another cocktail, and vanish into the evening and go downtown. When I did my first job with the Perpatones at the Hob Nob Room in the Coates Hotel in Virginia, I finally got to see where they were going. I was able to enter the nether-world of adult nightlife, and I liked it.

We set up in the corner of the bar. I knew many of the clientele: the bankers, lawyers and doctors, parents of friends, and some of the denizens of our small town who only came out at night. The men all dressed in suits and ties that would loosen as the night wore on. The women in dresses and skirts. And back then, everybody seemed to be smoking. The lights were low, bartenders in white shirts lit up from behind. Almost everybody danced, and when I saw my mother and father on the dance floor, they seemed to glide and float like Fred Astaire and Ginger Rogers and looked so handsome, in love and alive. Dancing, in this case cheek to cheek, is something you don't see much anymore. It was cordial, polite, and a great way to socialize, and something, to this day, I still miss.

Chuck and I put a new band together in high school called Damn Everything but the Circus, a name we borrowed from an e. e. cummings poem. Brian Vitali, my next-door neighbor and classmate, played bass guitar. He wasn't the greatest player but a real sweetheart of a guy, and he was movie-star handsome. The girls loved him, and he cut a striking figure with his long black wavy hair, goatee, and whiter-than-snow pearly teeth. Brian Maki played drums, had an expensive drum set, and sang as well. Chuck and I had both purchased real rock and roll electric guitars. Mine was a cherry red Gibson ES-330 that I bought from Bob Driscoll, the guitarist for the Small Society, and Chuck had a classic yellow 1968 Fender Telecaster, a gift from his grandpa.

I had written several original tunes for the band including "Back in the Backyard," which became a very popular tune among our crowd, who were all growing their hair, wearing bell bottoms, and tie-dyeing their own T-shirts. None of these tunes was headed to the top of the charts, and the less said about another original, "Boogie Tune-ite," the better. We played several tunes by a band from California called the Hoodoo Rhythm Devils, whose song "Crazy 'bout the Ladies" became our theme. We rounded out the set list with songs by the Band, the Doobie Brothers, ZZ Top, and others. We had our own sound guy, and we practiced and stored the equipment in my parents' garage. We played at high schools, Armory dances, and when the drinking age dropped to eighteen years old in 1974, bars and nightclubs.

Apart from getting booed off the stage at a junior high dance in

Babbitt, we played almost every weekend to great response. Playing gigs in the winter was absolutely brutal. We'd meet after school and pack our gear into a trailer in weather that would scare the hell out of Will Steger, the Minnesota explorer who took sled dogs to the North Pole. We'd drive through snowstorms, set up for a couple of hours, play for three or four, tear down, and head back home through sleet, rain, and snow. Coming home from a dance in Orr one night, in blinding snow and on a highway covered in ice, the trailer went off the hitch on the Gheen hill and ended up buried in the ditch. We left it there, kept our fingers crossed it wouldn't get stolen, and picked it up the next day, but not before most of it was covered in frost and ice.

Our crowning moment was at the WEBC Battle of the Bands at the Duluth Armory in the spring of 1974, the same battle of the bands that the Small Society won six years before. The Armory, a cavernous building of brick overlooking the shores of Lake Superior, had an interesting history. It had been used to house the National Guard in case of impending strikes on the range. After that, it began a more multidimensional role in the community.

My family had gone to the Duluth Home and Boat show there every year. The stage had seen the likes of Louis Armstrong, Gene Autrey, Johnny Cash, Sonny and Cher, Bob Hope, and Frank Zappa, a cross section of artists who could only have come from America. Buddy Holly played there two days before his final show at the Surf Ballroom in Clear Lake, Iowa. A young Bobby Zimmerman, down from Hibbing, was at that show. He stood in front of the stage, and after Buddy made eye contact with him, many think the symbolic and psychic torch of rock and roll was passed.

We were the last band, among five or six to play. We each had a twenty-minute set. The contest was based on crowd response, and we had invited a small armada of friends to join us. While I'd like to think we were the best band of the night, our friends who grew up cheering on the local hockey, football, and basketball teams, and now more into music than sports, took that hometown team and teen spirit to the next level. With a roof-to-rafters response that echoed throughout the room and raised the dusty ghosts of the Armory to whirl around us, we emerged victorious.

I also had a side group during high school. It was made up of three of my best friends, fellow seekers in the green pastures and tumultuous times of the early 1970s. I had known Terry Monroe (Dennis's younger brother) and Tim Lemieux since junior high. Kelly Hotchkiss, a recent transplant from the other side of the Range, arrived at our high school in 1971 and became a catalyst for this gang of four. We called ourselves the Bastards, and Kelly's mint 1957 black-and-silver Batmobile became our rolling clubhouse. Too young, for the most part, to go to the bars, we'd spend nights crossing the range on the back roads and, back in Kelly's basement, bond over music, books, magazines, and weed.

Mad Magazine, even more than *Playboy*, was a common denominator among budding hipsters in the mid-to-late-'60s. Equal parts social and political satire, Dadaist absurdity, and teenage slapstick, William F. Gaines's subversive monthly magazine soon gave way to *Ramparts Magazine*, Tom Wolfe's *The Electric Kool-Aid Acid Test*, Richard Farina's *Been Down So Long, Looks Like Up to Me*, and of course, Hunter S. Thompson's *Fear and Loathing in Las Vegas*. They were all a great escape from that tension-saturated decade and took a bit of the worry out of growing up surrounded by assassinations, the Vietnam War, the remnants of the cold war, the fear of the draft, amid the burgeoning age-of-Aquarius-style freedoms. We traded our books and magazines, much like we did with baseball cards when we were kids.

Kelly had a Tandberg stereo reel-to-reel recorder, and the Bastards would meld country, Middle Eastern, prog, Asian, jazz, English folk, and other general weirdness into improvisational streams of consciousness using guitars, saxophone, various woodwinds, kalimba, chimes, whistles, dog toys, found objects, beatnik bongos, and tape manipulation to create two sixty-minute DIY tapes, that even the local hippie fringe found a bit too far out. After successfully performing as the featured entertainment during an intramural speech meet at Roosevelt High School, we went looking for a paying gig. As luck would have it, we heard that the Pickwick, a country-western bar on Chestnut Street, had a band cancel on the all-important weekend. We talked to the owner, a local kingpin named Jack Blatnick who wore more jewelry than his wife, replete with the prerequisite pinky ring. When we told him that we had a saxophone in the band, Jack's eyes lit up, and he said, "I LOVE horn bands." Little did he know.

We had local poster artist Jeff Johnson do up a quick poster and handbill that we posted to every telephone pole in town, calling all of our friends as well. By 9 p.m. the place was packed with our underage friends who had snuck in the back door. By 9:10 p.m., the regulars were streaming out the front door. We tape-recorded everything, and at exactly 9:19 P.M., Jack came running up to the bandstand and can be heard on the tape screaming, "Get out of here! Get this MARIJUANA music the hell out of here!" The Bastards can be heard grinding a twisted bossa nova to a halt, laughing as we doused the incense, and started taking down the hanging wind chimes. We didn't get paid and years later the Pickwick burned down. Coincidence?

We grabbed the rest of our meager gear, our crowd, and headed down to Rollie's Bar, down the street, that had been on the downside of down-and-out for years. I am not sure that we told Rollie, a handsome Native American with a striking resemblance to Ricky Ricardo, what we had in mind, but we just walked in and pretended to own the joint. Before long, we were well under way handing out percussion instruments for those bold enough to grasp our time signature. Dancing in and on the bar ensued for the rest of the evening. At the end of the night, Rollie asked us, "What kind of music do you boys call that?" to which we responded, "Ehhh . . . Marijuana Music." He said, "What are you doing next weekend?" It was his best night in years, and though we never played live again, we had free tap beer at Rollie's for a long time, made it home base, and once the drinking age was lowered we were actually able to drink there legally.

VASELINE MACHINE GUN

Dudley was from Eveleth, Virginia's archrival in sports. He wore a head-band over his long hair and across his forehead and mostly wore sun-glasses day or night. He drove an old black hearse, a conveyance for his absurdist style. He always held his cigarettes between his third and fourth finger and would flick the ash into a rolled-up pants cuff. Though just a few years out of high school, he seemed an old and wizened sage. At the time there was at least one hotshot electric guitar player in every town. We knew them by name, by band, and by sound. But Dudley was unique, and the only guy I knew besides Dennis Monroe who specialized in play-ing acoustic guitar, finger-style. I was interested in learning that style, and he reached out to me. The teacher was ready, the student appeared.

He loaned me his copy of Leo Kottke's *6 and 12 String Guitar* on Takoma Records, the standard for all acoustic finger-style players from 1972 on. The album had a gorgeous cover, white script on black. Kottke wrote the liner notes, hilarious and surreal, describing the tunes such as "Vaseline Machine Gun," "The Last Steam Engine Train," and others. I learned several of them and they became the bedrock of my burgeoning acoustic repertoire. Kottke had a unique approach to the guitar, combin-ing Pete Seeger, Chet Atkins, and John Fahey, with a healthy mule kick of Dave "Snaker" Ray. He also had a wild imagination and twisted sense of humor evidenced by the song titles. His playing, for me, evoked a certain Midwest sensibility in its melancholy and had a power not usually associ-ated with acoustic guitar. One reviewer described his style as "being able to find all the inherent logic and beauty in the acoustic guitar."

Dudley had scored some tickets to Kottke's show at the Guthrie in Minneapolis, early in December 1972 and invited me and a buddy to the show. We headed out of Virginia in a full-blown snowstorm, determined to hear a master.

Against the setting of fresh snow, the exterior and interior lights of the Guthrie extended an edgy, urban welcome. Kottke was rising to the top of the ranks of well-regarded and nationally recognized acoustic gui-tar virtuosos. Many in that night's audience had seen him years earlier playing the folk clubs on the West Bank and had followed his career since. He was a hometown hero. To me as a guitar player, he was everything I aspired to be. We took our seats amid the sell-out crowd on the confetti-colored seats in the theater, ready for a taste of some of the finest live acoustic guitar playing.

Wally Pikal was the leader of a polka and variety dance band booked for the opening act. While most of us Minnesotans had heard this oom-pah-pah sound track before by countless bands at weddings and dances, no one anticipated the climax of his show, which he performed bouncing on a pogo stick while playing two trumpets. It was to be no ordinary evening.

Leo came out in a V-neck sweater over a grey T-shirt, brown corduroy pants, Wallaby shoes (Hush Puppies with an attitude), carrying a six-string and a twelve-string guitar, casual but cool. He opened the show solo with one of his signature tunes, "Vaseline Machine Gun," on twelve-string slide guitar, amplified and flooding the theater with sound. His right hand had the strength of Rocky Marciano, his thumb anchoring bass lines like a steel-driving John Henry, his fingers dancing deftly like Baryshnikov on strings. The slow songs had a lilting, lazy river feel and aching loneliness suggesting black crows in leafless trees, the mid-tempo ones proud and strong with an almost patriotic backbone recalling Lincoln dreaming of a more perfect Union, and the fast ones like jackhammer lightning, a million miles an hour, cascading waterfalls of shimmering notes, all twelve strings sending out rivers of sound. The rhythmic patterns seemed to have some third concealed hand at work, the rhythmic equivalent of rubbing your head and your belly at the same time. Absolutely stunning. While Kottke compared his own singing to "geese farts on a muggy day," his voice sounded to me like honey-colored oak, honest, strong, and soulful as when autumn envelops the Midwest, days getting darker one by one.

The sound in the room was unlike anything I had ever heard. Years later I would learn that while architect Ralph Rapson was designing this room at the Guthrie, he used rays of light to gauge how the sound would project and swirl throughout. I am not sure how he did that—he might not have been completely sure himself—but it worked. Previous performers, the likes of Horace Silver, Doc Watson, Ravi Shankar, Laurindo Almeida, and others, had painted a sonic imprint across the theater, allowing the next performer to stand a little higher on that mystic sonic plane. Now it was Kottke's turn.

He was also a sit-down comedian, funnier than hell, self-deprecating, like Mort Sahl with a guitar. A master storyteller with twisted tales of his childhood, he told of characters he'd met on the highways and byways, including a story about his short-lived career as a teenage golf caddy, and other disastrous jobs that somehow informed his decision to become a professional musician. Fortunately for us, none of those jobs panned out. For the second set he brought out Billy Peterson on upright bass and Bill Berg on drums, two top-flight session players who would but a few months later play on another Minnesota musician's record *Blood on the Tracks*. The show was recorded and came out on an album later that spring called, in a reflection of Kottke's worldview, "My Feet Are Smiling." It was one of the first records, but not the last, that would be recorded within those acoustically perfect and glorious walls.

It was the kind of evening where time both stood still and went by so fast you hoped it would never end, the perfect elixir of a master musician—magnificent sound, exquisite lighting—with an audience that hung on every note. It was an enchanting night in a beautiful room, one that stays with you forever but where you can only stay for a little while.

From the early lures of the deep and dark minor-key Finnish melodies of my grandpa's 78s in the evening light of their living room apartment above the Roosevelt Bar on Chestnut Street with the neon from the street below blinking as if on beat, to the twist and shout of the Beatles on the *Ed Sullivan Show* in black-and-white, to my parents' LPs like *My Fair Lady* and *South Pacific* playing during dinner, to Dad's eyes growing damp as we listened to Gentleman Jim Reeves on our Magnavox Astro Sonic stereo record player after dark, to polka bands playing at summer festivals and parties beside cool blue lakes and green city parks, to junior high dances with deejays playing songs like "Crimson and Clover," to Hendrix and B. B. King on television, and rock and roll bands at ski hills and local dances, to lying in bed with WLS Radio out of Chicago channeling the rhythms of the Windy City and deejay Clyde Clifford on "Bleecker Street" out of Little Rock on my transistor radio replete with background psychedelic sound effects, to the Preservation Hall Jazz Band and Carlos Montoya at the Duluth Arena, all pulling and tugging my young heart beating in time. . . .

Through them all, one song and show at a time, on the heels of a two-hundred-mile drive through a blinding-white snowstorm, I had arrived this night at this temple of exquisite sound and seductive light, wide-eyed, impressionable, and inspired. Something powerful was stirring. How could I not want to spend my life doing this? In a culminating moment, a snapshot between the shadows and lights of great masters whose paths give way to ours, the place where past meets future, I decided to become a professional musician that night. The three of us got back into the car now heading north, and I fell asleep in the backseat dreaming of the world to come.

CRY OF THE MUSKRAT

He was the new kid in town in the summer of 1973. I'd see him walking his little tan dog several times a week down the main drag. He had long hair, a ruddy complexion, and walked like he was going no place in particular. He was usually wearing a jacket, plaid flannel shirt, a beat-up pair of Red Wing boots, and if you walked by close enough, you'd notice the little dog had a somewhat menacing sharp tooth hanging over his lower lip. His name was Tim O'Keefe; the dog's name was Rip.

I heard that his dad was the new president of the State Bank in Virginia and had just moved the family here from Superior, Wisconsin. He did not fit my image of what a bank president's son might look like, but I had heard through the grapevine that he was one hell of a harmonica player. I had been playing harmonica on a rack for a few years with my acoustic guitar, but once I heard O'Keefe, I ended up storing my harp in a cardboard box along with a box of baseball cards, a signed Fran Tarkenton rookie photo, and other assorted memorabilia and didn't open it for a couple of decades.

Most of us got together, drank and partied on weekends, at keg parties in fields, at cabins, and in gravel pits. You could hoot and holler, pass joints, meet girls, cheerleaders, and hippie chicks and occasionally taste a bit of the forbidden fruit beyond the shadow of the fire, in your car or in the bushes. Occasionally, a fight would break out, usually between drunken knuckleheads, and they never lasted long, with never more damage than a bloody nose or black eye. The combatants would usually be back by the fire, sharing beer and laughs, before the party ended.

I pulled up to the kegger after a night shift at WHLB, a small radio station in Virginia, where I had gotten a job as the weekend deejay at the beginning of the summer. I arrived around midnight, party in full swing. There were a couple of dozen people gathered closely around a roaring bonfire surrounded by two steep rock and gravel walls in a pit just north of town. I heard a harmonica being played. It was the new kid in town and the main attraction, playing it, blowin' his brains out, and teetering dangerously close to the fire that was spitting orange sparks in every direction every time the wind blew around the corner.

He was amazing. Wearing the same clothes I had seen him in a few days earlier, playing at a hundred miles an hour, a whoop here, train whistle there, like the bastard son of the Harmonicats. The crowd was spurring him on, spilling beer out of plastic cups as they saluted him, the moon shining like a spotlight in the night sky. Toward the end of this tour de force performance, amid the thicket of birch trees and pines that surrounded the gravel pit, he started to fall backwards, in slow motion while continuing to play, and ended up completely on his back like the last log on the fire. He was quickly rescued, pulled from the flames, and he dusted himself off, stood up, and finished the solo. Yeah, he was completely hammered, covered in still-burning ashes, and he held his harp high in the air with one hand, while reaching for a beer with another. I left before I had a chance to say hello but knew our paths would soon cross.

I cornered him after the first day of school as seniors and told him I heard him play at the party a few weeks earlier, and that I was a guitar player. He carried a half a dozen harps in his pocket, and I told him I would bring my guitar to school. The next day after school we sat on the steps and played together until the sun came down and both of us had to get home for supper. I had met a kindred spirit, and though both from somewhat different musical backgrounds, we both enjoyed a variety of music and had been playing for more than half of our young lives.

We became fast friends. Winter comes early in northern Minnesota and was right around the corner. Music gave us something to do indoors that would get us through the brutal temperatures, sharing record collections, musical ideas, and high jinks.

My first real exposure to the blues was on the Johnny Carson show where I saw B. B. King, Jimi Hendrix, and others. For the most part, blues bands were scarce on the Iron Range. I had bought a B. B. King record at Dayton's department store in Minneapolis in junior high and enjoyed the feeling and the lift that electric blues had. I wore out that record and especially his signature song "The Thrill Is Gone." While I had heard names like Lightnin' Hopkins and Mance Lipscomb, I really had no idea about the world of acoustic blues music, or that you could play the blues on the acoustic guitar. That would soon change.

O'Keefe had a stash of records but spent most of his time listening to Little Walter, Muddy Waters, and others on a cassette tape player next to his bed, hour upon hour. It became the marrow in his bones, a compass through which he viewed life, and some sort of spiritual sound track for him. My first night at his house he played some stuff by Sonny Terry and Brownie McGhee, a duo from the South that had been championed by both Woody Guthrie and Pete Seeger. Sonny played harp, and Brownie used his Martin acoustic, as he would say, as his weapon against the world. Their style seemed to be tailor-made for us: one guitar, one harmonica, and two vocals. We loved their songs, and they all seemed within reach of our musical abilities. They became our blueprint and, eventually, our weapon against the world as well.

In addition to the guitar, I learned to play the autoharp, dulcimer, and banjo. Tim added a mean washboard and some mandolin. We dug anything that swung, sounded good, and gave us a reason to play. The first song we wrote together was called "Cry of the Muskrat" combining O'Keefe's Sonny Terry–like harmonica chugging over a bed of ragtime chord changes that I fingerpicked on my twelve-string guitar. We put together a set of about thirty songs, ranging from songs I learned from my grandfather, country classics, ragtime, blues, bluegrass, and a few other originals, and emerged from Tim's basement as the Bernie Scribble New Freedom Jug Band. Thanks to my grandmother we booked our first gig in the basement of the Unitarian Church for a coffee social, where six years earlier I played my first gig as half of the duo Paul and Christian. Bernie Scribble was my nom de plume for a weekly article I wrote for our high school newspaper, and whose motto now inscribed forever in the senior VHS yearbook reflected dozens of lunch hours enjoying the mild frontier of reefer madness: "When Reality realizes it's insane, and the Brain begins to dribble, the Universe will drop its drawers, and sing songs of Bernie Scribble."

We would eventually evolve into Metsa and O'Keefe, the only Finnish-Irish blues duo on the Iron Range. We played school assemblies, our high school graduation, house parties, and the occasional saloon gig where we actually got paid. We would have, and did, play for nothing. About a year later, we met rockin' Johnny Pasternacki, and Cats Under the Stars was born.

CATS UNDER THE STARS

I knew John Pasternacki since I moved to Horace Mann Grade School in the third grade. John was a year older than I. In Virginia to this day, people are referred to as Southsiders or Northsiders, depending on what side of town you live on. Johnny and I were Southsiders. We got to know each other a little better in high school. He was a superb athlete, lettering in both football and track. He still holds the Virginia Blue Devils record for longest touchdown run in a high school football game. His coach and teammates used to call him All the Way Pasternacki.

Pasternacki and O'Keefe were both working construction in the summer of '74 and met on a job site. When Tim found out John played guitar, he suggested he join us for a rehearsal, which at that time meant a couple of hours rehearsing at Tim's parents' house and a couple of hours getting greased and lathered at the Eldorado, a popular bar on Chestnut Street with lots of black leather booths, red carpet, and low lights, and one statue of a bullfighter. We developed empathically both as musicians and as friends. Pasty, as we called him, and I eventually developed a second sense of each other's guitar playing, much as O'Keefe and I had with his harmonica and my guitar. We had listened to many of the same records and had similar styles. Like Tim and I, we were able to anticipate each other's next musical move and provide a launching pad for the other's flight of fancy. It was not uncommon for the three of us to turn a three-minute song into a thirty-minute ramble, exploring all the rhythmic and harmonic ideas available. It was like picking up a friendly hitchhiker and transporting him to his destination by way of the back roads.

The first golden moment in time for any band is when they get together to just play, lock in on a song, listen to each other's ideas, and coalesce them into a whole. Those exciting shared moments of discovery begin to define both the sound and the direction of the band. We cribbed from a wide variety of musical influences and, with open ears and minds, let our sound develop organically with no set boundaries. We'd know we had it when we heard it, and we were in no hurry and developed our repertoire, one stoned rehearsal at a time.

We were developing a rhythmic telepathy with each other and would work on playing the different grooves, grabbing them by the neck, and literally beating them into the ground. Instead of tapping of a foot, we would be pounding our boot heels into the floor, wrestling folk, blues, country, and bluegrass tunes to the mat. And though no one would have mistaken us for the Three Tenors, we started to develop three-part harmonies, singing like lumberjacks around a campfire. We were having a ball, while traveling back in time discovering the roots of American music.

A few months later we added Skip Nelimark on banjo, and then we were four. We named ourselves Hot Walleye, a northern play on the popular acoustic blues band Hot Tuna, played a few weddings, and often shared the stage at parties with the Pike River Bottom Boys, an acoustic bluegrass and jug band from the area featuring Rodney Jackson, a colorful and charismatic character in farmer's jeans with a Santa's belly. Rodney would do a variety of loon, wolf, and moose calls that would bring down the house.

While reading *Crawdaddy* music magazine one day in 1973, I read an article called "Cats Under the Stars." It was written by Robert Hunter, the lyricist for the Grateful Dead. It was a stoner comedy article, had nothing to do with the Dead, and included grand metaphysical questions like, "What do you do with a pack of Lucky Strikes, and no matches?" and other meditations on the absurd. I thought it was a great name for a band, clipped it out, and put it in my wallet. I had it for more than two years when Hot Walleye got a call to play an outdoor gig at the gazebo in Northside Park, on August 17, 1975. We changed our name and debuted as Cats Under the Stars. With two acoustic guitars, a banjo and harmonica we played with treasured abandon, and knew we had something going on.

Though we practiced regularly at O'Keefe's house, his mother, Marge, never quite gave us her seal of approval. She used to call us the "fun and games boys," so we started to refer to ourselves as the Milton Bradley Gang. She always thought, ultimately, we were up to no good. She may have been right. We invited her to our first theater show at the Mesabi Community College Theater in the fall of 1975, and she gave us one last chance to redeem ourselves in her eyes. Pasty had started smoking Camel Straights. He had written a little ditty called "Humper's Rag" based on the sexual double entendre acoustic blues of the '20s and '30s and an ode to his favorite cigarette. The tune was a bit of a ribald affair, and when he got to the line (and we knew it was coming) about how they "go in both ways, even from the back," Mrs. O'Keefe's blonde beehive started on fire. While she always loved her son, I don't think she ever forgave Pasty, or the band, for that song.

The summer of '76 rolled around and the Cats were about to shed their acoustic skin and plug in. We got a drummer named Steve Sandstedt and took up a Tuesday night residency at a little honky-tonk in Biwabik, Minnesota, called the Tumbleweed. We were starting to add a little rock to our roll. We'd end most nights by taking the crowd to an iron ore pit, now filled with water, where we'd skinny-dip, drink beers, and carry on. It was summertime and the living was easy.

Tim and I also kept playing gigs as a duo, and in September 1976, Metsa and O'Keefe starting hitting the college coffeehouse circuit. I had inherited my grandparents' '68 dark green Dodge Polara. We pulled the backseat out and fit our PA system there along with the rest of the equipment and suitcases. O'Keefe didn't have his license, so I would drive while Tim would roll these foot-long handmade cigarettes of the Jamaican variety, carefully adding one thin Zig Zag paper at a time to these miniature masterpieces, delighting us for hours on end. We did a couple of shows a week and made about $300 per show plus room and board. We'd get done early and would always have a chance to retreat to a local watering hole and throw down a few. Once, after a gig at Moorhead State College, we retired to Mickey's Office Bar just before last call. The waitress asked us what we wanted, and we said on a lark, "Sixteen rum and Cokes." She brought them, and we drank them. We were young, hitting the road, and seeing the sights. We were making money as musicians, too, and though since then things have been as good, I am not sure they got any better than those first days when freedom rang as we rode and rambled.

In 1977, Pasty had moved to St. Peter, Minnesota, to go to school. O'Keefe, Gary Brekke, our bassist in the winter of 1975–76, and I moved into a house together in Minneapolis. The Cats had turned into a pretty good rock and blues band, taking many of our cues from Lamont Cranston, a very popular blues band in Minneapolis. Lamont Cranston was the inspiration for John Belushi and Dan Ackroyd when they created the Blues Brothers. We would reunite in Virginia on the occasional weekend for gigs about every six weeks. We weren't actively looking for gigs, but they'd somehow find us, and we'd end up in the strangest of places.

We got the New Year's Eve '77 gig through Big Bill Gordon, a friend of O'Keefe's: a biker's clubhouse in Quamba, Minnesota, out in the middle of nowhere, on New Year's Eve. Sure, what could go wrong with that? It was colder than a well digger's ass. We met in Virginia, borrowed a van whose heater was shot, and along with our new drummer, Joe Luoma, took off innocently enough to make our way to Quamba, a three-hour drive from Virginia. Bikers, for the most part, are some of the best audiences musicians play for, kindred rebel spirits, and we were looking forward to the gig.

The clubhouse was a double-wide, beat-up aluminum trailer, and there were at least a dozen bikers on Harleys with their girlfriends, who had somehow gotten there through the snow. We carried our gear up the steps and through the front door when we noticed the arm wrestling table next to it. It was only 7 P.M., and the middle of the table was already oozing with blood. We set up, and they were nice enough to give us plastic cups and access to the fifty-five-gallon keg of beer. They forgot to tell us it was spiked with LSD.

Barely into the first set the acid kicked in. Now Joe, Tim, and Skip had never done the stuff; John and I had, and at least we thought we knew what was coming. The room was starting to change shape, the faces of the bikers looking more horrific than some of them already were, and the broken window behind us was blowing in a thirty-degree-below wind, with snow starting to pile up behind the drum set. We held on for dear life, and it looked at times like we were playing forty feet from each other, and the sound was echoing off the far wall, coming back to us in a way where we weren't sure if what we were playing were actual notes, the echo off the wall, or some ghost band that had been murdered there on a previous New Year's Eve. The bikers took turns riding their Harleys up the stairs and into the trailer, revving them in front of the band when they weren't trying to arm wrestle. The floor under that table was becoming a small Sargasso Sea of blood. Somehow we made it through until 1 A.M. and were getting ready to pack up and get the hell out of there when the club captain came up and told us we weren't going anywhere. We closed our eyes, said prayers to each of our gods, and made it, barely, until 3 A.M. when the bikers paid us in full and released their prisoners.

We had gotten a hotel room in Mora, a small town where my maternal grandparents, Ernie and Evelyn Paul, used to live, with two rooms. O'Keefe took the floor. We passed out immediately and barely two hours later were awakened by the rancid smell of burning polyester. Tim went to sleep next to the floor heater, and his jacket was on fire. The room was filled with smoke, and while the sun was rising, we were in no shape to deal with it. We gathered our things and headed north. We had a six-night gig starting at Norman's Bar that night in Virginia.

Though we were crispier than a new bag of Old Dutch potato chips and had the collective IQ of a small ashtray, we were happy to be home. Norman's Bar used to be the Roosevelt Bar, the bar my dad's parents, Emil and Elna Metsa, owned and sold in 1965. The bar hadn't changed at all, but the rooming house and my grandparents' apartment upstairs were worn down from years of neglect. The bands who played at the bar stayed upstairs, and I doubt, back in the day, if my grandma would have rented to any of these heavy metal playboys. My grandparents' living room had been turned into a shrine, with black lights and posters, to Jim Morrison.

My grandparents now lived above the Magic Bar down the street. Below them was an electronic fix-it shop called Zimmerman's Electric, owned by Jack Zimmerman, Bob Dylan's uncle. He was friends with my grandparents, and when he found out I was a musician, he gave me a signed Dylan photo that I still have. My grandpa would be at Norman's at the start of our sets each night, in a white shirt, tie, and Stetson men's dress hat, sit at the bar, and buy the band a round every night we played. Though he was in his late seventies and had promised grandma he stopped drinking, he'd have his rare but usual Black and White scotch on the rocks, and we'd toast each other's health. He was a hell of a guy, a great grandpa, and the band and bartenders loved him. He'd always leave a fat tip as well, a tradition I have kept with bartenders to this day.

By 1978, we had all gone our separate ways. I had moved to Minneapolis and got an apartment at 441 Ridgewood Avenue, down the street from Tom Lieberman, a great young folk and blues musician, and the first guy I knew in town. He was playing in a new trio called Rio Nido, featuring Tim Sparks on acoustic guitar and Prudence Johnson, a singer from Moose Lake, Minnesota, who sang like a midnight nightingale, with blonde hair pulled tight in a ponytail, accented by a white gardenia that recalled Billie Holiday. She had one of the most beautiful voices I had ever heard. She moved seductively in floral designed skirts wrapped tightly around her and silk or cotton tops.

They would do regular gigs at the 400 Bar, playing their tightly arranged versions of songs by Cats and the Fiddle, the Boswell Sisters, Stuff Smith, Al Jolson, and Nat King Cole, among others. Three-part harmony, complex, tighter than the lips of Russian gangsters, highlighting Prudence's voice and Tom's playing with the Big Bill Broonzy bounce, and Sparks's solos, reminiscent of Charlie Parker and Jelly Roll Morton. Majestic and swinging music on the corner of Cedar and Riverside. The New Riverside Café, where they'd play as well, which was kitty-corner to the 400 Bar, used to advertise that corner as the "bio-magnetic center of the Universe." The nights they played it was.

I had just moved to town and had started to stake out my favorite bars and restaurants. One of my favorite restaurants, located at Seven Corners on the West Bank, was the Haberdashery across the street from Dudley Riggs's E.T.C., one of the oldest comedy clubs in the country, where I had gotten a job selling tickets. (At E.T.C., I got to meet legendary comedian Henny Youngman, a young comic named Louie Anderson, and satirist Paul Krassner, a roommate of Lenny Bruce's and a founding member of the Yippie Party.) The Haberdashery was openly gay owned and operated, not unlike the Saloon on Hennepin Avenue, which was the largest bar-restaurant operation in the state. The Haberdashery had an outlandish purple décor, waiters that would swish to and fro while taking orders, and a menu that included their special, available at all times, the Juicy Brucey.

On Halloween, my favorite holiday, I decided to go down to the 400 Bar and listen to Rio Nido. I knew my best new Minneapolis buddy, bartender Steve Baker, was working, and the joint would be jumping. The band was as usual superb, and many couples in the crowd wore dress-up outfits from the '30s and '40s.

It was hard not to keep your eyes on Prudence as she paid tribute to Sarah Vaughn and Billie Holiday, among others. She came up to me at the end of the night and said hello. I'd been sitting by myself, savoring that evening's performance in a bit of a Heineken glow, courtesy of Mr. Baker. After some delightful conversation I told her my birthday was November 1, All Saints' Day, the day after Halloween. She asked me if I liked pumpkin pie. Even if I didn't, I would have lied and said I did. She invited me to her house, opened a bottle, then two, of wine, and we danced closely by candlelight in the make-believe ballroom of her living room. We slipped upstairs to her bedroom, lit scented candles, and in a magic bed, covered with lush quilts almost Amish in style, waited for neither another season nor another reason to make a little whoopee. The sun tried to come up but we wouldn't let it, and when we did, it came up, shined over Riverside Park, and on us for almost five years as boyfriend and girlfriend. I got to hear her sing in a variety of styles and settings, including with the Cats and myself, gracing any musical style from Patsy Cline to Bessie Smith, with complete, singular, swinging authority. She'd light up any stage on which she'd appear, breaking many men's hearts in the process, and five years later, mine as well.

I had just started my own solo career in '78 and had also gotten a job teaching guitar at the Guitar Store, at Twenty-second and Johnson in Northeast Minneapolis. In a short time, I had thirty-five students a week and was doing solo gigs throughout the Twin Cities. I had developed a repertoire of jazz, blues, ragtime, country, and bluegrass tunes. I played both acoustic six-string and twelve-string guitars. I had also started to write original songs again.

O'Keefe was living in Duluth but would come down to Minneapolis every so often, and we'd play as Metsa and O'Keefe. In January 1979, we were doing a gig at a place called Butler Square Saloon in downtown Minneapolis. On our second night there, we were approached by a guy in a full-length fur coat, cowboy hat, and cowboy boots with spurs. His name was Chase Walker, and he was an agent and musician himself. He had a music agency called Moonwalker and was partners with a fellow by the name of Chris Moon, who owned Moon-Sound Studios on Twenty-eighth and Dupont in South Minneapolis. While Chase was interested in working with Metsa and O'Keefe, both Tim and I were interested in involving Pasternacki again, in a new, improved, and revived acoustic version of Cats Under the Stars. They offered us some free studio time in return for helping them put a fake ceiling in one of the studios. Deal!

We had rehearsed about six numbers at my studio apartment on Ridgewood Avenue the evening before the sessions. We arrived at noon the next day, set up quickly, and recorded most of them by 5 P.M. Chris Moon had been working with a young black kid from Minneapolis, and he was due in early that evening. Chris had given him the keys to the studio to let this very talented young man work his magic whenever he wanted. He came to the downstairs studio as we were packing up our gear. He was pretty shy, had a small afro, was wearing a black leather jacket, and shook his car keys in his right hand, as if in time to some song in his head. His name was Prince Rogers Nelson. We'd be hearing a lot more about this wunderkind in the next couple of years. In spite of a handful of other singer-songwriters who were dubbed such, after listening to him, observing him evolve, and eventually watching him perform live, to me Prince really was the next Bob Dylan.

Pasty and O'Keefe both moved to Minneapolis in the summer of 1980. They rented a little two-bedroom apartment on Clinton Avenue by the Electric Fetus, a great independent record store that was founded in 1968. The *National Lampoon,* among others, singled it out as having "one of the worst names for a business." I loved having my two best friends and band mates back in town, and we quickly got to work on creating our new repertoire, look, and sound.

I really loved Rio Nido's three-part harmonies and their take on classic swing, jazz, and blues tunes. My idea was that the Cats could do a similar take on that swath of material, find our own songs, and create our own identity. The other thing that appealed to me about a new sound was that it was something my mom and dad would enjoy as well.

We got together almost daily. We'd drink coffee, listen to records, and discover tunes we would enjoy doing. Cats and the Fiddle was a swing and jive quartet that was formed in the late '30s and were considered early pioneers of rhythm and blues. They had a great look and beautiful four-part harmony propelled along with swinging guitar and upright bass. They were definitely cool cats. Right away, we chose three songs of theirs to study and learn: "Killin' Jive," "Nuts to You," and "Hep Cats Holiday." We were also learning Mills Brothers' arrangements (one of my folks' favorite ensembles) as well as tunes by Bob Wills and the Texas Playboys, Sam and Dave, and the Everly Brothers, among others.

We had to chart the songs ourselves, slowing the records down and transcribing one vocal line at a time. Occasionally, we would either wear the records out or scratch them in the process of learning the songs. We'd run over to the Fetus, the Wax Museum, or Hymie's Record Shop, grab a fresh vinyl copy, and start anew. It was a painstaking process, but it worked. Like the rest of the different styles of music we learned and covered, it made us better and more complete musicians. For me, it continued building bedrock foundation from which my next flock of original songs would be able to take wing and fly.

Once we had a couple of sets, all that was left to do was figure out a good look. We decided on two sets of vintage tuxedos, one white and one black for each of us. This did three things: it fit into the '30s and '40s look of some of the bands we were covering, they were cheap and easy to find at used clothing stores, and it was easier to ask for more money if you showed up in the monkey suits.

Moonwalker Entertainment and our agent Tom Griffith (Pasty's cousin) started to book us at colleges, clubs, and private events. While we were traversing the country club circuit with the flashy tuxedos, we also got a house gig at the 400 Bar every Tuesday night, which lasted four years. We'd play our arsenal of swing and jazz tunes but would also include our folk, blues, and country songs. O'Keefe had started to play percussion, which added some punch to the trio. Pasty and I had also started to listen to records from the ECM catalog and were starting to get inspired by the likes of Pat Metheny, John Abercrombie, Ralph Towner, and others. While some of their stuff was a bit over our heads, we would start laying down our own progressive soundscapes with a hillbilly twist. A Tuesday night with the Cats was a walk through the streets and alleys of American music, off to outer space for a while, and then back home around the campfire from where it all began.

I had always written original songs throughout whatever outfit I was in. During my formative years, I was as interested in learning songs from other artists and playing in as many styles as I could get my head around as a way to broaden my perspective. From a strictly working musician's standpoint, it also gave me, and us, a chance to work in a wide variety of clubs.

My dream to play the Guthrie Theater finally arrived. Sue McLean, who booked the Guthrie, called us and asked us if we would like to open for Ry Cooder, one of America's preeminent musicians and musicologists. Musicians like Ry Cooder, Taj Mahal, David Bromberg, John Hammond Jr., and others had gotten us interested in and first introduced us to roots music, and they were also the portals through which we would pass to discover the original masters of folk, blues, bluegrass, and other types of music. Ry didn't tour very often, and he was using John Hiatt's band including John, Bobby King, and Terry Evans.

We wanted to give Cooder a gift as an appreciation for his music, and something that reflected our northern Minnesota roots. For some reason, as he was always pictured in a variety of headscarves and hats, we thought in our infinite wisdom that he might appreciate a birch bark hat.

When we gave it to him after his sound check, he stared at it silently for what seemed to be an hour and thanked us. We still laugh about that. We had a really wonderful set and enjoyed Cooder's show immensely. We went back to Pasty's apartment and toasted our good fortune. It remains one of our finest and most prestigious gigs.

Two other memorable gigs took place in St. Paul. We played the Prairie Home Companion Radio Show and went over very well. It was right before the holidays, and Garrison Keillor was nice enough to invite us over to his house, off Grand Avenue in St. Paul, for an after-show party. Pasty and O'Keefe wanted to get back to the bar and their girlfriends in Minneapolis, so as the leader I went over and spent the evening playing Pictionary at the Keillor household and listening to Garrison's young son Jason play a Christmas song on his trumpet.

The other memorable St. Paul gig was when we were booked at the Oz Nightclub. It was an odd gig to begin with since the place was usually a discotheque. We had taped a television variety show called *Nighttime Variety* for Twin Cities Public Television in downtown St. Paul earlier that day, a few blocks from the Oz. They had live entertainment that night, and when we got there in our white tuxedos, we entered a room full of at least three hundred women. Nice. It didn't take us long to figure we were opening for the Chippendales (the Thunder from Down Under) Male Stripper Revue. The women applauded politely after several tunes and then got a bit unruly when they realized we were wearing actual tuxedos and wouldn't be ripping off any breakaway costumes and shaking our money makers in front of them. They were as happy to see us leave as we were to go.

By the end of 1981, we decided to bring the electric band back as well, alternating between the acoustic trio and an electric quintet. We had hired a new guitar player named Jeff Cierniak who made his debut with the electric band in Ely on New Year's Eve 1981. We originally hired him as a bass player, but somehow he ended up playing guitar and Pasty switched to bass guitar. In a way it turned out to be a good thing, and Pasty turned into a powerhouse of a bassist, putting all those years of athletic training into holding down the bottom of the electric band.

Through Cierniak we met Kenny Jacob, soundman for Cierniak's annual acid-drenched Resistance Festival at the Odd Fellows Hall on Lake Street. It was an annual Halloween Bash that featured Dunk Ritter, a wacky architect who would put on a cowboy hat and Day-Glo, Jeff on a

Wally Burkes handmade electric guitar, a rhythm section playing psychedelic cowboy music (tongue planted firmly in cheek). It also featured a special appearance by Jeff's brother Johnny, dressed in nothing but a fluorescent green jockstrap, who did a version of "That's Life" by Frank Sinatra that made Sid Vicious's take on "My Way" look puppy tame by comparison.

Kenny became the Cats' soundman with our electric band. His dad was the head of the hematology department at the University of Minnesota, and he had two brothers equally as cool as him. Their family had a cabin in Ely, and he and I realized we had much in common. They kind of welcomed me into their family as the fourth son, and my relationship with the whole family got richer and more important to me as time went on.

The new electric Cats, besides our regular repertoire of blues, country, and rock and roll, were now getting into reggae as well. Someone had also turned Pasty and I on to the Wild Tchoupitoulas, a Mardi Gras Indian band backed by the Meters and the Neville Brothers, the first family of New Orleans music. They played a joyous music featuring call and response and those intoxicating New Orleans rhythms. We loved it. We had big ears, and wide eyes, and were ready to learn and play anything that was soulful and swung.

Mike Starnes, a New Orleans native who sold ads for *City Pages,* the alternative newspaper in town, had turned us on to live tapes of the Neville Brothers. We played those tapes until you could see through them and started learning several of their songs. Mike had gotten us a gig at the recently remodeled Moby Dick's. Moby's was a legendary nightclub at the corner of Seventh and Hennepin Avenue in downtown Minneapolis that featured a "whale of a drink" and would let people who had just completed thirty days of sobriety turn in their AA medallions for a cocktail. Its bouncers were huge, many of them wrestlers and boxers, whom you did not want to mess with; if you did, you'd get the ass kicking of your life and end up in a garbage can in the alley. Inside you'd find pimps, working girls, drug dealers, the occasional brave transvestite, working folk, and drunken college kids out for a good time, enjoying the largest collection of foosball tables in the state.

They had put a large stage in the west end of the room for bands they were starting to book. This was our first big show downtown. The manager, a nice fellow named Bobby Gold, with a bad permanent and covered in gold chains, gave me a tour of the stage. He pointed to the large rack that could hold a couple of dozen lights. I reassured him, "Bobby, don't worry. . . . We just have one light." By now we were starting to attract a fair number of Deadheads, as Jerry Garcia's record *Cats Under the Stars* had come out in '78, and everybody thought we got our name from that. We didn't play any Dead tunes but did love to jam, and we enjoyed the new people firing up the dance floor. The gig was a blowout, and we would go on to play there as long as they had music. On a break, I was taking a leak in the urinals, standing next to an old black cat who was a regular. The usual drug deals were going on in the bathroom, and occasionally you'd see the glare of a knife blade or small pistol as the dealers opened their jackets. The old cat looked at me, smiled, and said, "You can remodel the bar, but you can't remodel the people."

We started to play the Union Bar in Minneapolis during the week. On the weekend it had acts like Albert Collins, Lonnie Brooks, Gregg Allman and had featured Stevie Ray Vaughn in his first Minneapolis show in 1983, and Muddy Waters in one of his last. The Cabooze was the other big club in town that hosted acts like Delbert McClinton, Savoy Brown, Johnny Winter, James Brown, and others. It was not long before we were headlining weekend nights there. After a couple of drummers, our old drummer Joe Luoma joined us, replacing Rex Morriss, along with keyboardist Al Oikari, and we started to develop a big sound, a bigger following, and played more than four hundred shows in the next couple of years.

In the summer of 1982, Kenny Jacob invited us to do some recording at a studio at the Children's Theater in the Phillips neighborhood of Minneapolis. We had saved a little money in the band fund and decided on cutting a single featuring our reggae version of "Louie, Louie" and for the B-side a number I had just written called "Blue Ghosts." My old buddy Chuck Christianson, from Paul and Christian, was in town, and we brought him in to sing harmonies. After the second night of three sessions, I grabbed a cassette dub of the rough mix and went down to the Artists' Quarter, just a few blocks away, to see Howlin' Wolf's legendary guitarist Hubert Sumlin.

I got to the club for Hubert's last set. I sat down at the horseshoe-shaped bar next to Tom Surowicz, a local music critic. I told him that the Cats had just got done recording and that I had a cassette dub of the session. He suggested I go give it to Bob. "Bob who?" I asked. He replied, "Bob

Dylan. He's sitting in the booth by the corner." Sure enough, I looked toward the booth, under the window with the neon sign, and there was Dylan, back to the bar, wearing a polka-dot shirt, vest, and Ray-Ban sunglasses, the light from the neon shadowing his head like a barroom halo. He was with two beautiful women. I walked out to my car, got a Cats promo piece and the cassette, strolled over, introduced myself, told him we were from the Iron Range, and gave him the promo. He was very polite and seemed to get a kick out of the fact we were from his neck of the woods. I went back to the bar and wished to hell I had a camera to take a picture of Dylan reading the Cats promo.

Dylan was spending time at his farm west of Minneapolis and was popping up at various places around town, occasionally going over to West Bank blues god Willie Murphy's house to listen to records. Several weeks later, Sue McLean called us again and asked if we would like to open for Robert Hunter, the Grateful Dead's lyricist, at Duffy's, a cool little rock club in the Seward neighborhood where I would see acts like Captain Beefheart and Wendy O. Williams. It was an auspicious occasion: not only had we gotten our band name from the *Crawdaddy* article by Hunter, but also this gig was set on August 17, the seventh anniversary of our first Cats show. It was a lovely coincidence, and Hunter seemed to get a kick out of it as well. The show was a complete gas and put us one step further up the ladder.

We released the 45-rpm single on my new label, Monkey Business Records, whose motto was "Monkey business is our only business." It featured a logo of a chimpanzee in a top hat smoking a cigar. It is pretty exciting to hold your first record in your hands. We sent it out to a couple dozen reviewers and the radio stations in town that might play it. Robert Christgau at the *Village Voice* wondered why in the hell any band would release "Louie, Louie" as the A-side of their debut record and compared "Blue Ghosts" to the Jefferson Airplane. He gave it a B-plus.

It was going to be featured on a local music show on KDWB, a popular 50,000-watt station in the Twin Cities on a Sunday at 1 A.M. We cut out of our gig at the Payne Reliever on the east side of St. Paul early so we could catch it on the radio on the ride home. Excited as cheerleaders at their first state hockey tournament, we rode home together and had the radio cranked. The deejay introduced the record, said a little bit about the band, and started to play it . . . at 33 rpm. We called the station and got a janitor on the phone who told us the show had been taped earlier and no one was there. Damn! "Louie, Louie" was an up-tempo tune, and though we sounded a bit like a polka band on mescaline at that speed, it wasn't deadly. But when they played "Blue Ghosts," a slow ballad, it sounded like we were ten thousand leagues under the sea, in a wash of Romilar cough syrup and covered in molasses. It was but a small lesson in what my friend the great alto saxophonist Eddie Berger used to call "life in the shoe biz."

We'd play every kind of gig imaginable in the two years to come: clubs, parties, festivals, parks, and opening acts. We were enjoying a nice, new two-year run, but a rift was developing in the band. O'Keefe, the star of the band, Pasty, and I had been tighter than the Three Musketeers since we started to play together in 1974. Somehow Cierniak, a bit of a chatty Cathy, was pulling a power trip in this, his first real band and had created a divide: John and I on one side; Joe, Tim, and Jeff on the other. It had started to drain the fun out of a band that was, for the most part, nothing but that. Although I was the leader, booked all the gigs, rehearsals, and made sure we were always moving forward, I never took a dime for any of that and ran the band as a democracy. While I had been developing a solo act, my dream was to take Cats Under the Stars as far as we could go, together.

We had been playing a half a dozen or so of my new stash of originals, and I thought it was time to go back into the studio and record another Cats record. Pasty had a couple of great tunes, including a great nascent rap tune called "Under Grey Skies in a Buffalo Zone." Between our songs and a couple of choice covers, I thought we had the beginning of a full-length LP.

Kenny Jacob was a relative of America's greatest talent scout, John Hammond Sr. Kenny's grandpa on his mother's side, Fred Field, was adopted into the Cyrus Vanderbilt family and their fortune and was a cousin to Hammond. Fred, after visiting China in the early 1930s and becoming quite taken with the earliest and purest form of Communism, was given an ultimatum by Vanderbilt: "You have a choice, Fred. Take your inheritance or go to China." Fred went to China. That move, coinciding with Hammond's progressive political leanings, cemented their bond as cousins.

Hammond, I believe, was single-handedly responsible for American music as we know it today. He signed Billie Holiday, Count Basie, Big Joe

Turner, Teddy Wilson, Aretha Franklin, Pete Seeger, Leonard Cohen, Bob Dylan, Bruce Springsteen, and Stevie Ray Vaughn to Columbia Records. He tried to recruit an unknown Robert Johnson to his Spirituals to Swing Concert at Carnegie Hall in 1938. Though he didn't know at the time and couldn't track him down, Johnson had died a few months earlier. He recruited Big Bill Broonzy in his place, alongside Meade Lux Lewis, the Golden Gate Quartet, Helen Humes, Sonny Terry, and others. He would be responsible for overseeing the Robert Johnson posthumous reissues of his recorded work, *King of the Delta Blues Singers,* in 1961. Hammond's accomplishments will never be duplicated.

Kenny had been graciously pitching John Hammond to get him to listen to the Cats. I really appreciated Kenny's help with this. The acoustic Cats had opened up for John Hammond Jr. in the fall of '83, and he was impressed with the band. I had always thought John Hammond Sr. would be the one guy in the record business who could appreciate our amalgam of styles, the virtuosity of Tim O'Keefe, and our ability to play both acoustic and electric. Kenny was able to secure an audience with America's finest talent scout in June 1984.

Kenny and I arrived in New York City on a sweltering hot mid-June day. I hadn't been to New York since a family trip in 1963. I remember that trip vividly, as we bumped into an old babysitter of ours at the top of the Empire State Building. We also went down to Washington, D.C., for a tour of the town. Racial tensions were boiling over all around the country, and we were dumbstruck when our family (mom, dad, three kids, and cousin Merline) was refused service at a black restaurant. It confused and mystified us and stung a bit as well.

Kenny had set up our accommodations at his grandmother's apartment in Chelsea. She was on vacation and the apartment was empty. We were extremely excited about the meeting and almost too tired to sleep. There was no air conditioning in the fifth-floor apartment, so we kept the windows open, only to be attacked by mosquitoes throughout the night. Of every image I had had over the years about New York City—the *Ed Sullivan Show* in black-and-white, boxing matches from Madison Square Garden that my dad and I used to watch on television, the Brill Building, Carnegie Hall, Central Park, and Greenwich Village—I had never considered mosquitoes being part of the equation. Policemen Kojak and McCloud, yes, but not mosquitoes.

I had bought a new suit coat and tie for the visit and took the time to press my pants, shirt, and tie for the meeting. We were staying on Twenty-third Street and decided to walk up to 311 West Fifty-seventh, where Hammond's office was. We probably should have taken a cab but thought the walk would do us good. We got there five minutes before the 11 A.M. meeting, stood in front of the building, and walked up the four flights of stairs to John's office.

It was an old office and apartment building where once the great Hungarian composer Béla Bartók lived. We wound our way up the stairs and arrived at Hammond's office. We knocked, and Mikey, John's secretary, answered the door. For me, it might as well have been walking into Thomas Jefferson's office, as I held Mr. Hammond in such high regard.

There, behind an old brown desk, sat the man. He had a full head of hair, cut in a butch haircut, a loud plaid jacket and tie, and a smile that could light up the Chrysler Building. He was delighted to see Kenny, came around the desk, gave him a handshake and a hug, and shook my hand as well. He was a complete gentleman, and I expected nothing less. He and Kenny got caught up on family business for about ten minutes, when he suggested that we get down to business and listen to what we had brought.

I excused myself to the bathroom before the listening session. It was right next to his desk. I closed the door behind me, and in the old-style bathroom I saw a claw-footed tub filled with hundreds of cassettes. I could only imagine how many broken hearts and dreams were at the bottom of that. I said a little prayer, hoped mine wouldn't end up in that pile, and went back into the office where Kenny and John had set up the video machine and cassette player.

This was going to be my one big push for Cats Under the Stars. We had a cassette of both acoustic and electric cuts, including our single, and a video of the band playing at a very wild party. We opened with that, and in the middle of a percussion jam someone had passed a joint on stage, and it was in full view. John immediately said he didn't need to see the rest of that and told Kenny, "Don't show this to anyone else in the music business." Jesus H. Christ, talk about not putting your best foot forward. Kenny then started to play John cuts off of the cassette. They weren't indexed, and it took Kenny a while to find the tracks. John said, "Kenny, the next time you do this, make sure you know where the songs are." If it had been anyone else besides a relative, we'd probably have already enjoyed our fifteen minutes and been out the door.

We played John about nine songs. They included some of the swing stuff, some electric band tracks, and we ended with "Louie, Louie" and my song "Blue Ghosts." John listened intently, smiling when he heard something he liked, his right thumb and finger on his cheek, and his elbow on his desk. When "Blue Ghosts" was finished, he asked, "Who wrote that?" I said I did. John Hammond, one of the gods of American music, said, "*That* is what I am interested in." My heart was beating like loud African drums, and my eyes lit up like a jackpot light on a slot machine. All those years and tears, all those bars and scars, all that time walking on the tightrope, here I was, with my buddy Kenny, and we had landed safe and sound. Fucking A!

The meeting was coming to a close. John told us how much he enjoyed the success of his latest signing, Stevie Ray Vaughn, and how Stevie reminded him of T-Bone Walker. For some reason, we talked a little bit about pinball machines, and John hipped us to a great place called Playland in Times Square with old pinball machines that he liked to play after reading the *New York Times* on his way to work. What a classic and classy guy. He wished us well on the rest of our stay in New York and gave me his address and phone number and told me to stay in touch. His last words of advice as we left: "Paul, remember the next time I hear a song of yours, I want to be able to whistle it when I leave the office." That golden advice has always stayed with me.

Coincidentally, at about the same time, the Cats' cup had finally runneth over. I arrived at a gig at a place called Shenanigans in Dinkytown to find this typewritten note written on the back of a Cats Under the Stars Trio poster from Pasternacki taped to his bass amp and addressed to all of us: "I know this is rather short notice, guys, and I do apologize for the inconvenience, however someone has got to shut this party down, call in all bets, and face the music, so to speak. And so, this cowboy says goodbye to the Cats, invoking the sacred right as a founding father to cancel, rather than tarnish, an illustrious, if obscure, rock career, preferring to go down in a blaze of hype-less glory, as opposed to the ever-present and well-documented terrors of Dinkytown. Happy St. Patrick's Day. Later, Pasty, aka Johnny (mustang sally) Murphy."

So after seven years, this incarnation of Cats Under the Stars ended. Though I was crushed, Pasty had called it like he saw it, and the Milton

Bradley Gang with the two other guys was going down and wouldn't ride together again for another ten years.

Only time can reveal certain truths to you. In a way, I was just getting started, and in retrospect it was probably the best thing that had ever happened to me. This time, I was going to start doing things my way and then would have only myself to blame.

ONE MORE SATURDAY NIGHT

Jerry Garcia, lead guitar player for the Grateful Dead, was as good as America got on a Saturday night. On his best night, he went where no man had gone before. Beyond Main Street, beyond church, beyond the ballpark, bedroom, or boardroom, Jupiter and back and yet still down by the riverside, an electronic sugar shack where anything seemed possible. Trailed by hellhounds and at least a step or two ahead of Mr. Charlie most of the time.

The Grateful Dead was an experiment in rock and roll improvisation by way of Bakersfield and Brubeck. Trucking around the country with a hundred thousand pounds of sound and lighting equipment, and a lesser amount of drugs, they played with wild gypsy grace and abandon, a misfit pirate ship charting dark enchanting waters. Though often slagged as hippie has-beens, the Dead were at their core a biker band. Like bikers, they played by their own rules, sometimes damaging themselves and their music with their excesses in the process. Welcome to America. And like anyone who plays by their own rules, they were never moved by popular opinion. Whether with the Dead, or his own band, Jerry was always ready to jump whatever joint he was playing.

I had heard the Dead for the first time on a Saturday night in 1973. My friend Kelly told me that the Grateful Dead were playing in Minneapolis in a couple of weeks. At the time, I was only familiar with their work through their LP *Workingman's Dead,* and my only impression of them was that they were a slightly out-of-tune country rock band.

We called a couple of friends and plotted the "trip." This would be my first trip to the Twin Cities on my own without my parents, and we prepared for it, like thousands of other teenagers in America now under the literary and literal influence of Hunter S. Thompson's *Fear and Loathing in Las Vegas.* Kelly brought his homemade mini-bong made out of an old Shure 57 microphone, with a hose long enough to pass around the car. He had a bag of homegrown smoke and Tim had a bag of sinsemilla. Brian, my best buddy, had a bag of Panama Red, and I, working as both a deejay at a small radio station and playing gigs on the weekend, had scored a bag of the smoke of kings, Acapulco Gold. We could only hope that those four bags of grass would get us through the weekend.

It was about a four-hour trip to Minneapolis, and by the time we hit the city limits we were giggling like fools, higher than Chinese kites, and had the eight-track cranked to the Doobie Brothers, the New Riders of the Purple Sage, Elton John, or Wishbone Ash and were reveling in our newfound freedom. Right before the downtown skyline came into view, I noticed a highway patrol car right behind us, lights a-flashin'. Code Panama Red time. He pulled up in front of us, and I pulled up slowly and cautiously behind him. We waited for a minute. I took a deep breath and got out of the car, while my buddies were busy stuffing their crotch with their individual four-fingered lids. I walked almost to the back of the patrol car before I realized he had actually stopped the car ahead of us. Whoops. I tiptoed back to the 1959 baby blue Cadillac, and we were back on the road, laughing like the James Gang—the outlaws, not the band. Thank God for small favors.

On Saturday, we went to the Wax Museum, a great record store and head shop on Lake Street. This place was Richard Nixon's worst nightmare. There were long hairs in front of and behind the counter, rock and roll posters adorning the walls, and racks and racks of records that were destroying the minds of young America. My kind of place and my kind of America. We bought our tickets, at $5 each, and scored two hits of 4-way Orange Sunshine acid on the way back to the parking lot.

We got to the St. Paul Auditorium a couple of hours before show time. We carefully split up and dropped the acid and moseyed in. The tribes were gathering. Now it wasn't like there weren't hippies on the Iron Range. They stood out, and some had probably been to either coast, or some back from Vietnam, said to hell with it, grew their hair, and hung around back home, some of the veterans repressing memories that probably haunt them until this day. But these were real goddamn California hippies, just like the ones I had seen in *Life* and *Look* magazines. They dressed like modern gypsies, the men in long hair, the women longer. They smelled like a garden of patchouli, sat on Mexican rugs in the lobby, and some brought their dogs along for good measure. A swirly, whirly, cavalcade of colors, stripes, and tie-dye wraparounds. And the hippie chicks, oh my freakin' lord! Gorgeous goddesses from some forgotten time. They were all beautiful, and most of them braless. Each and every one of them, smiling at us and with us, giving this seventeen-year-old hope that he might have a chance at some sort of ecstatic sexual communion with one of them.

We settled into our seats and slowly adjusted to our surroundings as the carnival started to unwrap itself around us. The Dead were using what was known as the Wall of Sound. Visually, it was absolutely stunning, tons and tons of speakers stacked upon one another, up to the sky and back. Though we had been to dozens of rock and roll shows, we had never seen a sound system like this. It looked like the audio equivalent of the Great Pyramids. Pipes were passed, several jugs of wine as well, and Kelly's mini-bong was the talk of the aisle. The lights went down and the band started to play. I don't think I had ever heard a band play a song longer than five to six minutes. Their slow-motion version of Kris Kristofferson's "Me and Bobby McGee" clocked in at more than ten minutes. Of course, by now the acid had kicked in, and time became immaterial. At the end of the first set they went into their signature song, "Playin' in the Band," a twenty-five-minute tour de force, and I couldn't believe what I was hearing. This was psychedelic baroque music for this generation, the sound of LSD, on fire and on display, explosive, chaotic, sexual, vibrant, and twisting and turning down roads that Jan and Dean could only dream about. Dead man's curve for sure. And at the helm, none other than the man himself, Jerry Garcia, bearded and in sunglasses, caressing a Fender Stratocaster with a Hells Angels sticker, a wah-wah pedal, a Fender twin reverb, and a thousand watts of solid soul through a sound system that was crystal clear and louder than anything I have ever heard. He led the cavalry and charged through sunlit meadows, dangerous grease gravel alleys, mountain peaks, deep valleys, in swirls and curls, around and around. It was swinging jazz, played by a rock and roll band, conversing musically with each other as if in a Dixieland band. Here, standing before me in a black T-shirt and corduroy pants, was a true American master of the electric guitar. As a guitarist, I was hooked. As a teenager, beginning to explore a world my parents never told me about, because none of us knew it existed. While LSD was known as a very dangerous drug—and it can be, especially if you do it by yourself—I was among friends, thousands of them, most of them as pleasantly high as myself, and in control. And this was only the first set.

The second set ended with a tune called "One More Saturday Night," with a rave-up worthy of the Duke Ellington Orchestra, except ten times louder. At the end of the tune, a spotlight hit a mirrored disco ball reflecting lights from this electric Shangri-la around the hall, from Prohibition to the Promised Land, through my body and soul, and out back into the universe. By now everyone was on their feet, dancing and screaming, making out, and having a damn good old time. A made-in-America Saturday night. Let freedom ring.

I would have probably never met Jerry Garcia had I not met Steve Baker first. I moved back to Minneapolis in the fall of 1977 with the goal of getting a degree in the music program at the University of Minnesota. Previously, I had been studying classical guitar since 1976 at the University of Minnesota, Duluth, and attending classes at Mesabi State Junior College in Virginia since fall of 1974. Not so much a junior college as a high school with ashtrays. I was taking the usual fare, with an emphasis on music theory.

I would drive down to Duluth once a week to take lessons with a pipe-smoking, seersucker-suit-with-leather-elbow-patches-wearing professor named Robert Wander, who was a hell of a classical guitarist. Sight-reading music for me has always been about as fun as watching your ex-girlfriend dance with her new boyfriend, yet I managed to learn twenty to thirty classical pieces, and with my background in finger-style guitar playing I found a certain affinity for the style. The two-year academic program ended uneventfully enough, and in the spring of 1977, I applied for entrance into the University of Minnesota music program.

I was to be in Minneapolis early Monday afternoon for my entrance exams. Cats Under the Stars had a Saturday night gig at Elna's Bar in Ely two days before. After that gig, we were invited to a party with wild women and free booze, at a campground that required us to drive fifteen miles out of town and then walk in the dark down a mile portage, to a campsite. When we arrived, there wasn't a woman in sight, all the booze was gone, and our hosts were passed out in a tent. One of the guys in the band had picked up some weed called Alaskan Thunderfuck, and we smoked that until the sun rose over the lake. Shivering and cold, we doused the embers in the campfire and, still high, made our way back to the parking lot, our vehicles, and headed back to Virginia. I should have gone straight home to study and also should have passed on smoking that most powerful strain of monkey shit.

I left early for Minneapolis for my theory and performance exam

Monday afternoon. Fortunately, my performance came first. While I was used to playing in dimly lit bars, where the audience, after a cocktail or two, could be for the most part forgiving, this setting was way different. It was on a brightly lit stage with three professors in the first row with clipboards and red pens. I played a couple of pieces by Bach and felt, all things being equal, that it was a strong performance. There was a half-hour break, and then about sixty of us were led into a large classroom and were given our theory exam. The first question was "What is a Neapolitan chord?" Uh oh, I think I was either at the Magic Bar or Eldorado Lounge during that lecture. And it went downhill from there. I finished the exam in less than two hours, knowing I had completely blown it, and left the campus hoping that my performance exam would outweigh the theory exam, and they would have the good sense to admit me as a student. Two weeks later, I received a letter from the music school at the university bluntly stating, "Upon reviewing your exam, we strongly recommend that you find another field of study." I ripped the letter into a thousand pieces, threw an alarm clock smashing it against a wall, and went for a long walk, pondering my next move (though now I wish I would have kept the letter to include it next to the lyric sheet on my first LP). I blamed this episode on that curiously strong reefer, which I now refer to it as the "pot that kept me out of college."

I still wanted to please my folks and get that valued music degree. I moved down to the Twin Cities in September of that year. I found a place in South Minneapolis on Ridgewood Avenue, a little two-block street barricaded by Franklin Avenue and interstate highway 94. I found a studio apartment about the size of a baseball dugout and moved all my records, guitars, snowshoes, books, clothes, and a bible I received, and still have, from my church confirmation. Cabbies would refer to this neighborhood in the '60s as Psychedelic Alley, and in the '70s, the Swish Alps, as it bordered Loring Park, one of the homes to the gay community in the cities. Ozzie and Harriet Nelson wouldn't have felt out of place on this street, and neither would Ricky, if he had had a boyfriend. I would live in that apartment for twelve years.

The West Bank has a storied history in Minneapolis. A stone's throw away from the U of M campus, it became home to the Swedish and Norwegian immigrants at the turn of the century. A true bohemia. Not long after, home to a student population, and in the midfifties beatnik-run coffeehouses and bars like the Mixers, where you could see Bill Grimes, an older African American gentleman who enjoyed snapping a ten-foot bullwhip in front of the club on the weekends, and South of the Border, a black-and-tan joint where the pimps, prostitutes, and drug dealers would conduct their business. It was home to the likes of poet and professor John Berryman and other assorted working folk, and the gathering crowd of wanderers and dreamers.

The Scholar Coffeehouse and the Purple Onion opened in Dinkytown, a ten-minute bike ride from the West Bank, in the late fifties. They were the anchor joints for a budding folk music scene, and the site of Bob Dylan's Minneapolis debut when he was a University of Minnesota student and member of a Jewish fraternity nearby. In the late '60s and early '70s these two scenes merged into one and drifted southward to the corner of Cedar and Riverside avenues.

In the late 1960s the hippies planted their flag there, and it became a Midwest country cousin of Haight-Ashbury. In the '70s the New Riverside Café, a hippie co-op, and the Coffeehouse Extempore, which had opened in 1965, both featured top local folk, blues, and bluegrass as well as national acts passing through town. This helped shift the folk music magnet and ground zero from Dinkytown to the West Bank. There was a handful of great music clubs in the neighborhood including the Triangle Bar, the Tempo, and the Joint, among others. They all cranked up the volume, booking rock and roll, blues, and rhythm and blues bands. Folksingers walked the streets with banjos and guitars, and the songs of Pete Seeger and Percy Mayfield, among others, were never in short supply in any of the clubs, bars, and coffee shops. Richter's Drug Store was in the heart of the 'hood, and while older folks could purchase their prescriptions inside, younger folks would pick up their head stash for the weekend outside. A young red-headed blues sister named Bonnie Raitt planted the seeds for her career there. Willie Murphy, who produced Bonnie's first record, was the spiritual guru of the neighborhood, and his band Willie and the Bees, an R&B powerhouse, pounded out their juju one weekend after the next. They were the Mill City version of Sly and the Family Stone, with a little more grease in their griddle. Blues artists like Lazy Bill Lucas and Baby Doo Caston had moved here from Chicago and were inspiring dozens of future blues cats. Koerner, Ray, and Glover, the holy trinity of Minnesota folk and blues in various configurations, played all of these rooms, and you could find them winding down after shows at various neighborhood watering holes, most notably Palmer's Bar and the 400, both still up and running.

I skipped class one day and walked into the 400 Bar, at the corner of Cedar and Riverside. I ordered a shot of Southern Comfort on the rocks, my drink of choice, and sat by myself. I struck up a conversation with the bartender, a handsome, affable chap with a full blond head of hair and an Eddie Munster hairline. I told him I was new in town from the Iron Range. He introduced himself as Steve Baker, and from the tips he was pulling in, I could tell he was a popular cat. I found him to be extremely interested in a variety of subjects, but especially music, and he was very popular with the local musicians. On any given night at the 400 you could bump into local legends like "Spider" John Koerner, Bill Hinkley and Judy Larson, Pop Wagner, Dean Card, Cal Hand, Sean Blackburn and "Dakota" Dave Hull, Dave "Snaker" Ray, and traveling musicians who had played across the street at the Coffeehouse Extempore or the New Riverside Café, like Utah Phillips, Rosalie Sorrels, and Bill Staines. I loved it. That night, Steve served me several more shots, all on the house, and I realized that might have been another reason he was so popular with all the musicians. I had made my second new friend in Minneapolis.

Steve and I got to be really good buddies, and he was kind enough to invite me over to his house and to family gatherings if I wasn't able to get up north to spend time with my own family. He came from a family of eight children. He also had a large stash of live Grateful Dead tapes that were shared by his brothers and sisters. I had no idea that there was such a thing. In February 1978 he invited me to go to a Dead show in Madison, Wisconsin, along with his seven siblings and his father, Keith, who had come out of the closet after his divorce and would be joining us with his boyfriend. This was an interesting family, to say the least.

On the morning of the show, we got together at Steve's mother's house and caravanned down to Madison. We got there and checked into the Holiday Inn, across the street from Dane County Coliseum. Someone had given me an envelope full of miniature magic mushrooms. I had learned that swallowing the sacrament of psychedelics before a Dead show was kind of like the flu shots that sailors get before they sail with the merchant marine: it was something you didn't think twice about.

It was another epic four-hour show, and before I knew it, we were back at the hotel in time for the lounge band's last set. If the Bakers were no ordinary family, then this was also no ordinary lounge band. Though the shrooms were wearing off, it was hard to tell. The band featured two lead singers: one was almost seven feet tall in a ten-gallon cowboy hat, and the other a four-foot Mexican dwarf. I am not kidding you. We savored a couple of cold Heinekens at the bar and took one each back to our hotel room and then fell into a restful sleep.

The next day, we got up around 9 A.M. and had breakfast at the hotel restaurant. I had brought a cassette tape of a live Cats Under the Stars show, if I had the good fortune of bumping into someone who could pass it on to Jerry Garcia. It turns out the Dead were staying in our hotel. With nothing to lose and curious as hell, I dialed up the hotel operator and asked for Jerry Garcia's room. Lo and behold, she put me through. Jerry answered and, I thought, was fairly alert as it was only 10:30 A.M. I told him about the band and how we had the name since '75, three years before his record of the same name, and he invited me up to the room to drop it off. I had no idea I would get to enter the lion's den.

I knocked on the door, it opened, and there stood Garcia, aviator shades, black T-shirt, corduroy pants, and tennis shoes that looked suspiciously like the clothes he had on the night before. He had a warm radiant smile and seemed genuinely enthused about getting the cassette.

He was about to say good-bye and shut the door when the phone rang. He invited me into the room as he went to answer it. I stood next to the desk and surveyed the room. I looked at the bed and, so naive at this point, said to myself, "Man, what a guy, he makes his own bed!" He had an anvil briefcase on the desk that was open. Inside were about a dozen orange prescription bottles, some I am sure filled with genuine prescriptions, a huge wad of tin foil that I don't think he was using to wrap up the cold cuts, and a thick hard-covered book called *The Primitive Origins of Christianity.* The book reinforced one of the reasons I loved about the guy—that it is possible to be erudite, intelligent, but still want to play in a rock and roll band.

He got off the phone, and I handed him the cassette. I told him that if anyone in America could dig what my band was playing, it would be him. He smiled and held it. He then asked me what I thought of the show. I said, "It took a while to find the sweet spot in the room where the sound and the show converged." He smiled, warmth exuding off him like blasts from a potbellied stove, and said, with a flippancy that probably got him kicked out of the army, "Yeah, one fat lady walks into the room and blows the whole mix." That was funny, damn funny. He was a very easy guy to like. We made some more small talk. As I was about to leave, I felt in my pocket and realized I had a small stash of the mini-mushrooms left. In the spirit of Sonny Barger, leader of the Hell's Angels, who when asked if drugs should ever be legalized replied, "Of course they should. You should just never do them two days in a row," I offered them to Garcia. I laid them on the desk, and I will always remember him looking up to me with his flashing baby blues, the shades now slipped down to the bridge of his nose, looking me straight in the eye and saying, "Thanks, Paul. I LOVE mushrooms." I gently floated out of the room, at least a couple of feet above the magic carpet and floor.

FRANKLIN AVENUE

My grandpa was my best buddy. He'd take me to the cabin when I was just a kid to get it ready for summer when the family stayed there, or in the fall when it was time to shut it down. It was our private time. Occasionally, he'd bring along one of his old barroom buddies. I thought they were there just to help with the chores and cut wood but realized when I was older that Grandpa also wanted to help them dry out away from the bars and city life.

I'd sleep next to Grandpa in his cast-iron double bed, with the fading flowers stenciled on the headboard, and wake to a cozy warm cabin whose fire he kept lit and burning throughout the night, to the smell of toast, bacon, and eggs. It was heavenly then and, in the rearview mirror of time, even more so now. He'd set up a bowl of water and shaving cream, and we'd shave though I was years away from having whiskers, looking out over the boathouse, and our day would start. A little later, when I was around ten, he'd let me smoke one of his Tareyton cigarettes and smile while I coughed and turned green. I wouldn't smoke again until my late twenties.

He used to play accordion for dances when he was younger and would sometimes walk three miles through the woods in the snow to play a country dance. At night we would crank up the Victrola in the corner of the living room of the cabin. It was a wedding present for him and Grandma in 1928, and the bottom held a large collection of 78 records, old Finnish waltzes and polkas, that he would sing along to in Finnish. I'd sit by his side, way after my normal bedtime, listening to song after song, sometimes falling asleep in his lap or beside him, and then he'd carry me off to bed. He always called me Pauly.

Wherever we went he'd run into somebody he knew. When he owned the Roosevelt Bar in Virginia, he was well liked and respected. The lumberjacks (mostly Finnish) would come into town with their paychecks, and Grandpa would put their checks in a safe, give them a drinking tab, and, when they exhausted that, would send them back home with money left to take care of their families. When I was in high school, he'd call and ask me to drive him to one of the funeral homes in town. On these trips he'd always wear a white shirt and tie. Inevitably, there would be one of his old buddies, in a cheap casket, an old flannel shirt or a rumpled suit, and sure enough, we would be the only names on the visitor register. He never forgot his friends.

I had returned from Minneapolis in the spring of 1978. I spent the summer in Virginia playing bass for a country-rock band called the Hole in the Wall Gang and spent as much time as I could with Grandpa. I knew when I was leaving at the end of August it would be for good. The night before I left back for Minneapolis, he and I got together at the Magic Bar. The owner, Pete McDonald, got in the business bartending for Grandpa. He was there behind the bar. We had several drinks, and I told Grandpa how excited I was to be leaving for Minneapolis and how much I'd miss seeing him. I knew he'd miss me, too, but we kept our game faces on. We played a round of dice with Pete, and he ended up buying us our last round. I hugged Grandpa and told him I'd call him the next day. I went home, with a bit of a brandy glow, put my face in my pillow, and cried like a baby. I was finally leaving home.

The next day, my old yellow Dodge Dart with a black hardtop that I inherited from Grandma was packed to the gills, along with a small trailer filled with records, guitars, amps, and clothes. I kissed my mother good-bye, stopped by my dad's office and Grandma and Grandpa's to say good-bye, and drove out of Virginia, toward Minneapolis and my new life with the radio cranked, the windows open.

I stopped at Tobie's restaurant in Hinkley for a cup of coffee and a buttermilk donut. Grandpa had shaken my hand during our good-byes and had put a bill in it, which I stuffed in my blue jeans. I reached for it to pay the cashier, thinking it was a ten or a twenty, and the lovely young lady was surprised to see I was going to pay for my coffee and donut with a hundred dollar bill.

It was late afternoon when I arrived in Minneapolis. It took me just a few hours to unload, unpacking my stuff and placing it around the room, which was the size of two one-man submarines back to back. The apartment, in the twelve years I lived there, never really got any more organized. I set up my stereo first, a small Sylvania unit with even smaller speakers. I placed my boxes of records along the west wall and hung a portrait of Grandpa and me over them. My clothes filled the two small closets, and I set my guitars and a pair of snowshoes around the room. I would wear the guitars out but never wore the snowshoes again.

I was in Candyland, a sweet-toothed kid, and music was my sugar. My apartment was within stumbling distance of Orchestra Hall where I saw Andrés Segovia two weeks after I got to town. At eighty-five years of age, he'd just recently become a father and stared down a fan who had dared to cough. He played unamplified to the crowd of two thousand people who almost had to cover their ears because his guitar projected like a jet plane.

The Longhorn Bar was the music bar downtown. Natural Life, a group of Minneapolis jazz musicians that played a form of jazz fusion with a midwestern prairie twist, was upstairs every Sunday night. The Suburbs, a punk rock/funk/new wave band, and others headlined downstairs, gathering the soon-to-be chiefs and princesses that were to hold sway over the blossoming new wave and punk scene, the sons and daughters of the actual suburbs who got their rock and roll panties first twisted by listening to Kiss on the radio and television.

My new favorite music bar was the Artists' Quarter at Twenty-sixth and Nicollet, right in my neighborhood. It had a horseshoe-shaped bar at the entrance that always had at least one empty seat, as if just for you. There was music seven nights a week, a mixture of local blues and jazz bands, and the occasional jazz legend. In a year's time, I saw Tal Farlow, Herb Ellis, Charlie Byrd, and others, the crème de la crème of living jazz guitarists, and sat close enough to hear their amplifiers hum. Pianist and bandleader Jay McShann would rule the roost with a solo set when he passed through town. It was all so above my head and ears, and I soaked it up, a pilgrim to the holy waters of jazz. I also enjoyed avant-garde jazz performances by saxophonist Archie Shepp and pianist Cecil Taylor at the Children's Theatre, and Sonny Rollins and Bill Evans at Northrup Auditorium, that made my head spin. I would eventually fill my record crates with all their records.

I was attending night school at the University of Minnesota, trying to follow up my two years at Mesabi State and cobble together a music degree out of the deal. While the visual arts department at the U of M had a very progressive and cutting-edge program, the music department seemed to be more traditional and more for those who wanted to become band directors or get trained as classical musicians with the hope of landing a coveted job in an orchestra. Neither of those was on my radar, and I dropped out the night before my first finals.

Instead, I opted for private lessons from a variety of very cool instructors. Minneapolis–St. Paul was, and remains, a hotbed of great guitarists of all styles. And while Leo Kottke and Peter Lang led the acoustic finger-style brigade, guitarists like Adam Granger, Tim Hennessy, and Dakota Dave Hull would hold forth at various gigs from church concerts to Dulono's Pizza, gracing audiences with their flat-picking wizardry. For me, someone addicted to all things guitar, it was pure nirvana. Most of my teachers were professional musicians, working at night and supplementing their income by teaching lessons. I would do that as well.

I studied with Tony and Michael Hauser from the vaunted Hauser family (their mother was a dance instructor, their father a sculptor), learning classical and flamenco guitar from them, respectively. I studied jazz guitar with Mike Elliot. I took lessons at the West Bank School of Music. I went to guitar master classes by musicians like Albert Lee and Joe Pass at the local music stores. My favorite guitar instructor was Tim Sparks. Sparky was from North Carolina and had taken master classes with Andrés Segovia. He transferred that knowledge of finger-style guitar to the steel string and specialized in transcribing piano rags and jazz and blues songs, from players like James P. Johnson, Willie "the Lion" Smith, Fats Waller, and others. He was a genius, and the only guy I knew who had actually read *Finnegans Wake*. He was both erudite and streetwise, wore a mustache and hats favored by hipsters from the '30s and '40s. He was an encyclopedia of knowledge on a number of subjects, and his rap was as entertaining as his playing. I learned a dozen or so of his arrangements that I play to this day.

I also picked up a job teaching guitar at the Guitar Store in Northeast Minneapolis and had, at one time, thirty-five students a week. I also started working on my solo show. I have always been interested in all kinds of music, and my repertoire reflected that. I put together a little promo piece that said, "Paul Metsa: 6- and 12-string Guitarist and Songster." In a way, I thought I was following down the path of guys like Blind Willie McTell, a musician and songster from Georgia who recorded and played under a variety of pseudonyms (my favorite, Pig and Whistle Red). Musicians like him—and even to some degree, Robert Johnson, the King of the Blues—played in a variety of styles and could play requests from ragtime to polka, traditional tunes as well as tunes off the radio, for anybody who threw a coin into a hat. Their styles gave me a framework to develop my own style. Like Duke Ellington said, there are only two types of music, good and bad. I like to think I played the good stuff.

That winter I had seen an ad in the *Minnesota Daily*, the college newspaper for the U of M, for a bar downtown called the Skyway Lounge: "Wanted—musician, $30 a night." The next day, I grabbed my promo, a cassette demo I had recently made, and headed downtown to Eighth and Hennepin to meet the owner. The Skyway Lounge was a strip club in the heart of downtown. At the time, downtown Minneapolis was the entertainment center of the Twin Cities. Its sister city, St. Paul, while a good place to find a beautiful church to go on Sunday, rolled up its streets at dusk and hadn't seen any real action for years. The West Bank had its own scene but was more bohemian in nature, and Uptown Minneapolis was taking baby steps toward becoming the next hip destination.

I got to the club at noon and found the owner, Reggie Colihan, smoking a cigar between shots of breath spray and reading the newspaper in a corner booth underneath a picture of the Beatles. His hair was cut like Thurston Howell III, from television's *Gilligan's Island*. He was wearing a green-gold sweater over a tan turtleneck, khaki pants, and wing tips, and had a bit of a reddened whiskey nose. I introduced myself and sat next to him. Unlike most bar owners I have known who love music but musicians not as much, he was a real gentleman. He seemed to enjoy the fact I had made an immediate effort to reach out to him, and he studied my promo with amusement and deliberation. And then I asked him about the Beatles picture.

It turned out that Reggie had quite a history in the music business. He had owned Big Reggie's Danceland in Excelsior in the early 1960s and in 1964 booked the Rolling Stones, who played to a crowd of three hundred people. Reggie's other coup was booking the Beatles at Met Stadium in 1965. When I looked closer at the photo, there was Big Reggie, fifteen years younger, with cigar, in a sharkskin suit favored by music promoters and gangsters, right next to the Fab Four, standing over Paul McCartney's shoulder. I ran into a waitress who worked for Reggie for twenty years and she told me, "Reggie was the only guy who lost money on the Beatles."

Reggie went on to own the Uptown Bar in the early '80s and turned the neighborhood joint into a rock and roll club. The electric Cats Under the Stars used to play there. Originally booked by Mike O'Neill, and then Maggie MacPherson, it was the Uptown version of 7th Street Entry and would feature up-and-coming national acts like Nirvana, Pavement, Guided by Voices, the Smashing Pumpkins, Uncle Tupelo, as well as local upstarts Babes in Toyland, the Mighty Mofos, Curtiss A, the Jayhawks, and the Replacements. Anita Stinson, Mill City's favorite rock and roll mom, and mother to Bob and Tommy Stinson, worked there for thirty-five years.

Reggie took a shine to me and booked me for the upcoming weekend on Friday and Saturday from 7–10 P.M., after which I would bequeath my space toward the back of the club to the half a dozen strippers who would shake their booties until closing time. The gig paid $30 and all I could drink. I had come of age drinking on the Iron Range, next to steelworkers, carpenters, and bricklayers, and thought I could hold my own. Reggie gave me a run for my money. He'd send up shots while doing them in tandem with me at the bar. Toward the end of my set he'd come up, take the microphone, and I would back him in a Jerry Lee Lewis medley. Legend had it he once booked Jerry Lee, who had challenged him in a song-for-song battle to see who could outdo the other guy singing Jerry's hits. They say Reggie kicked his ass. I played there for a couple of months, had a hell of a time, and always took the backstreets home.

When I wasn't teaching and playing the barroom folkie circuit at night, I worked feverishly on my guitar playing. I couldn't sight-read to save my life but had a quick ear and could read tablature, and between Sparks and listening to records I was building up a nice little army of songs. I was also starting to write original tunes again. I kept a little notebook of chord changes, taped riffs on a cassette recorder, and wrote free-form poetry from which I'd cull ideas, keeping track of phrases and possible titles for future songs.

On my nights off I attended any kind of show or concert I could afford. The West Bank had a number of venues, including Whiskey Junction, the Cabooze, the Viking, the 400 Bar, where you could see national acts and revered locals like Willie and the Bumblebees, Doug Maynard, or the Explodo Boys. The Coffeehouse Extempore had national acts like Ramblin' Jack Elliott and Rosalie Sorrels, and local acts like Rio Nido, Becky Reimer and the Sky Blue Water Boys, and others. The New Riverside Café had national and local acts including reggae bands like Shangoya and was a cooperative that served vegetarian food on the main floor and workers smoking other vegetable matter in the basement. The Rainbow Gallery featured free-jazz artists like Milo Fine, Dean Granros, and Steve Kimmel. This club checked anything resembling a melody at the door. It was a rush to hear young radical musicians unfettered by any form or structure, blowing to their hearts' and souls' content.

The other center of the rock and roll universe was right in my neighborhood. Oar Folkjokeopus at the corner of Twenty-sixth and Lyndale in South Minneapolis, a record store since 1973, was fast becoming the Bunsen burner for a new and exciting rock and roll scene. Many of the up-and-coming punk bands had seen the New York Dolls at the Minnesota State Fair in 1974, which inspired them to go forth rocking into the night. I had seen that show as well. The Dolls were late, and when they arrived and started playing they were greeted by some with beer cans and burning paper airplanes. They were all wearing eye makeup and the bass player had on a pink tutu and bunny boots. Personally, I didn't know what to make of it but enjoyed the madness of it all.

Like all great record stores, Oar Folkjokeopus, had a great selection of records, both imports from the punk scene in England and elsewhere and racks of affordable used records in all styles. I'd take five bucks, walk from my apartment near Franklin and Lyndale, down to the Egg and I for breakfast, and stop by Oar Folk, as we called it, to purchase a record or two from the used bin, all of which are in my record collection now.

Peter Jesperson managed the store. He usually wore a white dress shirt with the top button fastened, like the Beatles wore, always tucked in. He knew more about rock and roll than just about anybody in town and, like most record store guys, was a complete fanatic. He had started Twin/Tone Records with recording engineer and partner Paul Stark in 1977, and they had already released records and EPs by the Spooks (featuring Curtiss A), Fingerprints, and the Suburbs. He also deejayed at Jay's Longhorn in downtown Minneapolis where the godfathers of the Minneapolis punk scene, the Suicide Commandos, held forth. National acts that could almost burn that place to the ground included the Ramones, Iggy Pop, the Dead Boys, and Richard Hell. It was a punk rocker's paradise, had a short run as Zoogies (which was upstairs, where Natural Life played) before it closed, and paved the way for First Avenue and 7th Street Entry, which picked up the slack.

At the Longhorn I saw the original Pat Metheny Group, with Danny Gottlieb, Mark Eagan, and Lyle Mays, and bebop tenor saxophone king

Dexter Gordon, who was enjoying a comeback and was enveloped in smoke from his Camel straight cigarettes, which he smoked until the tip was about to burn his hand, between long and luxurious solos. Though not standard fare for the club, both shows were quite memorable.

I enjoyed hanging out at Oar Folk and listening to Jesperson carry on about his favorite bands, including the one he couldn't stop talking about, the Replacements. I hadn't heard any of their music yet but knew that the blond-haired kid who looked to be about thirteen years old and hung out at the store on his lunch hour and after school was their bass player, Tommy Stinson. His brother Bob, the Replacements' lead firebrand guitarist, was a regular there, and I kept bumping into him at other record shops and guitar stores. Occasionally, we'd take turns trying out guitars or comparing record buys. I always found it fascinating when Bob would gush about Steve Howe, the guitarist in Yes, one of the bands that punk rock set its sights on and wanted to destroy. It was the sign of an enlightened mind that could keep two disparate ideas together at the same time.

I got to know Terry Katzman, one of the clerks at the store who along with two other important guys in the blossoming scene, Roy Freedom and Kevin Cole, did sound and spun records between bands at 7th Street Entry and First Avenue. Terry also did live sound for Hüsker Dü, ran their fan club, and helped out around Reflex Records, the Hüskers' record company. I'd often see Bob Mould, guitarist for the band, going through the record racks, studying liner notes and album artwork like a student at a local library. Simply put, there was an incredible energy around that scene at the time.

The telephone poles up and down Lyndale and throughout the neighborhood were covered with posters advertising bands playing at the clubs around town. Over the years, posters for bands like Wilma and the Wilburs, Things That Fall Down, Babes in Toyland, Loud Fast Rules, Tetes Noires, the Figures, Johnny Rey, Rifle Sport, Man Sized Action, the Mighty Mofos, Hüsker Dü, the 'Mats, and others graced those poles, channeling the thunder of the city's sound.

It was 1978, I was twenty-two years old, gas was sixty-eight cents per gallon, eggs forty cents a dozen. Jimmy Carter, after pardoning all the draft resisters in his first day in office, was barely a year into his first year as president. Son of Sam had been captured in New York City, and John Travolta and his new movie, *Saturday Night Fever*, ruled the world. But in South Minneapolis, all we wanted to do was rock and roll.

ELECTRIC HIGH HEELS

There are two great moments for a songwriter. One is when the idea or inspiration for a song drops from the heavens; you happen to run into a piece of poetic graffiti scrawled on a barroom wall, or you overhear something somebody says and realize it would be the perfect building block on which to write a song. The other is when you are strumming your guitar mindlessly, trying a new set of chord changes or riffs, when they finally fit together like a railroad man's handshake. When the calloused grip relents and the fingers open, a melody appears. Now all you have to do is wed the two.

I was at Palmer's one night, an ice-cold Grain Belt in front of me, a shot of brandy on the side. "Spider" John Koerner liked to read his morning paper there and a few times a week came down at night for a few cold ones. He was sitting at the bar minding his own business, as he usually does. As for many musicians in town, John was a true hero to me. I had bought his record *Spider Blues* in the early '70s and wore it out. He calls his music "1960s barroom folk," and twenty years later you could still hear him fairly regularly at many of the joints around town playing his twelve-string, harp on a rack, wearing plaid shirts, blue jeans, and stomping his foot in time like a steam-driving train, occasionally joined by his old running buddy Tony Glover, on harmonica.

I saw his glass was empty and offered to buy him a beer and a shot. I had seen him dozens of times, but never had a chance to talk with him. He has one of those ageless faces and didn't really look any different from how he did on the cover of *Blues, Rags, and Hollers,* the seminal album Koerner, Ray, and Glover recorded years before. Though shy, he can talk knowledgeably on a variety of subjects including film and astronomy. He had a done a record with Willie Murphy in 1967 called *Running, Jumping, Standing Still* that *Crawdaddy* magazine called the only psychedelic ragtime record ever made. It is a certifiable Minneapolis classic. We chatted for about fifteen minutes, and I asked him while I was recalling that record if he would ever play with a band again. He responded very matter-of-factly, "Anybody can play with me, but I can't play with anybody else."

Spoken like a true Zen master. I went home, paraphrased it, and added it to my now-finished song "Stars over the Prairie": "You can be with them, but they can't be with anyone." Thanks, Spider.

Kenny Jacob and I had booked several days at the Carriage House Studios, two blocks from my apartment, and a BB-gunshot away from Franklin Avenue. We were attempting to get eight songs recorded and mixed. We didn't have a huge budget but enough to get some of the best, and my favorite, musicians in town. I called Prudence Johnson, Willie Murphy, Tom Lieberman, Peter Ostroushko, Eddie Berger, and some others. Because this originally started as a Cats Under the Stars project, I invited Pasty, O'Keefe, Luoma, and Al Oikari to join me. The first group of musicians arrived on a Tuesday night around 6 P.M., got set up, and by 7:30 the tapes were rolling.

It was my first time recording in a twenty-four-track studio. The room sounded great, and the engineers were really good. The magic can happen if you are prepared, confident, and have superb musicians. We recorded the rhythm tracks first, and I was amazed at how good it sounded. After the first session, Kenny and I walked out onto Franklin Avenue, the sounds still in our heads, the cars driving by almost in silence, their headlights bouncing off the incandescent and rainy street, the bushes, flowers, and oak trees blossoming in the midnight wind.

I am not an arranger. I always trust the musicians to react in an artful and inspired way to the song. The best musicians are very rarely wrong, and the ones on these sessions seemed to understand almost instinctively what to play. For the most part all of the songs and solos were done in one or two takes. Like Allen Ginsberg said, "First thought, best thought." We recorded everything in three nights and mixed and mastered on the fourth. The night before the photography sessions for the front and back cover of the LP, I stopped by a grocery store on the way home from the gig. The headline on the cover of *Weekly World News*, the newspaper that was always reminding us that the UFOs had landed and Bigfoot lives, read "Child Raised Like a Cat." Perfect. I grabbed that and read it while we got the back cover shot. With the master tapes, cover photos, and lyric sheet, we were off to meet the man who was going to ship it to the pressing plant.

While we waited for the record to get done, I had put an ad in *City Pages* for musicians for the Paul Metsa Group. The new group was a bit of a reconfiguration of the Cats; I kept O'Keefe, moved Pasty to guitar, and Cierniak to bass. Joe Luoma would be on drums, and Al Oikari on piano. I was looking for another keyboard player, and maybe a sax player. The paper had barely hit the streets when I was wakened by a knock at my door at 7 A.M.

I put on a bathrobe, rubbed the sleep from my eyes, and opened the door. There stood a 350-pound black guy, as big as Rosey Grier, in sunglasses with a younger woman by his side. His name was Charlie Alcox, and he said he was a keyboard player and singer. I invited them in and stumbled to put on a pot of coffee. He held a copy of *City Pages* in his meaty right hand and his girlfriend's hand in his left. She led him in through the door, down the short hallway, and it didn't take a rocket scientist to see that he was blind.

Charlie said he was new in town, arriving just two days before from Alabama. I have loved black music since I was a kid. I worshipped Stevie Wonder, the Staple Singers, Ray Charles, Odetta, Richie Havens, Motown artists, and more. I had always felt an affinity with these rhythms and the music. Like a lot of black musicians I would get to know, Charlie came up in the church. I was slowly starting to wake up and grabbed my guitar and, like a cat next to the mouse hole, was dying to hear him sing. I asked him if he knew "Amazing Grace." He started to sing and had a heavenly voice, the vibrato of which almost blew apart the snowshoes in the closet.

He took off his sunglasses. His eyelids covered his eye sockets, like brown drapes at an abandoned movie house. Due to a disease, his eyes were removed when he was four years old. His mother suggested that he as a child find a vocation to help overcome his disability. He chose auto repair. That worked out well for him, and me, too. After he started to play with the band, he would crawl underneath my pickup truck when it needed repair, listen to the music of the engine, and diagnose the problem. His girlfriend and I would laugh when we went to the auto parts store, and Charlie would amble through the aisles, to the astonishment of the clerks, and grab a bit haphazardly at the parts that were needed to fix the problem. He remained not only one of the best keyboard players and singers I ever had, but my best mechanic as well.

To round out the group, I hired Cleveland Gordon on percussion. Cleveland used to sit in with the Cats at the 400 Bar on bongos and kalimba, a small hand-held instrument the size of a cigar box sometimes called a thumb piano. He was from Ocho Rios, Jamaica, and at least ten years older than I. Over a homemade dinner of jerk chicken, washed down by cold Red Stripe beer in bottles, we laughed about some of those nights. During his tenure, he remained a calming figure, wise sage, and great friend.

My debut LP, *Paper Tigers,* came out in October. I was at the Egg and I, flirting with the waitresses and having my usual: two over easy, crispy hash browns with Swiss, wheat toast with a side of peanut butter, coffee, and water. I opened *City Pages* to the record review section, and there was *Paper Tigers,* with a stunningly good review. I read it enough times to memorize it. Now, over the years, I have developed a theory that rock critics had more to do with destroying rock and roll than record companies. My theory is that they operated in ideological packs, none of them wanting to seem less hip than the other. Ultimately, it seemed, they all wanted to work for, and started to sound and write like, the self-professed Dean of Rock Criticism, Robert Christgau of the *Village Voice.* Concerned only with bands that seemed on the cutting edge, they overlooked some very good bands in the process. By 1984, the national music spotlight was on Minneapolis, highlighting bands like the Replacements, Hüsker Dü, and Prince. I was able to catch part of that wave, due in no small part to the momentum those acts created.

In October the Cats did one last big gig, the Last Meow, at the Union Bar. The place was packed tighter than a carton of Marlboro reds. In the regular bob and weave of the dance floor, young hippies were doing the Seaweed, waving their arms wildly with a back-and-forth sway like floating ocean flowers. Older couples, arms around each other, held on for dear life. We went out in grand style, louder than an open hemi-fueled stock car race on a newly tarred track, and wrung every note of joy and power we had built up over the past decade.

We debuted both the new record and the new band at the Union Bar on December 19. I added a sax player Merlin "Bronco" Brunkow, who was a little older than we were and played in variety bands. We introduced him as the Polyester Polish Playboy because of his preference for polyester shirts and bell-bottoms. He'd show up to the gigs on his Harley, when it wasn't snowing, with his sax strapped to his back, take the stage, and blow his horn in gusts of lust and frenzy. The crowd loved him. Charlie Alcox, sitting behind his keyboards and synthesizer like a black statue of Buddha, was featured on several Motown tunes and would blow the house down with everyone's favorite encore, Prince's "1999." I was out front now, growing ever more confident with my electric guitar playing, the band humming behind me like a jet ready for take off, sending my original songs soaring. As the gigs progressed, I'd often find the audience singing the chorus to many of the songs. There is *nothing* better than to have a great band play your own tunes. On a good night, it is as good as sex and, in my case, usually lasted longer.

The band rarely retreated to the dressing room on breaks but would mingle with the crowd at the bar or join those outside in the intoxicating mist. The crowd was an amusing amalgam of characters. The Union Bar, our most regular venue, was near the University of Minnesota campus, and the college kids would arrive first, putting off another night of study. The nights would slowly build with couples enjoying a night on the town, working folk, as this bar was home base for many of them, bikers, and old and new friends and fans, creating an amiable and courteous blend of humanity, all of whom were out for a good time.

I met Pygmy one night on a break. He always wore a tie-dye T-shirt, had brown curly hair, and always danced by himself in a free-form style that sometimes suggested he danced to the beat of another drummer, not necessarily the one who was on stage. Pygmy came to all of our shows, and the night I met him I asked him what he was up to. He said, "I'm joining the army." I said, "Pygmy, I don't really even know you, but something tells me you aren't really army material." He disappeared all winter and showed up that spring, with a buzz cut, and still in one of his omnipresent tie-dyes. I said, "Pygmy, I thought you were in the army." He replied, "I'm AWOL." My intuition was correct, and he proceeded to dance the night away, lost in the reverie that only dancing can provide.

Everybody in the band was single, and it seemed like Minneapolis had the prettiest girls in the world. I met the love of my life there. Pasty, the best-looking guy in the band, always had a small brigade of beauties watching his every move. Bronco, though he had a girlfriend, collected more numbers than the Census Bureau, and the rest of the guys weren't complaining either. I was dating a few women I met on the dance floor, although some of them just wanted to take me home to read me their poetry. Eventually, I met a beautiful ballet dancer at the Union Bar, whom I fell in love with and would go out with for seven years.

There was also another woman whom I will call Lonesome Suzi. I couldn't help but notice her. She was at every gig I did. I was playing six nights a week in various configurations. She was pretty in the way that prisoners find attractive after several months in lockup. She had wheat-colored hair, usually covered by some sort of cowgirl hat, tight clothes that would light up the life of on-the-road truckers, skin as pale as Marianne Faithfull when she was going out with Keith Richards, and enough eye makeup to last several Halloweens. Spooky but sincere, in an odd sort of way, and in love with a guitar player she didn't even know.

One night at about 3 A.M., I was in my apartment having a beer and watching a rerun of the *Rockford Files*, when I heard a knock at my door. My apartment had a security door, and I figured it was a neighbor. I opened it, and there she was. It looked like it had been raining, and her eye makeup was running down her face. Hell, she might have been crying, for all I knew. I started to go out with my new girlfriend, and for the most part was a pretty faithful boyfriend, but I wanted nothing to do with this damsel in distress and had to threaten to call the cops before she left. Fortunately, she did.

Lonesome Suzi showed up the following week at a gig I was doing at the Five Corners Bar on the West Bank. At the end of the night, after squaring up with the guys in the band, I went back to the stage and found her wrapping up my guitar cords and packing away my guitar. I was exhausted and was going to a little postshow party, and she was so insistent I took her along for the ride. I stayed at the party for about an hour, and we got back in my pickup truck and headed back to the Five Corners to drop her off at the car. She had other ideas and was bound and determined to go back to my place. I told her, in no uncertain terms, I had a girlfriend and was not interested in anything she had to offer. We pulled in front of the bar and I asked her to leave. She wasn't going anywhere. I eventually had to grab her black purse, hand-decorated with cheap rhinestones that represented some sign of the Zodiac, place it in the middle of Cedar Avenue, and hope she would jump out to grab it. She did, and I took off toward Ridgewood Avenue faster than Wile E. Coyote. Groupies, while they sound great on paper, can lose their luster faster than ramen noodles in cold soup.

A week later I got a call from Lonesome Suzi's mother asking me why I was not there for dinner. Really? Her daughter told her we were an item and had invited me to dinner. I explained to her mother that I had a girlfriend, didn't even know her daughter, and asked her to please lose my number. A few days later her mother called and asked me if I was "sending satanic messages to her through my music." I got very pissed off and told her, "Your daughter needs help, and I am assuming you may need help as well." At that point if I had been able to send satanic messages to Suzi, I might have. I found out later that Suzi had been committed to six months of serious lockup at a mental health facility. Thank God.

Winter rolled around and it was time for a new project. Winter in Minnesota, if you are a musician, can be the most productive time of year. Like most musicians, though not all, I did not skate or ski and spent most of my time when not playing gigs inside a warm apartment writing songs, booking gigs, occasionally braving the arctic blasts to meet my buddies at local bars. My cash flow had improved considerably. On a good weekend night, after paying the band, I'd have five or six hundred dollars in my pocket. Add this to the bill or two I'd make on the other gigs four or five times a week, and the next thing you knew I was making real money.

I wrote a new tune called "59 Coal Mines." It was a song written about a fictional old miner named Lucky and reflected the layoffs around the country in a variety of industries. Union busting was becoming popular again in the harsh and bright light of Ronald Reagan's Morning in America. In retrospect, it should have been called Mourning in America—trickle-down theory, my ass.

I was a child of this sort of American progress, the third generation of Americans that was predicted by Thomas Jefferson when he said, "I am a farmer, so his son could be a banker, so his son could be an artist." As the artist, I was delighted to infuse a song with my political beliefs. There are many so-called political songs that are not worth the paper they are written on. I did not tread here lightly. A song also has to stand on its own musically, or it belittles the cause. I thought "59 Coal Mines" was a strong song.

I booked some time in the brand new Metro Studio space and brought in most of my band, including two gospel singers that Charlie Alcox knew. I called Cal Hand, who played in the legendary Sorry Muthas, the Twin Cities most acclaimed jug band, and was a featured player on several of Leo Kottke's records. Cal brought his dobro and pedal steel, which at the time was out of fashion even on most country records. We cut the song in two sessions. It was the first session at the new studio that would later host everyone from Paul Shaffer, bandleader of *Late Night with David Letterman*, the Jets, Greg Brown, and local headbangers

Slave Raider. It was a great place to record. My friend ECM recording artist Steve Tibbetts (whom I met when he was a record store clerk and over the years was generous with his advice) was kind enough to help hand-edit it using a razor blade on the two-inch master tape. The song swung heartedly.

The single received great reviews both in town and in a handful of music papers around the country. The *Boston Rock* compared it to Woody Guthrie, which thrilled me to no end. Somehow it ended up in the hands of Joe Brown and Frank Riley at Venture Booking in New York City, and the next thing I knew I had a gig booked at Folk City in the heart of Greenwich Village in New York the following June, hallowed ground for folksingers.

The gig was the third week of June. I had started working with Harvey Van Horn, a Duluth native, who was trying his best to manage me. We were going to be staying with Jerry Disrud, a Minnesota native who had been living in Rego Park, Queens, since 1973 and whom I had met through his childhood buddy Jeff Cierniak. Jerry picked us up at LaGuardia airport and we drove to his place to clean up. I always like to check out the room I am playing ahead of time when I can, and we were set to drive into the city at sundown.

New York City occupies no small place in the American psyche. It was the very top of the pyramid for anyone who ever dreamt large, a destination for millions of immigrants on their way to the new country, and once those immigrants spread around America, for their sons and daughters. I was no different and felt my heart beat faster and kept the window of the Jeep rolled down as we headed toward the city. I didn't want to miss a thing.

I have never been to the Grand Canyon, but I have never seen a sight as elegant as the lights of Manhattan, sparkling as far as the eye could see, as we entered the Queensboro Bridge. I felt like Dorothy and her charge when they finally spotted Oz. I knew this bridge. Simon and Garfunkel wrote a tune about it, the "59th Street Bridge Song," that I first heard when I was ten years old. I told Jerry, "Slow down, you're moving too fast." I was both seduced and hypnotized by the iconic view.

We went immediately to Greenwich Village. We passed by the Lone Star Cafe at Thirteenth Street and found a place to park just down from the arches at Washington Square Park. We roamed lazily into the park by the fountain and stopped to have a cigarette. I imagined all the folksingers who had gathered around it over the years and in my head heard a quiet cacophony of banjos, mandolins, guitars, and fiddles.

We ambled through the park on the way to Folk City on Third Street, just east of Sixth Avenue, the Avenue of the Americas. We walked past Ray's Pizza and Bleecker Bob's record store, and then there it was, with a white hard-plastic canopy over the entrance, and in big plastic red letters, FOLK CITY. It had a marquee enclosed in glass next to the window. Upcoming shows: Ferron, Suzanne Vega, Livingston Taylor, Melanie, and more. I would be on that stage the next night playing a triple bill with Peter Holsapple from the dB's and a new band from Austin, Texas, called the Wild Seeds. It was all a bit overwhelming—time for a stiff drink.

We headed one block east and took a right on MacDougal. It looked like every photo I had ever seen of the street but now in color, and at night, the time New York becomes New York: tourists speaking in different languages, college kids, couples in love walking hand in hand, tipsy businessmen now out of the bar and adjusting their ties for the cab ride home, some wiping lipstick off their collars, and people who actually lived there sitting on stoops, smoking cigarettes. I walked slowly so as not to miss anything, imagining the millions of footsteps that had gone before me. Walt Whitman, I knew you had been there, too.

We walked by the Café Wha?, Minetta Lane, the Minetta Tavern, and Cafe Reggio, where people were drinking coffee and playing chess, and then headed toward Bleecker Street. A half a block up, at 114 MacDougal Street was the Kettle of Fish, the kettle-shaped sign still hanging above the door, and the red neon BAR sign still in place and lit by the door. We walked in to a floor covered in sawdust, hand-drawn charcoal caricatures of regulars covering the walls. Kerouac is remembered in a Kodak moment next to that red neon sign and had gotten his ass kicked right outside this door. Just about every folk singer I had come to adore and worshipped as a kid played at the Gaslight underground, right next door, and came up here between sets and after the show to toast one another, and then probably talk behind each other's backs. We had a beer and a shot at the bar and pretended we were from another time.

The next day I got to Folk City in the afternoon for the sound check. The sound guy, who I remembered as the doorman the night before, was a musician himself. He was skinny, with a mop of black hair that reminded me of Maynard G. Krebs. His name was Pat DiNizio and in the months and years to come, he would soon be blasting over pop and college radio with his band the Smithereens.

That night the room was full, as was the bar. Jerry and Harvey sat at the bar and were soon joined by Kenny Jacob, who had taken the train from Boston for the show. The stage wasn't very large. The wall behind the stage had dark red-velvet wallpaper with a black pattern that wouldn't have been out of place in a New Orleans cathouse. There were Xeroxed photos of Tom Paxton and other folksingers who had graced that stage, and the Folk City sign in plastic letters behind it. The original Gerde's Folk City was three blocks east, but this incarnation of the place was brimming with its spirit. The significance of the place was not lost on me, and I approached the stage with reverence and confidence.

I played almost everything off of *Paper Tigers*, mostly with my eyes closed, and finished my forty-five-minute set to a very sweet round of applause. In spite of everything you have heard about New Yorkers, they are a very hospitable bunch and kinder than you have been led to believe. They also love creativity, art, and wild abandon, and they encourage and support it. I think I had a bit of all three that night, and they responded in kind. Robbie Woliver, proprietor of Folk City, bought me a beer after my set, and my friends bought me several more. I felt like a cat after the canary.

I woke up early the next day, and Harvey and I took the subway into Manhattan. After several hours of sightseeing around the city, we walked down to Bleecker Street and thought we'd grab a beer somewhere. We walked past a saloon called Mills Tavern, looked in the window, and thought we'd check it out. It was an old school saloon, an oak bar with a mirror behind it. An old black tomcat slept on the end of the bar barely noticing the customers who were starting to fill the bar at happy hour. The place reminded me of dozens of bars on the Iron Range. To top it off, they had Pabst Blue Ribbon on tap for just $2 a glass. I read years later that Dylan wrote several songs there, which made complete sense. Who says you can't go home again?

While there, I had booked myself another gig in August at the Speakeasy, a small club on MacDougal Street across from the Kettle of Fish. I came back to New York a couple of months later for that gig. I got to town a couple of days before it and met two friends of Jerry's who would become great new friends of mine. They were Jerry "Big Fish" Fishman and his son Scotty. They were native New Yorkers and welcomed me like a long-lost cousin. Big Fish had become very successful in the clothing business and some referred to him as the Frank Sinatra of the garment industry. He is mentioned in Pete Seeger's book *How Can I Keep from Singing,* and when Pete met him he was coming up in the world. Pete mentioned that he was unique as the only Jew he knew who sold Chinese food on a pushcart with wind chimes on the streets of Manhattan. I knew I was in good hands when he told me that he had also befriended another young midwesterner years earlier named Johnny Carson.

His son Scotty was my age and was starting to run his dad's business. Scotty and Disrud had become acquainted years earlier at Cody's Bar, a country western joint at Sixteenth Street and Sixth Avenue. They were trying to ride the mechanical bulls. Neither fell off, and this unlikely pair bonded over their mutual love of Johnny Cash. On the evening of my Speakeasy gig, Scotty was hosting a party and couldn't make it down. In the type of hospitality he afforded his friends and in his usual fashion, Scotty sent me down to the show in a white stretch limo. After splitting up the door proceeds from the gig, and after subtracting the people on the guest list, I made one dollar. The owner of the club, patrons, and other folksingers were more than a little amazed when I pocketed the money, hopped back into the limousine, and headed back up to Scotty's party. Only in New York, New York does this happen, a town so great they had to name it twice.

John Hammond Sr. couldn't make it to either the Folk City or Speakeasy gigs. I had been in touch with him, sending him demo tapes of new songs. We chatted several times on the phone, and that meant the world to me. We talked about the songs, how I could make them better, and at the end of the conversation, he always asked me about the weather in Minneapolis. During that time he came to Minneapolis for an event hosted by the Walker Art Center where he was interviewed by his old friend legendary jazz deejay Leigh Kamman. We had dinner at Harry and Lila Jacobs's, Kenny's mom and dad's house, and the next day I was honored to give Mr. Hammond a ride to the airport. He smiled widely when I arrived. He wasn't used to riding in a pickup truck.

I got to know Hammond's son, John Hammond Jr., in 1983, when Cats Under the Stars opened for him at William's Pub in Minneapolis. I still consider him to be the finest solo act in the business, somewhere between Robert Johnson and Elvis Presley. He is also one of the nicest men in the business. After Leo Kottke, John became the next model for my solo act, and I've always tried to summon the one-man-band power that Hammond Jr. has always displayed. I would always tell John Sr. how much I enjoyed John Jr.'s playing, and he'd beam with the smile of a very proud father.

The last time I met John Sr., his office was in the Black Rock Building that housed CBS Records in 1986. I considered him to be the greatest talent scout in the history of American music. He had done more to shape our musical landscape through his signings and championing of a variety of artists than any one man you could name. At the time, Mr. Hammond was not in a signing capacity anymore but was more of a figurehead. Columbia Records owed a great debt of gratitude to him for helping build the company into the powerhouse that they had become. A month after the meeting, I called Mr. Hammond and he told me that CBS passed on signing me. While I spent more than a few nights dreaming of being signed by the legendary John Hammond, some of them in a cold sweat, I wasn't completely crushed when I heard the news. I was playing regularly, had won a couple of Minnesota Music Awards, was enjoying life, and making some money as well. I still remain greatly honored by his interest, and it feels good to know that in his eyes I must have been doing something right.

I would always go and see John Hammond Jr. when he played in town, and I opened a few of his shows. He was playing at Wilebski's Blues Saloon in St. Paul the night his father died. I also saw him play at the Fine Line Music Cafe in Minneapolis the night his mother died. That night, when he got to the line in "Kind-Hearted Woman" by Robert Johnson, "I've got a kind-hearted woman, she'd do anything in the world for me," it cut to the bone. It was one of the most emotional musical moments I've ever witnessed. May both of his parents rest in peace.

PARTY TO A CRIME

My friend Billy Alcorn used to say, "Hang around the barbershop long enough and you are bound to get a clip." What he meant was, dabble in illegal substances long enough, and they will eventually bite you in the ass so hard you will be seven ways from Sunday before you realize what hit you. It all of course starts out innocently enough.

I remember when I first moved to town and was hustling like hell to find gigs. I would drop off cassette demos, some promo material, and wait for the phone to ring, and wait for the phone to ring, and wait for the phone to ring. Occasionally, I would stare at it and try to will it to ring. I did it so often, I am surprised it just did not levitate itself. Eventually, after the Cats dissolved, and *Paper Tigers* came out, and I had formed the Paul Metsa Group, the phone rang, and rang, and rang.

I never turned down a gig. Occasionally, this didn't work out as well as I would have liked. I got a call from the 7th Street Station in St. Paul. They told me they were starting to have folk music at their club and asked me to kick off the first weekend of music. What they didn't tell me is that it had been a strip club for several years before my debut there. I arrived and set up on a small stage with a dozen or so wooden chairs right in front of the stage. I should have known something was up when I went "backstage" to find these orders tacked to the wall: (1) Always carry your driver's license with you; (2) No changing in front of the customers; (3) No pissing in the garbage can. I started my set at 9 P.M. to a full house, the chairs in front of me now filled by men in their fifties and sixties, some who might have been wearing raincoats, socks and shoes beneath white fleshy and hairy calves. The club had started the music series but had forgotten to advertise or tell their regulars that the strippers would be no more. The crowd started to defect after my third song, gracing the exits into the jungles of East St. Paul through the dimly lit doorway. Sensing the impending doom, I hit the opening chords of "Leaving on a Jet Plane," and by the end of the song I had the room to myself. I played one more night there, to a bartender and a waitress, and that was the end of that.

Every so often after a gig, I would swing by SuperAmerica at Twenty-second and Lyndale to grab something to eat on my way home. I kept running into this guy, always wearing the same sport coat and sometimes the same shirt. He seemed to be always smiling, bantering with the clerks, and running his hand through a head of uncombed hair. I guessed he was an entertainer of sorts who kept the same hours as I did. We'd always nod to each other on the way out, and I had a feeling we would bump into each other somewhere, before closing time.

I got called to do a benefit for some union group, at the hall across from the Ford plant in St. Paul. There were several acts on the bill, and sure enough, there was my SuperAmerica buddy. He was a comedian and his name was Tom Arnold. The gig was in the early evening, and I had my regular Sunday night gig later at Bird's in Dinkytown. While we were hanging out in the basement dressing room we started to chat, and I asked him if he had any weed on him. I was frazzled from a week's worth of gigs and was looking for a little pick-me-up to get me through that gig and on to the next. He said, "Well no, but I have something better." He laid out two lines of cocaine, both of which could have reached across the river and back into Minneapolis. Sufficiently recharged, I played my three tunes and invited Tom to my gig after the benefit had ended. Tom showed up at Bird's around midnight, took the stage before my last set, and was hilarious. He took out one drunken yahoo who had started to heckle, slicing and dicing him into one hundred small and bleeding pieces. I had made a new friend, and that new friend invited me back to his place.

I had done cocaine several times before, but I was never a big fan of it or any kind of connoisseur. I had never purchased it and could take it or leave it. Tommy had a pocketful. We spent the rest of the night finishing the stash, which ran out somewhere around noon the next day. Though I felt like going home, it was my day off, and Arnold wanted to make one more run to his dealer's place on Lake Minnetonka. I should have said no. It was my first cocaine sunrise but would not be my last. I had a pocketful of cash, a truck back at my place not far down the street, and Tom was a pretty engaging conversationalist and very funny guy, and persuasive in a twisted Perry Mason sort of way. I had made two new friends that night. We decided to hitchhike the six blocks back to my apartment to get my ride, both of us in sport coats, and me with a guitar slung over my shoulder. The owner of the market next to the record store Oar Folkjokeopus was outside sweeping his sidewalk at noon when the sun shines the brightest. He looked at us and said, "You guys aren't fooling me, just a couple of entertainers trying to get home." We got back to my apartment and pickup truck, made the run, and called it quits right after midnight later that evening. I had dipped my toe into rejuvenating waters of cocaine, having no idea that but a few years later I would be pulled ten thousand leagues under the sea.

Wavy Gravy once called cocaine "thinking man's Dristan," and initially you would feel better looking, smarter, with the strength of Samson in fifteen-minute increments after a couple of snorts. Its effect was immediate: colors were more vivid, your cigarette tasted better, your drink richer and more robust, conversation more enlightened and more intense, and you felt like you had entered some sort of secret club, a circle of hipsters who knew more than anybody else. The reason people do drugs is that they are very enjoyable at first and make you feel good. Unfortunately for me, coke had a surprise behind Door Number Three. It turned out to be a handshake with the Devil, and only the Devil knew when he was ready to let go. But even the Devil, when you first meet him, seems like he is on your side. And at first, it never occurs to you that it is indeed illegal.

For all intents and purposes, cocaine was legal in Minneapolis in the mid-1980s. It was a kind of currency. It seemed everybody was doing it in my universe of musicians, bartenders, bouncers, and booking agents. I was making enough money to afford a $25 quarter-gram every now and then, though usually got turned on by the cocaine cabal, which included every strata of society that was involved in this sort of illicit pleasure. It starts with whoever has it and is willing to share or has a little to sell. Damn near every nightclub in town had its resident dealer. Not hired by the club, mind you, but the guy sitting at the end of the bar and, many times, not using it himself. Unbelievably, some of them stayed in business for years. Some got out while the getting was good, investing their money in legal enterprises. Some have coffee cans of cash stashed in the woods. The rest are retired, in prison, or dead.

Most of casual users were productive members of society: lawyers, doctors, insurance salespeople, the occasional off-duty cop, mechanics, secretaries, car salesmen, city workers, nightclub employees, and a percentage of musicians like me. Like illegal gambling or cockfighting, one connection leads to the next. You'd meet them sometimes in the bathroom stall at some club and then usually get invited to an after-party somewhere. Or you'd meet them at a party and later end up in the bathroom stall at some club, cutting lines off the toilet paper dispenser with them. Everybody gets at least two good years in the cocaine rodeo. The majority of us would eventually get kicked off the powder pony, hit the steel wall right around the corner, and end up face down bleeding on the pavement. It was all invisible and harmless at first, but when the darkness finally appeared and the karmic hammer was about to come down, I found myself moaning to the gods who had given me this illegal lift and felt Father Time calling in his marker. And that is what cocaine is really: you are buying time from the future to use in the moment. And when you get to that point in time that you have already used up, to paraphrase Gertrude Stein, "There is no there there."

In the meantime, life was great. Tom and I got to be great pals, partners in what seemed at the time to be victimless crime. The comedy scene in Minneapolis was one of the best in the country. Many of the local comics had house gigs at Scott Hanson's Comedy Gallery at Eleventh and LaSalle, including Lizz Winstead, Jeff Cesario, and Joel Hodgson, who all went on to national acclaim. The national headliners included Jay Leno, Jerry Seinfeld, and an up-and-coming housewife from Colorado named Roseanne Barr.

Musicians can be a tough crowd, always tougher on their fellow musicians than they are on themselves. Comics are worse, way worse. They, like musicians, are brimming with insecurity but need targets at which to aim their slings and arrows. If you don't believe that, go to a party with a roomful of comedians. It can be tremendously entertaining, as long as you aren't a fellow comedian. They are amazingly competitive, constantly working out their bits on each other. One would take a bathroom break or go to the kitchen to pour another drink, and those caustic comments would target them behind their back, and the others would gnaw at them, like rabid and hungry dogs going after the last strips of meat on a bloody carcass.

Tom, though very competitive, was a bit different. His act was called Tom Arnold and the Amazing Goldfish Revue. He owned, at the time, one sport coat, one mattress, and a plastic sandwich bag of swimming goldfish that he would take gig to gig. He would dress them up in miniature pope hats, ride them through flaming toothpicks, and the like, using them as props. He would use this bit as a fulcrum, to wisecrack about society and those in the audience. He could improvise like a son of a bitch, insulting anybody in the room, and would follow it up with his standard line, "I mean it in a good way." Tom has been slagged by some as a gold digger for his marriage to Roseanne Barr. That's bullshit. I was there the night they met after Roseanne watched his opening set for her. She was in hysterics. We hung out afterward at Tom's house, and I felt love was in the air. At the time, they were perfect for each other.

For me the best comedy comes straight from the heart and right off the top of the head. I grew up listening to the records of Redd Foxx, Woody Woodward, Lenny Bruce, Bob Newhart, and Lord Buckley. I loved the television appearances of Richard Pryor, Woody Allen, Mort Sahl, and Jonathan Winters, and the writings of everyone from Bennett Cerf to Paul Krassner. I've always loved to laugh, and the one defining trait of my entire wide circle of friends is their sense of humor. Like Lord Buckley said, "When a person is laughing, he's illuminated by the full beauty of a human being."

After meeting Tom, I got to meet a variety of the touring up-and-coming comedians he was opening for, or he'd take me along to see the show. We went to see Sam Kinison at his first show in town. We went back to Tom's place for a bash, and then to someone else's house where Tom, Sam, and I sat up most of the night with our medicine. In spite of all of its drawbacks, coke can be a great ally for conversation. We didn't do all that much, but how I enjoyed talking to Sam about music, comedy, life, and his time as a preacher. Unlike his stage persona, he was a very gentle man—he spoke in a soothing voice, well versed in a variety of topics—and he remains one of the most revered comedians of my generation. I will always treasure that night. Sam later became a huge star, hung out with rebel rock and rollers, and was unapologetic about his drug use and love of strippers. When I visited him backstage at his show at the Guthrie Theater a year later, Sam had on a silk bathrobe, a headscarf, and beside him a tank of oxygen. At one point he sneezed, and his road manager and fellow comedian Carl LeBove said, "There goes $3,500." Even Sam laughed at that one.

Cocaine makes strange bedfellows, not that you could ever sleep on the stuff. Keith Richards said, "The first time I had a line of coke, I felt like a new man, and the first thing the new man wanted was another line of cocaine." It actually starts easier than that. You do a line, or two, and go on to do whatever you were doing with a little more vigor. In my case, it was playing another show, writing some more tunes, or just hanging out with some new and intriguing friends. On my first few dates with the seductive white lady it seemed pretty innocuous, and something that was life enhancing and fun.

One of my musician buddies used to say jokingly, "I do another line of coke so I can write another song, so I can make more money, so I can buy another line of coke." This doesn't happen overnight. And it wasn't like I was doing it every night, and rarely during the day. You make a little more money, you buy a little more stuff, most of which you are sharing with your new friends. Slowly but surely you start to enter the second ring of Dante's Inferno. You meet a (literally) higher class of dealers, most of whom turn you on because you offer them a portal to a guest list, a great table at the club, or in kind introduce them to your other friends, in my case musicians, who would offer them perks as well. And before you know it, your old friends are dropping off like 55 mph speed limit signs in your rearview mirror, while your new friends say 70 mph, full speed ahead. I stepped on it, pedal to the metal.

Eventually, a couple of years into the white and dusty circus, I started ending up at parties with people I had nothing in common with, except that someone had powder in their pocket. I had gotten in way over my head without realizing it. To quote the old Doobie Brothers record, "What once were the vices now were the habits." At every party now where coke was the main attraction, there was the "room upstairs." This is where the very serious proposition of getting high went on. I had always stayed away from that one. Once, I ended up at a party in South Minneapolis at a house owned by serious punk rockers. I opened the door to the room upstairs to see legendary hard-core punk rocker GG Allin and another guy tying their arms off, ready to shoot up. I hightailed it the hell out of there and should have known then that this road I was on was not going to take me to the Promised Land. GG Allin died from a heroin overdose in 1993.

I knew better. And so did most of my oldest friends. Many of them tried to talk to me about it, but I thought I was just fine. I had the world on a string. My girlfriend knew as well, and like many who have friends, family, or loved ones in over their heads with drugs and/or alcohol, she felt helpless. For some reason, I felt like I was the bastard child of Pete Seeger and Keith Richard, and proud of it in a way I still don't completely understand. Like a dog that could lick its balls, I did it because I could. It came with its minor victories: ecstatic gigs where I completely jumped the joint, some good songs I wrote under its influence, and a few lifelong friends who made it through this hell ring of fire. Those times, which tattooed our tattered hides, are far enough in the rearview mirror now. They've made me more thankful for a normal lifestyle that I now share with straighter friends and family who enjoyed that lifestyle all along. I hope it will all be a cautionary tale to my nephews and nieces.

The parties got more raucous and darker. I was spending more nights over at Tony the Hat's, in the basement of his party house in South Minneapolis that he shared with his sister, who lived upstairs. I would occasionally rehearse there as well. They dealt blow, with a cookie jar of powder upstairs, and Tony sold it a gram or two at a time. He was a hockey player, a northern kind of cat from a northern town. He broke his leg in a bar fight the summer he was going to be drafted to the NHL, forever ruining his chances of playing professionally. That may have put him on this path. Tony had a lurid magic that intrigued me. He had great taste in music. He was tougher than hell, with a pretty good sense of humor, and he had cocaine cleaner and stronger than any I'd ever had. We connected on several levels, and I can't say it was all bad. I wrote dozens of tunes over there when I should have been home but wasn't. Yet I had no idea at the time that my career was slowly crumbling, longtime band members leaving, and my audience dwindling. The relationship with my girlfriend, the love of my life, and most of the other things I believed in, was disappearing, one line at a time.

There were glimpses that I was in over my head. My brother, wife, and family had invited me to their home in Rochester, Minnesota, along with my mom and dad, for Thanksgiving. I called them Thanksgiving morning, lied, and told them I was having problems with my car. I was up for a day or two and had no physical or psychic strength to make it down for dinner. I pulled it together and left the next morning. I got to the house and noticed two pillows by the doorway in the entrance. When I asked why they were there, my brother's wife, Dianne, told me that Jake, one of my four nephews and eight years old at the time, had stayed up waiting for Uncle Paul and fell asleep by the door. It broke my heart into a thousand pieces, and I should have known then it was time to straighten up and fly right. If only it had been that easy.

I never felt I was addicted. I just had tremendous access to cocaine, and because I rarely turned it down, it surrounded me like an ever-tightening straitjacket, one party at a time. To this day, there are gaps in this time frame I can't account for. I was losing my sense of reason and self-respect, but also, most important, my God-given intuition—the warning light in my soul that would flash red in times of impending danger. I was floating on this powder cloud and thought that my songs, guitar playing, and bandleading would balance out my late-night dance with the Devil, and everything would be okay. Good God Almighty was I wrong.

ROBOTS ON DEATH ROW

I took a month off of doing cocaine and was doing whatever gigs were left. In a moment of boredom I called Tony the Hat and said I'd stop by. It was a mild evening, but I picked up a quarter-gram for the hell of it, stuck it into my jeans pocket, and after a couple of whiskey Cokes went to bed in their upstairs bedroom. That night, a mule from Milwaukee came in and picked up a couple of ounces from Tony's sister. All I knew is that he used to work for the Beach Boys, taped the blow to his chest, and drove off. It was late. I stripped naked, as it was a hot July night, and went to bed on the couch in the ground-floor bedroom.

I heard the commotion in the kitchen immediately. "Get the hell out of my kitchen!" Then I saw the flashlights beneath the door of the room where I was sleeping. I opened my eyes to see two uniformed cops, one man, one woman, left hands on flashlights, right hands on their guns. They ordered me onto the floor, face first. I knew immediately what was happening: this was a major bust. I laid down, bare ass toward the sky, and my face smothered in multicolored shag carpeting. They cuffed me in tight white plastic handcuffs, and I was barely able to breathe. They left me there for at least an hour, while they perused the rest of the house, arresting the lady of the house, her brother, and her boyfriend. I knew we were fucked.

There were eight to ten cops in all. They had been keeping an eye on the place for several months, and though I was doing straight time on my own, I just happened to stop by the night before. Karma had caught up with me. After about an hour, after they had handcuffed and sent the brother and boyfriend downtown in squad cars, they let me get up, naked and cuffed, and now standing at the top of the stairs leading to the basement. They asked me where my clothes were and, knowing I had a quarter-gram in the pocket of my own pants, I pointed to a pair of swimming trunks and a Golden Gophers sweatshirt next to it. One cop dressed me in those, and they led me to the living room. The lady of the house and I sat there, both cuffed, while the head of the squad asked us where the rest of the cocaine was hidden. Though not in uniform, his gun was strapped across his chest and a large flashlight in his hand. He explained that the more we told him now, the easier it would be on the both of us. I kept my mouth shut. These guys were out of the Wild West, and I realized if you are cuffed, and they aren't, they have the advantage. After an hour or so on the couch, the doorbell rang, and it was WCCO television on the front porch. Now I knew why guys who get busted walk out of the front door with windbreakers over their heads. Fortunately, the cameras left before we were led to the back door to the squad that took us downtown.

We arrived at police headquarters and were driven down the eastern entrance to the basement. I had walked by here a dozen times but had no idea where it led. They split us up. I was led to a holding cell. They unhooked the cuffs right before they put me in. I now found myself in a holding cell the size of two Volkswagen vans. There were six to eight guys who had been recently arrested, half black and half white. I mentioned out loud how tight the cuffs were, looking for sympathy but finding none. Most of these guys had been there before. I was there for several hours and saw one Native American guy getting dragged past the door, screaming for mercy, while it looked like he was getting a righteous ass kicking by the cops taking him to a room downstairs. Maybe they had their reasons. This was where all the time in the future I had used ahead of time ended. I had several hours to ponder how the hell I got here and how I was going to get out, now languishing in the last ring of Dante's Inferno surrounded by other inmates with lifeless eyes and tattoos that looked like they were made with jackknives and bottle tops. I was on my own, lonesome, and a long way from home.

They give you one phone call. Of course, I had to call my father and tell him exactly what happened. He taught me to always tell the truth, and I knew this truth was going to be the hardest thing I would ever have to tell him. He picked up immediately with the good cheer I could always count on when calling home. He and my mother were having dinner. I let him know what had happened, as I held back tears of fear and disgust at myself. He told me three things: your mother and I will be there tomorrow, I love you, and this is the last call you will ever be able to make to me from jail. He put my mother on, and she told me she loved me, and then my time was up. I hung up the phone and was led back to the cell, silent tears falling like black rain.

Later that evening, I was brought to the sergeant at arms, where you traded in your street clothes, your watch, money, and anything else for your prison pajamas and slippers. The cop knew me and asked, "Metsa, what the hell are you doing here?" I could only answer, "Officer, wrong place at the wrong time." He shook his head, gave me my thin blue prison wear, took my wallet and belongings, and put them in a plastic bag. Hopefully, I'd be able to get them back in my lifetime.

Next up was the sheriff's deputy who would lead us to our cells. He couldn't have been older than thirty, and his uniform fit him and gave him the authority of the man in charge. They had rounded up a dozen of us and led us two by two to the jail cell. I stood next to a black guy named Hollywood who, though I didn't know it at the time, had a rock of crack cocaine between his teeth. It wasn't his first time in lockup. He started to sing, right around the corner from the cell, and without looking back, the young sheriff said, "Metsa, what is he trying to do, audition for your band?" Christ, man, I wish I knew.

When those cold iron cell doors behind me closed in the holding cell, a sound I remember to this day, it sounded like the last ring of liberty's bell, all hopes beyond this be damned. We entered a larger room, holding about a dozen of us. We each had our own cot, a communal shower, and at 7 P.M., the jailer arrived with stale ham sandwiches on white bread. I wasn't really hungry but managed to wash it down with water from the drinking fountain.

My dad had called a cousin of ours who was a detective at the Brooklyn Park police department. I was able to meet with him for ten minutes or so and tried to explain the situation. He had checked with the front desk and let me know I was going to be charged with possession with the intent to distribute and, worst-case scenario, could be looking at a couple of years in the big house. It turned out that the cops had seen my van enough times to consider me part of the operation. The nightmare had only just begun.

My folks came down the next day. There are times when you are with your parents that you still feel like you are a teenager. This was one of them, though now I was thirty-four years old and wearing jail pajamas. I hugged them both and did not want to let my mother go. My cousin had let my folks know what was up and what needed to be done. They had brought bail money, and I was released that afternoon. We went back to my apartment. I took a shower after two days without one, but I could not wash away the shame. We went to Market Barbeque down the street, and my appetite returned. I ate everything on my plate, as well as what my mom and dad offered me off of theirs.

My dad, God bless him, did not read me the riot act but instead asked me matter-of-factly what I thought needed to be done. I explained my fall from grace, leaving out the darker and dirtier details, which he did not need to hear. I told him what I really needed was a break from the clubs and the characters who'd provided the felonious temptations that led me astray and finally broke my back. The plan was for me to move out of the apartment I had been in for a decade, move back up north, and regroup. I was fine with that, and a summer at the cabin sounded almost ambrosial. I found someone to move into the apartment, which meant I didn't have to move my twenty-five crates of record boxes as she enjoyed listening to them. I'd get them later. I had a couple of buddies come over to help me pack my van (I was amazed at how much stuff I had accumulated and somehow managed to fit into that studio apartment). I had a lawyer friend of mine offer to keep an eye on the case, and with that I hit Highway 35, headed due north, kept one hand on the wheel, the other hand with fingers crossed, hoping that somehow this was all going to work out.

I got to the cabin in the early evening as the sun was setting on Wake-Em-Up Bay. The sauna had been lit, the loons were out, and the checkered half-moon that rose to the east over the almost-crimson waters was the prettiest moon I had ever seen. I went to bed early and got the best sleep I had had in days. I was almost ready to dream again.

I spent the next day unpacking the van: guitars, clothes, paperwork, and a couple dozen of my favorite cassette tapes. It was the end of July and I was looking toward August, a month of rest and relaxation. That was cut short when my father arrived that evening and told me he had gotten me a job starting at 6 A.M. the next morning. Good-bye guitar town, bricklayer's assistant here I come.

I hadn't worked construction in more than twelve years, and the job was right in Cook, Minnesota, twelve miles from the cabin. They were building an addition to the Cook High School, where my brother is now principal. My job was to take care of, or tend, four bricklayers. This entailed making sure they had all the brick and block they needed, as well as wheeling dozens of wheelbarrows of wet cement to them, all the while ducking under the red scaffolding that surrounded the work area. These were all union bricklayers who worked at lightning speed. It was exhausting work, and I also had to endure taunts from a couple of the newer bricklayers, who were probably hungover and loved giving the new tender shit when their supplies didn't arrive at the exact moment they were expecting them. I got back to the cabin after the first day on the job and fell asleep in my work clothes. I slept on my back, with my arms crossed. I woke up at 5 A.M. and could not pull my arms apart, my muscles frozen in place. After about five minutes, I was able to stretch and extend them, the blood slowly running back into each arm. It took another five to shake out the muscle cramps. Karma can be a real bitch.

After several days I started to get the hang of the job, my body slowly getting back into shape. I became good buddies with a couple of the older bricklayers, and then the two younger ones, and actually started to look forward to going to work. I was making a little more than $5 an hour, but at least I was not handing it over to the street dealers selling cheap cocaine cut with baby laxative after my shift was done. I was sleeping like a baby, eating well, taking a daily sauna, and was enjoying time with mom and dad, my brother, his lovely wife, and their four young boys who started to see the Uncle Paul they remembered. I was starting to remember who the hell I was and where I came from. Things were definitely on the upswing.

The summer was coming to an end, as was the job. I had a difficult decision to make. Was I able to move back to the Twin Cities and jumpstart my first comeback and not yield to the nightly allure of cocaine available by way of creatures of the night that still shadowed the saloons like human lamprey? In retrospect, making a living playing the guitar in nightclubs didn't look quite as bad as I thought when I left Minneapolis six weeks earlier. Winter was also right around the corner, and I had worked construction while the snow flies, ice covers the highway, and all my favorite birds had flown south. My mind was clearer, I was in great shape, and I was ready. All I had left to do was tell Dad about my decision.

My father told me when I was young and wanted to become a musician that the profession was rife with those with a predilection for drugs and alcohol. He called it a "great avocation but not a good vocation." While I had had a good career, putting out records, winning awards, and traveling the country, my latest series of escapades more than reinforced his perception of the business. In retrospect, he certainly wasn't wrong. Yet I was a professional musician and had the strength, the *sisu*, to overcome these latest roadblocks, and there wasn't really anything else I wanted—or, really, was trained—to do.

It was the beginning of September, the time of year for me that represents the start of the new musical season. Colleges are back in session, people are back from their cabins, and most people are ready to shake it, not break it, in the nightclubs. I was going to meet my dad at their house in Virginia and have lunch. He arrived with a bag with a couple of hamburgers and French fries. He is always impeccably dressed: snazzy sport coat, Windsor-knotted tie, light blue shirt, pressed slacks, shined slip-on black dress shoes, black mason ring on right hand with diamond, old classic wristwatch, gold wrist chain, lapel pin, and a full head of wavy brown hair combed a bit like Elvis, with just enough hair gel to keep it intact. He is business, and he means business.

We put the hamburgers and French fries on a plate, and I could tell he was not going to eat any of his. Long story short, he was telling me it was time to get out of the music business and get a real job. We had gone through this ten years before, and then as now I held my ground. While taking over my dad's insurance and real estate business, which came with two thousand clients in a town of ten thousand, would have been a bit of a cakewalk, I always thought that I wanted to make my own way in life, and music had always been my first and forever love. I recalled that the first time I told him I wanted to become a professional musician, against his wishes, was the day I became a man. I thanked him for everything he had done for me, including getting me out of the slammer and setting me up with work, and he realized I was as stubborn as he was. He hugged me, told me he loved me, gave me $20 for gas, and I hit the road back to Tinytown.

LIVING IN A HOUSE OF CARDS

I met my girlfriend in 1984 at the Union Bar. I was standing by the ticket taker on a break when she came up wearing a gorgeous red wool jacket and her brown hair cut in an angle right above her shoulders. She looked absolutely beautiful. She asked, "When are you going to take me out?" She wasn't being forward and seemed genuinely interested in me. She told me she worked at a Baskin-Robbins ice cream shop in Uptown, and we exchanged numbers. I stopped by the next day for a cone, and she looked even more adorable in her pink ice-cream-lady outfit. We went out that weekend.

I found out she was a ballet dancer, her dad a printer, her mom a housewife, and she had two brothers and a sister. She lived in Nordeast Minneapolis, the Twin Cities' version of the Iron Range. I fell in love with her almost immediately. I went to see her dance in the *Nutcracker Suite* at Northrop Auditorium during the holidays, and when she pirouetted across the stage, I fell in love with her again. She was absolutely divine, brilliant, shy, and had a wicked sense of humor. Though seven years younger than I, she was the kind of woman I used to dream about. In short, my kind of gal.

When I moved back to Minneapolis, I was staying on friends' couches and, without a lot of money in my pocket, was looking for a place to live. My girlfriend talked to her parents, and they were kind enough to offer a bed in their basement. My pockets weren't loaded with pride either, at that point, and I graciously accepted their offer. I stashed my belongings around town and moved in. I started to pick up some gigs and would usually try to sneak in quietly after work, trying like hell not to wake up their two Dalmatians, though not always successful at that. It was a welcome landing pad. I figured I could make enough money to find my own place in a month or two and tried not to disturb their home life too terribly.

In the meantime, I still had the possession and distribution charge hanging over my head. I always thought I would have made a pretty good lawyer, and I had at least a half-dozen friends who were. My good friend Mary was an outstanding attorney and offered to help me out. After explaining to the prosecutor that my van was at Tony the Hat's house because I occasionally rehearsed there and had left some of my equipment, the charges were dropped to "being in a disorderly house." This was an old law, put on the books back in the day to nab guys who were spending time in a gambling house, buying prohibition liquor, or frequenting working women. She got that charge dropped as well; for that I will remain eternally grateful. I got lucky.

While that major headache disappeared, my van was on its last wheels. I eventually had to junk it and was getting to and from gigs with my band members. It wasn't the end of the world, and after what I'd been through, it seemed like the proverbial fly on the elephant's ass: just another roadblock to my first comeback. I took it in stride.

One morning I got a call from the Internal Revenue Service. They had tracked me down through one of the clubs I was playing. I was not yet fully awake and thought perhaps I was dreaming. I wasn't. The monotone voice on the other end said, "We have gone through your tax returns for 1985 and 1986, have audited the clubs you played, and believe you have underreported your income by $100,000." I almost passed out on the spot.

Fortunately, the University of Minnesota Tax Law Clinic had a program for poor souls like me who were unprepared for an audit if a student could learn something from the case. I called the professor in charge of the project, Katherine Sedo, and she invited me in. I grabbed what papers I had at the time and met her and a student named Dennis Pelowski who was going to take my case—I was a musician without a clue and with the bookkeeping skills of a drunken librarian. We had no idea at the time that this audit would take more than two years before resolution.

A few days after I received the call from my friends at the IRS, I had bumped into a friend of mine named Tommy Rye at a gig. Tommy was a bright-eyed, bushy-tailed kid from Glenwood, Minnesota, who started coming to shows at a place called Birds in Stadium Village, right off the U of M campus, where he was a freshman. He went on to work with the Rolling Stones and Bruce Springsteen and is now working with U2. He was living in a carriage house behind an old spooky mansion at 1818 LaSalle South, in the Loring Park neighborhood and said there was a one-bedroom apartment available in the main building.

Loring Park was named after Charles Loring, a state Supreme Court justice and the father of the Minneapolis Park System. A statue of Norwegian violinist Ole Bull greets visitors at the northeast entrance of the thirty-two-acre park, a tribute to a man considered to be one of the first international music superstars. Ole had the speed and agility of Niccolò Paganini, was a friend of Franz Liszt, and a mentor to Edvard Grieg. He was also a hero to Norwegian immigrants and played Minneapolis several times in the mid-1800s. When Ole died, he was escorted home to Norway by twelve steamships.

The mansion was built by Sumner McKnight, a lumber and real estate mogul in Minneapolis in the early 1900s who made his fortune harvesting the white pines from northern Minnesota. McKnight sold the house to the Newell family, who went on to create the SuperValu grocery store chain. It was built in a Romanesque design featuring Lake Superior sandstone, with woodwork of oak and sycamore carved in Victorian style. The ceilings boasted angel designs, inspired perhaps by Michelangelo, though not as ornate, and painted by a lesser artist on a shorter ladder. At the time it was built its perch on a slight hill overlooked the farms that surrounded it. It was on the cusp of downtown Minneapolis and stands as a remnant from the time when the Mill City was the world leader in flour production and lumber milling.

My apartment was on the third floor in what was once the ballroom. It had been divided in two, with a bedroom on the south side and the kitchen and bathroom to the north. Perfect, really. One of the Newell family's wives had added a skylight in the high ceiling in the 1950s for an art studio, and light poured into the kitchen.

I moved in, bag by bag and box by box, huffing and puffing up all three flights of stairs that wound through the mansion. I made a trip up north and retrieved my grandfather's old metal bed frame, the one that he and I slept in when I was a kid at the cabin. That felt good. I also hauled down my twenty-five crates of LPs that my best friend Kelly had taken care of while I was in transition. His wife once threatened to divorce him over this, as they took up as much room in their house as the rest of their furniture. Like the great friend that he is, he held fast, and they remain married to this day.

My landlady was named Babe. She was in her mid-eighties when I moved in, stood just under five feet tall, with thick glasses and hair in a bun. Babe lived on the first floor. Her favorite entertainer was Danny Kaye. Babe's brother Horace, when he was dying, told her, "Take care of the house." And she did. Her kitchen had twenty-foot-high ceilings and her bed was in the corner, near a table that always had a banana and box of oatmeal on it, ready for breakfast. When I would come in late at night after gigs I could hear the music of her brother Horace playing the old pump organ (which was still in the living room), homemade performances recorded on a reel-to-reel tape machine. The music seeped through the sycamore woodwork and under the huge oak doors and filled the entryway with a fluttering, wavy, almost subterranean sound. The room at the mansion came with a sound track, all for $330 a month, including utilities.

I was happy to be back in my old neighborhood. My old apartment on Ridgewood was a couple of blocks away, and Franklin Avenue but a block and half away. I was within six blocks of the Guthrie Theater, and while I had already done shows there opening for Ry Cooder with Cats Under the Stars, then JJ Cale, Leon Russell with Edgar Winter, and the Neville Brothers, in the next couple of years I would also get to open for Lyle Lovett and Roseanne Cash, walking to the gig with guitar slung over my back. I started doing mostly solo shows around town, with occasional band gigs with a collection of different players.

I met a guy named Max Kittel who offered to manage me. Max put me into the studio with T Lavitz producing. T was the keyboard player for the Dixie Dregs, a jazz-rock fusion band from the South. Lavitz was my age, a monster keyboard player, and a great producer. We went into Creation Studios and cut six songs. One was a new tune called "Franklin Avenue," an ode to my old/new neighborhood, with the chorus, "I believe in loud guitars and everything will come true, and I had all these dreams first on Franklin Avenue." We also reworked my song "Slow Justice" with a new arrangement, and it ended up on *Legacy II,* a Windham Hill–High Street compilation record that featured Patty Larkin, Greg Brown, Cheryl Wheeler, and others.

Meanwhile, back at tension camp, Dennis and I were entering our second year of the tax audit. The agent assigned to the case was a rookie who wore a pocket protector and wing tips with white socks. We should have known this was going to be a tough slog when the very first question he asked was, "What is a gig?" Fortunately, I had paid most of the musicians and sound and light guys out of a business checkbook that included a few thousand cashed checks and had kept track of what cash I had paid. Unfortunately, I had to go back to each individual and have them sign an affidavit stating they had received the money. Had I sent them the 1099 forms as independent contractors, it would have prevented this. I didn't, though I do now. Some did it willingly, some were really pissed off, and two didn't sign at all. Some lessons are learned the hard way.

Two and a half years later the IRS still wanted to nail me with a tax bill for several thousand dollars that included penalties and levies. The professor helped me fight for every last dime I had claimed in deductions. During the last meeting with the IRS, one of their top dogs said, "Metsa, you are a folk rocker. How can you claim $900 in clothing expenses? Don't you guys just wear T-shirts and blue jeans?" I had brought to the meeting a half-dozen suits I had purchased at vintage clothing stores to wear at my gigs, including a totally wacky bright-orange ensemble purchased from Lucy in the Sky with Diamonds, a store in Austin, Texas. I shut the door (the clothes were hanging behind it), which revealed the orange suit, nearly blinding this most civil of civil servants on the spot. I got the deduction. He made a few calculations and concluded, "You owe us $270 from 1985, and we owe you $113 from 1986." Two and a half years and hundreds of hours later I wrote the IRS a check for $157 and went on my way. I was thankful for Dennis Pelowski, Professor Sedo, and the University of Minnesota Tax Law Clinic. Along with learning how to better run that part of my business, Dennis and I developed a lasting friendship and have been to gigs all over the country together, and we always have that story to tell when we meet a stranger at a bar who wants to know how we met.

Terry Katzman was one of the unsung heroes of the Minneapolis rock scene. He was one of the first supporters of and later managed Hüsker Dü, and he ran a record store called the Garage D'Or at Twenty-sixth and Nicollet. Unlike most record store employees of that time, he had absolutely no attitude. He talked fast, in a staccato rhythm that suggested he was always excited about the music he was talking about, and was a wealth of knowledge. Bob Mould, Hüsker Dü's major domo, David Savoy, the Hüskers' next manager, and Terry were always very welcoming and kind to me. They understood that I, like them, was a DIY guy, and that we shared that bond. Even when Hüsker Dü was, along with the Replacements, the premiere indie rock band in the land, Bob would always take time and interest in what I was doing and gave me advice like a big brother, even though he was younger than I was.

Back in the mid-1980s, fans were either in the Hüsker Dü camp or the Replacements camp. I had seen a couple of Replacements shows and always seemed to walk in when they were falling into a drunken and hammered puddle of flesh and feedback. I loved their records, though, and Paul Westerberg is one of the greatest rock and roll singers and songwriters of all time. The Hüskers were always four to the floor, and Mould played and sung like a man possessed, a finely tuned thrash rock silver machine.

The one thing I never understood about punk rock, or the rock insiders, was the elitist attitudes they held toward each other, or especially toward bands that played other styles of music. Because my band Cats Under the Stars was considered a jam band, before there was such a term, and therefore had some sort of connection to the Grateful Dead, I was always suspect. My buddy Monty Wilkes, who decided to become a soundman at a Grateful Dead show in Madison, Wisconsin, in 1973 at the ripe old age of twelve, told me, "I was a punk rocker. I was supposed to hate all hippies." Monty mixed my very first show under my own name at the NorShor Theatre in Duluth, in October 1984, when I opened for Taj Mahal. He went on to become the sound guy for the Replacements, the Pixies, and other punk bands and also spent six years working as front-of-house guy for Britney Spears. He also road-managed Nirvana and recently got off tour with the Scissor Sisters.

I always adhered to the "Spider" John Koerner philosophy, whose one record simply states, "Music is just a bunch of notes." Interestingly enough, many of the punk rockers who saluted the Clash, the Sex Pistols, and the Ramones have now discovered folk, blues, and country at middle age. That backbeat is not so bad after all. An article in the *Village Voice* a few years back by a writer who had returned from a CBGBs reunion of bands in the East Village said, "The show was great, and it was the first time I have seen a Mohawk with a bald spot."

Terry Katzman suggested to me that I should put out a compilation record with my first album, two singles, unreleased tracks, and some live stuff. It was a great idea. I gathered fourteen songs in all, put together with a great new band featuring Jimmy Anton, Emmanuel Kirakou, Jesse Wheeler, and my old buddy Al Oikari. The title of the CD originated on a return trip from a Dylan show in Davenport, Iowa, in 1990, when I passed by an old fifties-style motel with a bright aqua neon sign that said Radio Motel. I booked the CD release party for Halloween night at

Bunker's Bar in downtown Minneapolis, the day before my thirty-sixth birthday.

The morning of the show I woke up early and looked out the window at 1313 Mockingbird Lane, which is what I called my pad at 1818 LaSalle, an homage to the Munsters' TV mansion address. It was starting to snow, nothing new for that time of year. I went back to bed, woke up, more snow. As the day wore on, it was starting to ominously pile up. I left early for the gig to avoid having to call in a sled and a team of huskies to get across town. It turned out to be a record-breaking snowfall, one of the top five weather events in Minnesota history. There were six people in the club, two who had arrived by snowmobile. Earlier in the day I had looked forward to copies of the *Radio Motel* CD flying out the door. I ended up giving six away. I didn't want to break my fifteen-year string of consecutive gigs without a cancellation, so we played a couple of tunes, I bought the band, bartenders, and the chosen six a round of drinks, and we all headed home. Rather than dwell in self-pity, I grabbed a snow shovel and spent the next several hours digging stranded motorists out of the snowy streets and planned for a quiet birthday.

WHISTLING PAST THE GRAVEYARD

Bucky Baxter was one of the original members of Steve Earle's band, the Dukes, a white-lightning-fueled band of renegades that backed Earle for several years and threw down live performance like escaped prisoners, bloodhounds on their trail. Steve was one of the best of the new brand of songwriters out of Nashville in the mid-'80s, who stomped on the old Music City set of rules and ground them into dust with their boot heels. He was also a friend, disciple, and running buddy of Townes Van Zandt, one of America's greatest songwriters. Townes was man of God-given talent, Jesus in the Jerusalem that was Texas songwriting, honest as the day was long, cursed with some sort of death wish, perhaps depression mixed with a double shot of booze and drugs. He died at fifty-two, on New Year's Day, 1997, on the anniversary of the passing of his hero, Hank Williams.

I met Townes several times. The first time, in the basement of Folk City, I went down to say hello and he was sleeping, head resting on the wall, guitar in the case beside him in a low-lit, dark-green room. It reminded me of the Lincoln Memorial. I knew he was royalty and let him rest. My favorite time was when Guy Clark and Townes were in town the night before a show and came into the Five Corners where I was playing, on a drunken search to find "Spider" John Koerner. As luck would have it, Koerner was across the street bartending at Palmer's. When the bars shut down, we went to the Radisson Hotel downtown and had a guitar pull. In deference and respect, I would only play a song on every third pass of the guitar. Townes could be an ornery son of a gun when drunk, and he was that night. Between yelling "No cussing!" and playing those timeless songs—as deep as songs get—he and Guy were enamored with Spider's playing. Guy was fabulous as well. Townes took me to task for playing a new song I had written. For my last turn, I played my tune "Jack Ruby," and he said, "Now there's a damn good song!" An hour later, I left the room, the sun slowly rising on the streets of downtown Minneapolis, and people making their way to work.

I paused, smiled, and knew I had witnessed something very few people will ever be able to enjoy.

I had seen Steve Earle with the Dukes in '85 at First Avenue in Minneapolis. Steve looked strung out, his skin translucent, a silent yellow with a shade of faded and borrowed blue. Still, he sang like he had one leg chained to a devil's post and the other ready to kick you square in the balls. It was high-octane powerful medicine for this songwriter. The band sounded like a cross between Waylon Jennings and the Rolling Stones—loud, relentless, and poetic, my favorite kind of rock and roll.

In 1989, on the last night of Riverfest in St. Paul, an outdoor music festival on the shores of the Mississippi River, the Paul Metsa Group opened for the double header of Steve Earle and the Dukes and Bob Dylan. Though we were on the second stage, I could have hit the main stage with a slingshot. We ended at 6:30 P.M., Steve and the Dukes came on at 7 P.M., and Dylan at 9 P.M.

Steve and the Dukes played a great set. My buddy Billy Alcorn, a great songwriter and wonderful friend, knew a couple of guys in the Dukes, and we got backstage and he introduced me to Bucky. While Steve and the Dukes were on the road opening for Dylan, toward the end of his set Dylan would invite Bucky up to sit in with them on pedal steel guitar. Dylan offered him a seat in his band in 1992, where he stayed until 1999, playing steel and mandolin, singing harmony vocals, and recording with Dylan on *Unplugged* and *Time Out of Mind*. Some Dylan aficionados still consider his tenure in the band the high-water point for that Never Ending Tour.

While Bucky has always been reverent and tight-lipped about Dylan, there is one story that I feel I can share. Baxter was flown out to Los Angeles by Dylan's management to be considered for a chair in Bob's band. He arrived at the office in Beverly Hills at 10 A.M. He sat on one side of the desk, and Dylan and his manager on the other. I always imagined this as Shakespeare himself auditioning actors for *Hamlet*. Dylan was of course wearing shades. They made him an offer and Bucky said, "That's not a lot of money, Bob. I am already making that with Steve Earle." Dylan quickly replied, "Be a lotta money to somebody." Bucky took the gig.

Dylan was booked for a five-night stand at the Orpheum Theater, a theater he and his brother used to own, in Minneapolis, October 1992. Bucky got in the night before, grabbed a cab, and asked the cabbie where the best music in town was and told him to step on it. The cabbie brought him to my weekly stand at the Five Corners on the West Bank, where I was toward the end of a run that included 237 consecutive Tuesdays. Bucky remembered me. After the second set, before he had to leave, he approached me and we chatted. He offered to produce four songs of mine at his studio in Nashville, for the righteous price of $2,500, musicians included. We exchanged numbers, and he also put me on the guest list for the Dylan run.

The Dylan shows were of epic proportion. Each night included an opening act of Minneapolis's finest, including Willie Murphy, Ray and Glover, and the Jayhawks. He was about to enter a newfound path to glory, after four years or so in the wilderness, in the process rediscovering who he was. I remember one particular night he walked on stage looking like the fifty-some-year-old gentleman that he was. Walking off stage, after that incendiary show, he looked like he was twenty-one again, floating like a feather, stinging like a bee. He did a one-handed pass through that magnificent Jew-fro, with a stage-light halo bleeding through. The power of music and art, the rediscovered golden pathway of a blessed and dogged artist, transformative in a way beyond space and time. Back in his hometown and once again a hero.

Bucky's offer was an honor and very exciting as well. A chance to record with some world-class musicians, in Nashville, and do it right. All I had to do was come up with $2,500. The following Wednesday I was doing a gig at a place called the Buffalo Gap across the street from Nye's Polonaise Room. It was one of twelve bars at the west end of a new entertainment complex called Mississippi Live. I was getting paid $800 a night for a trio. The place was decorated like some Mexican whorehouse, with a small stage in the corner of the room.

Around this time, I happened to meet a guy named Paul Mandell. He had been coming to see me for years and on this night offered to buy me a screwdriver or two as I sat next to him at the bar. I have been lucky to have a steady audience for a long time, and while I always remember faces, I sometimes forget names or never get to know some of these folks personally. Not unlike anybody you might meet at a bar, after a couple of drinks we were like old lost cousins, bonding through the courage that a little alcohol gives to honest men. We shared stories, and he mentioned that he had just come into some money. So point-blank, I asked him if he ever thought about getting into the music business. Like my mother always told me, never be afraid to ask a question, as the only thing they can do is say no. He didn't. In fact, after I told him about Bucky's offer, he was genuinely excited to help—and just in time. The gods of music work in mysterious ways.

I called Bucky and told him I had secured financing. He called me later that evening, having scheduled four days at the studio he owned with Garry Tallent (Springsteen's bass player) for the third week of September. I was flying on a cloud and grateful for how quickly fate can turn on a dime. I never really have had any grand plan for my career, and most of the best stuff always just seems to happen, the winds of luck and circumstance blowing sometimes through doors you didn't even think existed.

I have scads of paper with song ideas written on them: envelopes, backs of letters, airplane sickness bags, hundreds of bar napkins with lines, words, images, and occasionally complete songs, some scrawled so illegibly even I can't read them. I still love writing on an old-school typewriter. I write letters to friends and poetry to real or imagined girlfriends, composing off the top of my head sometimes pages at a time. Inevitably, I will go back and find a great line or two that I can use later in a song.

This practice came in handy in 1991. I had gotten home from a walk around Lake of the Isles, the most beautiful lake in Minneapolis, almost a three-mile walk with dips and turns, a couple of old stone bridges, and a view of charming houses in the city. I had started walking around it when I first moved to town because it reminded me of home with the water, ducks, and geese. It was the perfect way to spend an hour writing songs or poems in my head, plotting my strategy to take over the world with my guitar, or just relaxing.

The phone rang and it was someone representing the thirty-fifth anniversary of Southdale, the first enclosed shopping center in America, in Edina, the richest suburb in the Twin Cities. They were doing a CD featuring local musicians and asked if I had any original songs about Christmas. Initially, I felt this was about as alluring as having my girlfriend sleep with my bass player and was just about to blow them off. For the hell of it, I asked them what the job paid, and they said $2,000. I answered them faster than you can say, "WTF?" and said, "I think I have something around here somewhere." They needed it by the end of tomorrow's workday and had a two-hour session already booked at a studio downtown the following afternoon. I told them to count on it, and I would see them at the session.

I went to my pile of mad-dashed napkins and envelopes stashed in my desk drawer and proceeded to look through this disheveled battalion of ideas and inspiration. Sure enough, midway through I found a bar napkin with the title "Christmas at Molly's" scrawled across it. Molly's Bar was a little beat-up hideaway on the northernmost end of Tower Avenue in Superior, Wisconsin, or Soup Town as we called it. Closing bar time was 2 A.M., an hour after Duluth's. So after a gig in Duluth, I'd usually go with other like-minded and thirsty folks across the John Blatnik Bridge and beat ass to Molly's Bar.

It was run by Molly herself, a grand old dame who bought it when she was thirty-three years old, the divorced mother of her only son, Oscar. She was now in her eighties and still worked the bar. She had seen it all and would dispense gypsy wisdom, with a wise twinkle in her eye, and let you buy her at least one shot of top-shelf brandy in return for the advice. The bar itself had an old pool table, out-of-the-way antique curios, and an old tin advertising sign for the Barnum and Bailey Circus from the late 1930s, which is exactly the decade you felt you were in when you entered those dark wooden doors. I would always invite my audience over to hang with me and would give a special shout out to Molly when I did interviews on KUMD, the local community radio station. Molly's had an interesting history. It was one of the first gay bars in the Twin Ports and had been since the 1940s. A retired sheriff, when writing a book about Superior for a small town press, said of the joint, "Molly's Bar was where sailors would go to eat, drink, and be Mary." Funny guy, that sheriff.

Anyway, I went to work on the tune and came up with a sweet set of chord changes in ¾, a great time signature to write a story song. The last phrase of the chorus came to me first: "Pass the malt and mistletoe, it's almost Christmas day." The idea for the song came to me quickly. It would be about a sailor, fresh off an iron ore freighter, who stumbling through town on Christmas Eve sees a light or star in the sky that leads him to Molly's tavern, his experiences there resembling the spirit of Christmas within a tap house. Twelve verses later, I had her. The sun was coming up, the hookers and dealers in the neighborhood had long gone home, and outside on LaSalle Avenue were the fresh faces of business men and women and students on their way to school. We cut it in two takes, and the engineer, Chuck Love, now an internationally renowned deejay, added a perfect overdubbed twelve-string part, and it remains one of my favorite original tunes. For years it could be found on the old Wurlitzer jukebox at Molly's. Molly was delighted, and I don't ever remember having to buy another drink there again, though I would always pay for a six-pack to go.

One night after a gig, I was home, had taken a couple of tokes to mellow down easy, and was working this little blues riff over and over on my guitar in front of a near-muted television replaying the nightly local news. The mayor of Bloomington was complaining about how his city's property tax was being raised for the grand temple of mindless consumerism, the Mall of America: "Everybody else gets the benefit, and we are left whistling past the graveyard." Whistling past the graveyard, DING! I had never heard that phrase before, but it fit exactly into the riff I was working on. A couple of minutes later I had the answer to that phrase, "When you are whistling past the graveyard . . . and the graveyard whistles back." A meditation on mortality. Less than an hour later I had six verses and never had to change a line. The best songs write themselves.

During my writing spree of the early '90s, I was ready to tackle my new tune "Jack Ruby." At around this time, I read a newspaper article that said Jack Ruby's brother was selling some of his brother's artifacts to settle a tax lien. Included in this tainted treasure trove were Ruby's pistol and his Cavanagh hat. Voilà, the hidden key! "Jack Ruby, Jack Ruby in a Cavanagh hat, whoever taught you to shoot a pistol like that? You walked in the basement and stood in the back, Jack Ruby, Jack Ruby in a Cavanagh hat." To paraphrase the Nashville line, "Don't bore us; get to the chorus." This tune would be my version of John Hardy, a story song about an American antihero. I got all my JFK books off the shelf, spread them around the living room, and spent the next couple of days telling Ruby's life story. After several rewrites I felt like I had captured the essence of the story. At the time, I had no idea that just a few months later I would get to debut "Jack Ruby" at Farm Aid V in Dallas, Texas, just five miles from Dealey Plaza, the site of the crime of the century.

I arrived in Nashville on September 21, 1992. Bucky picked me up at the airport, a small suitcase and guitar in tow. We went out for dinner and back to his place for an early night, the sessions starting at Moondog

Studio the next day at noon. After breakfast, I drove Bucky's car and followed behind him on his Harley to the studio, a converted garage in a quiet neighborhood. The engineer, Tim Coates, was there, and Bucky and I smoked a few heaters, waiting for the rhythm section to arrive.

First in was Garry Tallent, Bucky's partner in the studio. To my eyes and ears, Garry was as responsible as anyone for the steam-engine power behind Springsteen's E Street Band. Like most of the great musicians I had met thus far, he was a humble man, unassuming and a complete pro. George Marinelli, a remarkably versatile guitarist currently playing with Bruce Hornsby and the Range, showed up next with several guitars, both acoustic and electric, and was to provide many of the comic highlights that kept the sessions light, engaging, and merry. Last, the drummer showed and went immediately into an isolation booth to set up. It was actually happening, and my heart started to beat a little faster than normal.

It took about an hour to chart out the four tunes we were going to tackle in the coming days. I gave the guys my charts, and they translated them into the Nashville shorthand that is a second language to most top-shelf session cats. A little after 1 P.M., we were all set up. Everyone had a space throughout the studio that separated each of us, and I was placed in the largest room with my acoustic guitar, out of sight of the rest of the players. Before we started actually recording, I had to pause and reflect on my good fortune. Behind the wall in front of me were ace musicians from Dylan's band, Springsteen's band, and Hornsby's band. I said a little prayer of thanks to my mother and dad and told myself to just enjoy the ride. I had been in such a hurry over the years that I had missed priceless experiences in life, with family and in music, because I thought I had to be somewhere else for whatever reason. Now all that anxiety and expectation had disappeared, replaced by a feeling of complete calm. I knew the songs were good, ready, and waiting, and Bucky had my back as well. Gentlemen, start your engines.

Three hours later, we had four rhythm tracks completely finished. Welcome to the Nashville Express. We listened to the playbacks, and I walked to the grocery store feeling like Clyde Barrow after a successful bank job. We reconvened after dinner to start working on the solo and vocal tracks. Rhythm and arrangements are the bedrocks of getting great tracks, and we had those suckers nailed to the floor with railroad spikes.

Over the next few days, we put the fairy dust on the songs. Watching

Bucky and George cut their solos was as fun as making out with your first girlfriend. None of the songs was more than two takes, and any of their solo takes could have been used. For the most part, we used mostly first takes. That is how good these cats were. Bucky brought in the Britt Sisters to throw in a little harmony vocal sass, and a keyboard player, a first-rate session player as well.

A couple of mornings before the sessions I'd drive downtown and go to the Ryman Auditorium. They had not yet started to remodel the place, and the front door was open. Both times, I was in there by myself and was able to sit in the pews, walk both onstage and backstage, close my eyes, float back into time, and imagine the magic that radiated from here, the grand mother ship of American music. I'd say a silent prayer to the gods of music and head back to the studio.

By Saturday morning we were tying up loose ends, I was leaving, and I hadn't received the check from Paul Mandell in Minneapolis. Bucky knew I was good for it, but most musicians like to get paid immediately after the gig, almost before the paint dries. I called his roommate on Friday to find out that he had gone duck hunting in northern Minnesota. This was in the dinosaur days before cell phones, and I was at a loss as to how to track him down in a hunting blind. Fortunately, he was hunting on a lake in a small town with one liquor store. After a couple of calls, I found the number of the store, talked to the clerk, and described Paul. He knew exactly who I was talking about and said he usually comes in around 8 P.M. I left Bucky's number, and sure enough Paul called us that evening. He would wire the money on Monday morning, and Bucky and I went down to his local watering hole and celebrated an inspiring week of work.

I got back to Minneapolis and invited Paul over to hear the tracks. I told him Bucky offered me the same deal on four more songs, and what started out as a demo project was on its way to becoming a great album, Paul's pocketbook abiding. We listened to the songs a couple of times through, and we called Bucky later that evening and scheduled another four days of sessions a month later. That kind of generosity comes around about as often as true love, and when it does, it's almost as rewarding.

I got back down to Nashville in late October. We had the same players tuned up and ready to rock. There were a couple of tunes I thought could use a little different harmony vocal sound. I remembered that my old girlfriend Prudence and her boyfriend Gary Rue (also a singer) were now living in Nashville, running a bed and breakfast. Prudence and I had had a terrible breakup, and I hadn't spoken to her in almost a decade. Though she was surprised to hear from me, she and Gary came down and graced several tunes with their pristine pipes. It was great to see her again, she looked as beautiful as the day I met her, and they were both gracious and kind. I learned early on that the key to success is to surround yourself with musicians who are better than you are. These new tracks confirmed that and spoke for themselves.

Whistling Past the Graveyard came out a few months later on my own label, Raven Records. I had always joked that "I am the president of my own label, the only artist on the label, and I rejected my last record." Not this baby. While I was proud of my other records, this one was special. It was radio ready, featuring well-known players, and the tunes were some of the best I had ever written. I invited Bucky up to play the record release at the Cabooze Bar in Minneapolis. St. Paul Mayor Norm Coleman came down to introduce the show, and Bucky played his ass off. It was a dynamite way to end the year. New records always take on a life of their own, and at the time I had no idea this one would take me to Los Angeles, the City of Angels. California, here I come.

FERRIS WHEELS ON THE FARM

I have probably given away more records than I have sold: to the press, to bartenders to square up a tab, and to interesting people I'd meet in my travels. I would save what money I could from gigs for the recording projects and was always lucky enough to bump into friends with a little extra cash in their couch cushions to help move the projects along. When the musician is ready, the investor will appear.

I recorded my second single, "Ferris Wheels on the Farm," in 1986. It was my take on the disappearance of family farms. The chorus went, "And you know Grandpa used to have a nightmare, it was when the twister took the barn, some city slicker sellin' snake oil in the cornfield, tore down the windmill and put Ferris wheels on the farm." The artwork, done by John Hanson, a very respected graphic artist around town, featured a provocative silhouette of a farmhouse and Ferris wheel on the front cover.

The problem I'd run into was once the recording and pressings were done, I was usually out of money and energy to properly promote them. I'd do what I could, get a handful of reviews, and place the new stack of vinyl next to the old stacks of vinyl in my closet. If my place ever burned down, the closet area would resemble something like the La Brea Tar Pits in Los Angeles.

This record enabled me to do a headline CD release party at First Avenue, a place that remains one of the greatest rock clubs in the world. I had opened there for Richard Thompson, Joe Ely, Billy Bragg, Jane Siberry, and others, and had witnessed barn-burning shows by Link Wray, Black Uhuru, Iggy Pop, Metallica, and dozens more. First Avenue hired the opening acts, and I suggested the Kingpins, a new rock band in town, and the great Dave Ray. Both the club and I were honored to have Dave Ray on the show. Amazingly, it was the first time Dave played the club. He left right after his set, and Steve McClellan, the booking genius in charge of the room, tracked him down at his house gig at St. Anthony Main the next night, and personally brought over his cash to him. This was significant, as Steve worked eighteen hours day at the club and was rarely seen in public, but it showed Steve's respect for this hometown blues giant. It also gave Steve a chance to glimpse a bit of the world outside his cramped office, filled with posters, tickets, and work papers.

The single didn't make the Billboard Hot 100, which I didn't expect it to. Independent musicians put out records to get a little airplay, a few reviews, gigs, and build catalog. And most important, making records has given me a chance to capture myself in real time and make an artistic and sometimes political statement as well.

I love to read newspapers at breakfast. When I was at the Egg and I, I'd peruse the Minneapolis *Star Tribune,* St. Paul *Pioneer Press, City Pages,* and whatever else that had been left. Once there was a copy of *Midwest Singles* that featured lonely romantics of all types and stripes. In the back was a section that featured those in prison looking for love. I remember this one: "Enjoy crossword puzzles, black-and-white movies, crocheting . . . serving sixth year of a life sentence." Love like hope springs eternal, and like somebody once said, if love is blind, then why the hell is lingerie so popular? But I digress.

One morning I had read in *USA Today* that Roseanne Barr and her new husband, Tom Arnold, were going to be hosting Farm Aid V in Dallas, Texas, in March 1992. I thought I'd give my old buddy Tom a call and see if he might be interested in sending a copy of "Ferris Wheels on the Farm" to Farm Aid founder Willie Nelson for a chance to play on the show. He did just that, and two weeks later Tom's secretary called and had gotten us the gig. He also offered to fly me and my guitar player, Emmanuel Kiriakou, down to Texas and pay for our lodging as well. I didn't know exactly what to expect, but knew I would be playing in front of the largest crowd of my career. That's what friends are for.

We got to Dallas the afternoon before the big show. We were staying in the hotel that housed many of the musicians, and most of them checking in had cowboy hats and guitar cases. My buddy Tom Latimer had driven up from Austin and was coming to tag along, take photos, and enjoy this marvelous and mind-blowing couple of days. Emmanuel retired to his room, and Tom and I drove over to Texas Stadium, in Irving, to secure our credentials and check out the stadium with the hole in the ceiling, which many Texans thought was built so "God can watch his favorite team"—or maybe his favorite cheerleading squad.

We found the Farm Aid temporary offices in the bowels of the stadium. We got our passes and saw the lineup included cherished Lone Star acts Asleep at the Wheel, the Texas Tornadoes, Kinky Friedman, Double Trouble, to name a few, and other national acts like the Highwaymen,

Lorrie Morgan, Steve Earle, Johnny Paycheck, Joe Walsh, Lynyrd Skynyrd, Paul Simon, and the triumvirate of founders, Willie Nelson, John Mellencamp, and Neil Young. A lineup of distinguished and august luminaries, many of whom were my favorite musicians, and I was completely knocked out to be sharing the stage with them.

We walked out onto the empty field from the end zone where the stage was built. There was a band setting up. We walked past them, down the length of the field, back into the other end zone, and into the hallway where the Cowboys enter. As a kid your fantasy is to walk out of a hallway like this onto the field and hit the bases-loaded homer in the bottom of the ninth or kick the winning field goal from the forty-yard line with seconds left in the game. My fantasy was to walk onto that stage tomorrow, in a stadium full of people, and play two tunes, "Slow Justice" and "Ferris Wheels on the Farm," the song I was invited down to play.

Or was it? Texas Stadium was about five miles from Dealey Plaza. Might JFK's motorcade have driven the highway past this area on its way to the parade in downtown Dallas? What would happen if I replaced the second song with my new tune "Jack Ruby," which asked the questions: "Did the Warren Commission mean what they say, or did the Mob or oil money get in the way? Did the shadow of Cuba darken the day, in Dallas County, the land of LBJ?" I guess I'd have to sleep on that one. I was reminded of the old Bob Wills song "Big Balls in Cowtown."

When we got halfway back down the field toward the stage, we realized it was Paul Simon rehearsing with Willie Nelson's band, sans the Red-Headed Stranger. Tom, myself, and two security guards were their only audience. We stood on the fifty-yard line, listening to this sound check/rehearsal. Willie's band, most of them with him since the Alamo, were trying to get the groove to "The Boxer" with the lyrics "In a clearing stands a boxer, and a fighter by his trade." Simon was trying to fingerpick the tune and lead the band at the same time. Willie's band can follow Willie, and maybe only Willie, like bloodhounds on an escaped convict's trail. They were having a harder time with the folkie from Forest Hills, New York. After several unsuccessful attempts at the song, Simon unplugged his small Martin guitar, shook his head, and left the stage. Tom and I left the gridiron grinning and headed back to the hotel.

We had a Texas-style dinner of chicken fried steak, a side of okra, and several cold Shiner Bocks at a roadhouse at a strip mall and went back to the hotel bar. Inside, the place was jumping, lots of cowboy hats and boots. If you want to have a great party, invite a couple dozen or so musicians, their wives and girlfriends (I think one good old boy had both in tow), roadies, writers, and record company guys with expense accounts, add whiskey, and stir. It was a hoot. At about midnight a guy walked through the door, in a cowboy hat, colored glasses, a fine set of boots, and new blue jeans with the Nashville crease. It was Sir Douglas Sahm, the original cosmic cowboy, one of the true godfathers and gurus of the Texas music scene.

Doug was a true child prodigy. As a kid he opened for Hank Williams at the Skyline Club in Austin, Texas, at Hank's last show. He would die two weeks later. Rumor has it that Sahm was offered a job on the Grand Ole Opry, but his mother wanted him to finish junior high instead. He was instrumental in creating Austin, Texas, as we know it, and along with Willie created a bridge between the hippies and the rednecks, allowing the lion to lay down with the lamb. He helped put the electric Tex in Mex and was at Farm Aid V to play with his band, the Texas Tornadoes, featuring Augie Myers, Freddy Fender, and Flaco Jimenez.

He worked the bar like he owned it and went table to table shaking hands, as if he knew everyone in the place. He sidled up next to me as there was an open spot at the bar. I bought him a Chevas scotch on the rocks, a tall double, and introduced myself. He radiated goodwill and had an aura about him, or maybe it was the reflection underneath a bar neon light. He invited us to join him at his table. He'd tell a story or three, and the rounds came to the table as if on schedule between stories, bought by his fans, admirers, and disciples throughout the bar. By closing time, I had gotten a true tutorial in the history of Texas music, by a master of it and, between the Chevas and Shiner Bocks, felt duly christened.

I woke up with a slight hangover but felt my headache was a small price to pay to hang in that kind of company. I put on my green and tan cowboy boots (if you can't beat 'em, join 'em), a sport coat I had borrowed from Doug Nelson, one of the best-dressed musicians in Minneapolis, and a pair of matching sunglasses. Tom, Emmanuel, and I convened in the lobby, got in the car, and drove to the gig. We got to the stadium and with our parking pass parked next to several of the band buses. I got out of the car, in awe of the size of the stadium, and watched thousands of people march toward the ticket gate. Usually at gigs like these, I would be standing in line waiting to buy a ticket. Not today.

We entered the private entrance, walked down a couple of hallways, a block or so apiece, and checked in at the musicians' table. We got our

VIP passes and headed for the backstage area, and I pinched myself and waited to wake up from this dream. I came to quickly when I saw that we would be the fourth act up, after Double Trouble, Stevie Ray's old backup band. We would have time for two songs. Once I started to actually comprehend the magnitude of the event, I realized that it was no time to be timid. I mean, what would Woody Guthrie do? I decided that I'd do "Slow Justice" and debut my new twelve-verse saga about the JFK assassination called "Jack Ruby." Besides being shot myself, I really had nothing to lose. I remember the closing line I had received from a letter from Jimmy LaFave a couple of years before, the red-clay rambling son of Oklahoma, now living in Austin, Texas: "Throw caution to the wind." I was just about to.

While we were backstage we saw Neil Young. He was wearing a leather jacket with fringe just like you would expect him to wear. He was wheeling his severely handicapped son in a very touching way, nothing more than a loving dad taking care of his kid. It reminded me of two old friends, both band members, who also had disabled children and still lived on the Iron Range. I had a moment, while I was thinking of them, when dozens and dozens of gigs floated through my head—from Carol Flaim's thirteenth birthday party at the Gun Club in Virginia with my band the Positive Reaction when I was twelve, playing bass with Tony Perpich and the Perpatones in junior high, Damn Everything but the Circus's high school dances, and all those gigs with Cats Under the Stars. And now I was backstage with Neil Young, ready to play Texas Stadium, amid some of the greatest musicians in America, and for a damn good cause. This, my friends, is what it is all about.

We walked onstage after a brief introduction. The stagehands were seasoned pros and treated us no differently from any of the stars of the show. Any friend of Willie's is a friend of theirs. I plugged in my Takamine guitar, strummed a simple G chord, and was flabbergasted by what I heard. A hammer-of-the-gods sound, louder than I had ever been. While the sound of that first chord still resonated throughout the stadium, we kicked off "Slow Justice" and nailed it to the wall. While the applause rang from the more than twenty thousand people who were there, the Texas sun dazzling through the hole in the roof, I started the three-chord intro to "Jack Ruby," took a deep breath, and started: "Jack Ruby, Jack Ruby in a Cavanagh hat, who ever taught you to shoot a pistol like that?" All twelve verses, as loud as if the Blue Angels were flying overhead. While they liked the first tune better, I think most of those not applauding were still trying to figure out what this Yankee just sang about.

We went up to the greenroom where dozens of musicians were hanging out waiting to go on. I bumped into Steve Earle and Austin guitar god Charlie Sexton. Steve was looking a little rough, in dark shades and blue work shirt, tuning his mandolin, and Charlie looked like a movie star with wavy dark black hair, chiseled cheeks, tuning his guitar. Somebody had turned us on to a couple of drags of righteous gage, and we started to giggle when the entire Dallas Cowboy cheerleader squad came in, with pom-poms and followed by none other than the easiest rider of them all, Dennis Hopper, who was there to introduce a few of the acts during the televised portion of the show.

I wanted to tell Dennis about how my parents escorted my underage buddy and me to see *Easy Rider* at the Maco Theater in Virginia in 1969. Fortunately, we did not sit next to them but felt their discomfort rows away, especially during the scene where Peter Fonda and Hopper drop acid and go skinny-dipping with their girlfriends. The counterculture was arriving in the Queen City one movie and record at a time. Hopper was gracious and accepted my latest CD "Radio Motel," although he passed it on to one of his assistants before he left and probably never heard it. The den mother of the cheerleaders noticed Tom and me and asked if we would like a photograph with the "girls." That would be an affirmative, ma'am. And in a moment, captured on film and featured on my next Christmas card, are Tom and I amid the beauty, hot pants, and pom-poms in a picture that most of my feminist friends have never forgiven me for.

Willie Nelson welcomed the crowd, sat in with several bands during the day, wearing shades, a headband, and his guitar, Trigger, held fast to his chest with its red, white, and blue knit guitar strap. My favorite West Texas troubadour, Joe Ely, worked his magic, a true crowd favorite. The Texas Tornadoes played a rousing set and had them dancing in the aisles. One of my favorite electric guitar players, David Grissom, playing with John Mellencamp (who I first heard with Joe Ely) slashed and burned his way through Mellencamp's set, playing a gold Paul Reed Smith guitar, leashing wave upon wave of tremolo in true Texas-roadhouse spirit and style. These were hometown heroes, playing in their home state, with a crowd that liked to party and had been for most of the day. A majestic Lone Star communion with the faithful, all digging deep into the heart—beating loud and proud—of Texas. The rest of the forty-five acts were treated with equal respect and enthusiasm and were welcomed with the appreciation that the state of Texas has always had for musicians.

The stadium was full, the moon was rising over the field, and the audience now in the dark, occasionally visible from the glow of the massive stage lights highlighting a parade of entertainers whom most of us had never seen in one performance in our lifetime. We had bumped into a very drunk Joe Walsh trying to kick open the doors of the elevator going down to the stage, and minutes later he was onstage playing "Old McDonald Had a Farm." E-I-E-I-O.

There were two acts left before the encore. Lynyrd Skynyrd came out to a standing ovation— shit kickers, rednecks, and hippies melting together in a rebel yell choir. Opening for Neil Young was not lost on them, and their version of "Sweet Home Alabama," their last song, was played with a full gale force, throwing down the gauntlet to their host. Neil came out, with his great band, and no sooner had set foot on the stage before he went into a colossal version of "Southern Man" that reminded the band (who was from Jacksonville, Florida) just who was putting on this show. I was glad I played "Jack Ruby." There was revolution in the air.

I saw Tom and Roseanne briefly before the encore, gave Tommy a big hug, and told him how thankful I was for getting me on the gig. My good buddy had come far since I'd seen him years before, at the corner of Twenty-sixth and Lyndale, holding a small bag of goldfish, waiting for the bus. Though we were on before the nationally televised portion on the CMT television network, Tom had also made sure one of our songs was taped and placed into the prime-time broadcast. My parents, in Florida with their best friends Chuck and Kay Dellago, watched it on television and toasted their son from afar.

All the musicians, Native American dancers in full regalia, the Dallas Cowboy Cheerleaders, two guitar players from Minneapolis, and other celebrities were invited onstage for the encore. The stage lights were on full blast, lighting the stage in a vast rainbow of color. The audience was on its feet. The show had raised hundreds of thousands of dollars for small farmers across the land. Nobody was having a bad time. Like the chosen leader of this tribe, Willie Nelson led the assembled throng and the audience, now forty thousand strong, in a three-song medley that ended with Hank Williams's "I Saw The Light." By the end of that show, everyone had.

CITY OF ANGELS

I met Kim Fowley at the South by Southwest (SXSW) Music Festival in 1993. Fowley was a Zelig-type character, based in Los Angeles, who'd influenced hundreds of projects over the years, starting with his recording of "Alley Oop" in 1960 under the assumed name of the Hollywood Argyles. He was most successful with creating the Runaways, the teenage all-girl group based in rock and roll and sexual fantasy that featured a young Joan Jett. He resembled Willem Dafoe, though taller. I bumped into him after he'd just wrapped up a panel session. I introduced myself, we chatted briefly, and I gave him a copy of my new CD *Whistling Past the Graveyard.*

A month later my manager Tom Korstad got a call from the City of Angels from a man named Steven Machat, a friend of Kim Fowley's in the music business. Machat liked the record and was going to fly into town to meet us and catch a gig. He had a nice list of credentials; the most interesting to me was that his father was a lawyer for both Leonard Cohen and Phil Spector. Plus, it is hard not to like anyone that takes an interest in your music, and the thought of playing in Los Angeles was thrilling. I had been there once in 1982, staying at a friend's second-floor apartment. On my first day there I was using the john when an earthquake hit. I thought it was an elaborate joke. It wasn't. I can honestly say it scared the shit out of me.

Like his father, Machat was also a lawyer, but he didn't dress like one. He was handsome, tanned, wore a Rolex, monogrammed T-shirt, and fitted Versace jeans over black engineer boots. He looked cool enough to me. My mother happened to be in town and arranged to attend the gig. Machat treated her kindly, which endeared him to me, and after finding out she had a great voice, he thought it'd be a wonderful idea to have her sing harmony on a future recording. I wish we had done that.

To Tom and Steve's credit, they managed to secure a showcase gig at the legendary Troubadour Club in Los Angeles for August as well as funding for me to bring my band out there and put us up for awhile. We stayed at a residency hotel on Larrabe Street, a stumble down from the

Viper Club, the hot new hangout on the Sunset Strip in West Hollywood. The hotel had a cast of characters that included businessmen, journalists, rock and rollers, and a couple of charming young gay guys who loved to party. One was a trustafarian from Europe who got by on monthly payments from his family, and the other, a television producer with an unfortunate toupee but a wicked sense of humor.

We had a week to prepare for the gig. My buddy Tom Arnold, now writing for his wife Roseanne's television show, was master of ceremonies. Bucky Baxter happened to be in town rehearsing with Bob Dylan in Studio City and would be at the gig. Tom and Steve had hired publicist Norman Winter, an older version of comedian David Brenner, who helped grease the skids for Elton John's American debut at the Troubadour and had worked with everyone from Michael Jackson (beginning during the *Thriller* days) to the producers who brought *Jesus Christ Superstar* to the silver screen. It was Tinseltown in warp-ten motion: though completely surreal at times, it felt as though my star was on the rise.

The Byrds met at an open mike at the Troubadour in 1965. Years followed with the L.A. debuts of Buffalo Springfield, Joni Mitchell, Gordon Lightfoot, James Taylor, and Kris Kristofferson. Richard Pryor recorded his debut record there, as did Tim Hardin and Van Morrison, and Waylon Jennings graced the stage during the filming of *Cisco Pike*. It was there that John Lennon and Harry Nilsson got booted from a Smothers Brothers show for drunken heckling, and where Janis Joplin had spent her last night on earth. A performing artist's hallowed ground.

I would stay in Los Angeles for six weeks, but for now my only goal was to make sure we were rehearsed. I couldn't sleep at all the night before the gig, so I went for bacon and eggs at Ben Franks on Sunset Strip—the restaurant with a copper-colored and off-center triangular modernistic roof where Tab Hunter used to bring his "girlfriends" before he came out of the closet, the one Frank Zappa sang about, and where Slash probably met more than one of his connections. There at the table I tried to calm my nerves with a couple cups of strong coffee, like that was a good idea.

The Troubadour gig was sold out. Tom Arnold had been shooting the movie *True Lies* with Arnold Schwarzenegger that afternoon. He showed up in time for the local NBC affiliate to come in and film a live interview with us, two entertainers still trying to get home, that was broadcast on the early evening news. Tom took the stage and announced to the audience, "Paul thinks I am here to introduce him, but actually ladies and gentlemen . . . this is an intervention." Perfect. It broke the ice, and we played a seventy-five-minute set with one encore that went by quicker than the night I lost my virginity to a girl whose last name was Wild. Great gigs are almost impossible to remember. If you are doing it right, you get so lost in the moment and in the grace of who you always wanted to be that the memory of it is superseded by the moment itself. And that is reward enough.

I retired to the dressing room to clean up and congratulate the band. Perusing the autographed pictures of previous performers that lined the purple-painted walls, I was proud and humbled. I took out the silver necklace from under my shirt that my mother had placed around my neck as a good luck charm before I left Minneapolis and hung it proudly on the outside. Then I poured a double shot of Jack Daniels straight up in a plastic cup and went downstairs to mingle and press the flesh.

We gathered around the bar in the music room, and I made the rounds floating a couple of boot heels above the ground. Bucky and I shared a shot and I thanked him for the work he had done on *Whistling Past the Graveyard*, the record that had slingshot me here. Next up was the unlikely duo of Frank Stallone, Sylvester's brother, and Elliot Easton, the left-handed guitarist for the Cars. The three of us exchanged numbers, and we'd all get together in the days to come. Then I was introduced to Elliot Mintz, a well-coiffed man in a white shirt and pink tie who was the publicist for John Lennon and Yoko Ono. Toto, we're not in Kansas anymore. This was Los Angeles, the city of angels and angles, at the intersection of Devotion to Music and Plain Dumb Luck. Life was good.

The band left for Minneapolis the next day. I prepared for another five weeks' stay, ensconced in my one-bedroom hotel apartment, ready for whatever this city of dreams was ready to deliver. Tom, Steve, and I had created a new record label, the logo of which (ominously) was a guy in sunglasses and a Sam Spade raincoat reaching into his pocket. Machat had set up distribution through a smooth jazz label he was connected to, and all I had to do was wait for the money to roll in. And so I waited.

The Viper Room, a two-block walk from my place and owned by Johnny Depp, had opened just a few months before. It was across the street from Tower Records on the corner with lights and yellow window coverings bright and inviting and whose walls were splashed with posters of my Minneapolis buddy and electric guitar master Slim Dunlap's new record *Old New Me*. I spent several evenings perusing their record collection and imagined that my disc would soon be there as well, next to Slim's, among the thousands of other titles.

Frank Stallone called me, put through by the front desk, and offered to pick me up for a night on the town. He was a musician, songwriter, and actor like his brother Sylvester. He had also written "Eye of the Tiger," the theme song for *Rocky III*, a hair-metal tune that can stick in your head like a psychic bed bug whether you want it to or not. We went to the Palm, a steak house and martini joint on Santa Monica Boulevard.

Frank and I ordered fried calamari, two shots of Cuervo, and a couple of Heinekens. Austin native and former Texas law student Dabney Coleman was sitting at the next table. (His latest movie, *The Beverly Hillbillies*, was released that year.) There we were, throwing down a shot of tequila, with Milton Drysdale in the next seat. Frank was like the Margaret Mead of Hollywood, a sociologist of stardom, who hipped me to the ways and means of this city that had destroyed a thousand people for every one it made a star. He told me forthrightly that anyone in the music world if asked their age shaves five years off the real number; if in film or television, they shave ten. I was thirty-eight years old.

I had met Marc Percansky at a record store in Minneapolis in 1984. Now, almost twenty years later, he was living in Los Angeles and making his living as a magician. Perhaps he had a magical means of support as well, as he was the only magician in town who drove a DeLorean, the stainless steel car with gull-wing doors that opened to the sky, featured in the movie *Back to the Future*. We'd hang out regularly. One of his dreams came true when I stumbled over and introduced him to Patricia Arquette who spun him around the dance floor at the Viper Club. Several nights later, on a moonlight cruise through Laurel Canyon, we stopped at Harry Houdini's crumbling estate. We walked slowly up the stone stairway covered with fallen, brittle leaves to do nothing more than to observe the place the world's greatest magician called home. This midnight moment, cloaked in eerie silence, was interrupted by fierce and unexpected howls from what sounded like the menacing hounds of Baskerville. But the estate was abandoned. We ran like hell.

Occasionally, I'd rent a car and drive through Laurel Canyon and go to visit Tom Arnold who was working on the set of the *Roseanne* show in Studio City. I had bought a cassette of the *Mamas and Papas' Greatest Hits* and would blast their song "12:30 (Young Girls Are Coming to the

Canyon)" as I drove through, passing the Laurel Canyon Grocery store, just beyond the hill where Graham Nash met David Crosby and Steven Stills by way of Mama Cass. It wasn't hard to move and groove in a Beach Boys state of mind, with an L.A. cowboy boot on the gas pedal, four to the floor. After all, I was in California.

Elliot Easton had called and invited me to his house to write some songs. He lived a little bit outside of Los Angeles, in a swanky home that suggested he had done well mining the new wave world with his band the Cars. He was a great guitar player, and like many musicians I had met over the years who had played a variety of disparate styles, he had a great grasp of the American Songbook and was a joy to work with. We drank tea and had to go outside to smoke and by the end of the afternoon had finished a song called "Love Is a Dangerous Highway," which one day I still hope to record, providing I can find the cassette.

Stallone and I got together a couple of times a week and would frequent the Viper Club and Barney's Beanery, a roadhouse bar like one might find in the hinterlands of Wisconsin. Janis Joplin had her last meal there of chili and beans, and Jim Morrison would lord over the room as the Doors' office was right around the corner. Frank and Sylvester looked so much alike that after Frank and I downed a couple of shots, in those moments when sobriety slips away and the warm glow of whiskey takes over, Rambo was at the roadhouse.

I spent an afternoon with Jason Korstad, Tom's son, at the iconic Capitol Records building at Hollywood and Vine. We had been invited by producer George Acogny, a friend of Steve Machat's. We were led through the storied hallway, with black-and-white photos of Frank Sinatra, Nat King Cole, Dean Martin, and Judy Garland, under the Quiet sign that has been there since the studio opened, and into Studio A, the room where Frank Sinatra recorded so many of his classic sides. One could imagine Frank in a suit, shirt opened at the collar and tie undone, fedora tilting to his left, snapping his fingers and leading the band. Mind blowing and beautiful, and the refrain of "Summer Wind" danced in my head as we left.

Soul Asylum had always been one of my favorite Minneapolis bands. I knew the guys in the band since their days as Loud, Fast, Rules. They were literally on a "Runaway Train," the single from *Grave Dancer's Union* that would go triple platinum. Jason and I were invited to the Hollywood

Ready to take on the world from Virginia, Minnesota. My grandpa Emil bought me the Gibson amp and made the microphone stand. *Photograph by Bess Metsa, circa 1967.*

To paraphrase the Rolling Stones, "What can a young boy do but play in a rock and roll band?" The Positive Reaction at Carol Flaim's thirteenth birthday party at the Gun Club on Silver Lake in Virginia. Left to right: Chuck Christianson, Gary Pagliaccetti, Mike Weiss, and me. *Photograph by Linda O'Leary, circa 1968.*

Paul and Christian, the Iron Range's answer to Simon and Garfunkel, at Goodman Auditorium, ready to play at a junior high assembly, circa 1968.

Damn Everything but the Circus performing at the Virginia Armory, 1974. Brian Vitali on bass. *Photograph by Chris Canelake.*

My grandfather Emil Arvid Metsa and me in 1976. The best friend I've ever had, he told me, "It is either right, or it's bullshit," and later, "Kill 'em with kindness." *Photograph by McKenna Studio.*

Ready to strike out into the world of show biz with the 1955 Martin D-28, which I still have, and in boots that I don't.

PAUL METSA

6 & 12 STRING
GUITARIST AND SONGSTER

Digging deep at the 400 Bar on the West Bank in Minneapolis with the Cats Under the Stars trio, circa 1983. O'Keefe would occasionally run the tip jar to Palmer's Bar up the street, and when unsuspecting patrons would ask where the money was going, he would answer honestly, "To the band at the 400." We were there four years. *Photograph by Al Frick.*

Cats Under the Stars, a.k.a. Minnesota's best-dressed fishing band, circa 1976. Left to right: Steve "Skip" Nelimark, John Pasternacki, Tim O'Keefe, and me.

The Paul Metsa Group, circa 1985. A magnificent group, including (from left to right) Jeff Cierniak, Al Oikari, Merlin "Bronco" Brunkow, Charlie Alcox, me, Cleveland Gordon, and Van "Joe" Luoma.

Under the awning at Folk City in Greenwich Village—the Garden of Eden of folk as I knew it. I had arrived. *Photograph by Harvey Van Horn, circa 1985.*

Playing E chords with Ken Kesey in the basement of the Walker Art Center in 1991. I was his lead guitar player, and his rehearsals were nothing more than these words: "Play no riffs of chords from the last ten thousand years, and end with heavy noise." *Photograph by Jeff Forester.*

Backstage at the Guthrie Theater with J. J. Cale, who was showing me the old Nashville axiom, "There is no money beyond the twelfth fret."

Bookended by two of the best musicians in America: at the left, Garry Tallent, and at the right, Bucky Baxter. Moondog Studios, Nashville. *Photograph by Dick Blin, circa 1993.*

My most cherished photograph: with Senator Paul Wellstone at a protest. We met many times. He represented America at its best—honest, righteous, and powerful. *Photograph by Joey McLeister, circa 1991.*

The City of Angels. Headlining at the club that was the West Coast's entrance into the promised land. Beyond that, only the ocean. *Photograph by Larry Smith.*

Backstage at the Troubadour after the gig: a quartet who could have been brought together only through Hollywood with a sense of humor. Left to right: Tom Korstad, Steve Machat, me, and Tom Arnold. *Photograph by Norman Winter and Associates.*

Farm Aid V, Dallas, 1993, five miles from Dealey Plaza. Playing "Jack Ruby" to forty thousand Texans, ending with the verse "Did the Warren Commission darken the day, or did the mob or oil money mean what they say, shadow of Cuba darken the day, in Dallas county, the land of LBJ."

The favorite picture of all my feminist friends: my new background singers, the Dallas Cowboys Cheerleaders, immediately after the Farm Aid V gig, with Emmanuel Kiriakou and my new wing man, Tom Latimer, in the background.

My crowning moment: my sold-out show at the Guthrie Theater on January 31, 1994. A ten-piece band on one of the greatest stages in America. *Photograph by Elleni Fellows.*

My song and my *sisu:* between my beloved mother and my father at the after-show party at the Guthrie Theater. It was the last time my mother would see me play. *Photograph by Billie Failletaz.*

To Paul with love, nora

Pete Seeger, the granddaddy of us all, leading once again all of us in song (on the night that would have been my parents' forty-fourth anniversary—take what you have gathered from coincidence). Among the performers are Joe Ely, Ramblin' Jack Elliott, Jimmie Dale Gilmore, Pete Seeger, Arlo Guthrie, Jimmy LaFave, Bruce Springsteen, Billy Bragg, Dave Pirner, me, and Nora Guthrie. *Photograph by John McCally.*

The night I met Nora Guthrie, daughter of Woody and Marjorie Guthrie, in New York City, February 9, 1995. Marjorie saved everything for us to treasure. *Photograph by Parenteau Guidance.*

With the pride of New Jersey, Bruce Springsteen. When I told him, a week after this photograph was taken, that as a bandleader I dug it when he fired the E Street Band at a show in Minneapolis, he said, "Damn, that is the first time I heard that!" We understood each other.

Grizzled and weathered folksinger pictured here with Gordon Lightfoot, Superior, Wisconsin, 1997.

The toughest guys I know. From left to right: Jason, Jordan, my brother John, Jacob, and John-Paul with Road, their dog, near their home in Rochester, Minnesota. *Photograph courtesy of the* Rochester Post-Bulletin.

Between two of my favorite Minneapolis rockers. From left to right: Karl Mueller, me, and Dave Pirner. Eli's Bar, Minneapolis, 1998.

Martini Gulch, Nye's Bar, 1996. One downed martini and two on deck—and that was the first set. Tom Lewis on upright bass. *Photograph by Sean Beggs.*

With Scarlet Rivera after a recording session run by Kevin Bowe at IPR in Minneapolis, September 2010. Scarlet is a master musician with perfect pitch and a gypsy of the highest kind. *Photograph by Doug Webb.*

With Sonny Earl, my partner every Friday for fourteen years. According to the *City Paper–Nashville,* "Masterful guitarist Metsa and slashing harmonica soloist Earl function as a contemporary version of Sonny Terry and Brownie McGhee." *Photograph by Lynn Richter, circa 2008.*

The three wise guys. From left to right: Aaron Neville, me, and Willie West, backstage at the Dakota Jazz Club, Minneapolis, December 4, 2010. *Photograph by Patty Gambucci-West.*

With Big Jay McNeely during a recording session at the Silver Ant Studio, Minneapolis, October 2010. *Photograph by Darin Back.*

Star Lanes bowling alley in Hollywood where their record company was holding a party, and the same place where they would later film *The Big Lebowski*. It was a gratifying reunion, all of us so far away from home at the west end of the rock and roll highway.

Karl Mueller, whose wife Mary Beth was a good friend of mine, prowled the stage with his bass hanging from his slim body in a way that reminded me of Paul Simeon from the Clash. After their first appearance on David Letterman, I saw Karl just days later working in the kitchen at the Loon Bar and Restaurant in downtown Minneapolis, exhibiting a true Midwestern work ethic. A humble, handsome, and truly funny guy, who died too young in 2005. A gentleman of few words—most of them funny and all to the point—his last words to his lovely wife after she found him hemorrhaging after a valiant battle with throat cancer were, "You've got to be fucking kidding me." We all miss him.

It seemed everybody in L.A. was working an angle: for a movie or television role, record deal, or to cast new lights on the sparkle of their lives. Most of the servers and bartenders in town were referred to as MAWs (model, actor, whatever). I bumped into one couple from Montana who were sure as shootin' that Hollywood would soon be knocking on the door of their cheap hotel—because their script had been blessed by a Native American tribal chief. There was enough silicone in town to float the Hindenburg, and streets were full of lifted faces that resembled Old West outlaws ready to be hanged and taking their last breath.

My two gay buddies from the hotel, whom I had dubbed Oscar and Felix, invited me to clubs and parties, most of which, as usual, had free food and booze. I wasn't complaining. At one party in the promontories of the Hollywood Hills we drove up to the front door and were met by a valet and an armed guard with an Uzi submachine gun and a thermos of coffee. Once inside we were surrounded by a bevy of supermodels and half a dozen Middle Eastern men twice as old as the women. From there the view of the lights of the city made it feel like we were hanging from a cloud.

They also took me to a private disco that didn't open until midnight, with a sound system that vibrated loose some of my back fillings. The mirrored ball and psychedelic lights raining on the dance floor reminded me of the 1967 LSD-soaked movie *The Trip,* directed by Roger Corman and written by a young Jack Nicholson. I was getting a bit discombobulated by the lights and went to sit down next to a man who looked like

Tarzan but with longer hair. It was Fabio, the bodice-ripping novelette male model, who turned out to be a pretty nice guy. Next to him, circled by Sumo wrestler–type bodyguards, was a lithe black guy I realized was Prince. I wanted to say hello and ask if he remembered me giving him the new Cats Under the Stars 45-single at the SuperAmerica at Twenty-second and Lyndale a decade before. Like the supermodels at the party in the Hollywood Hills, he looked past me as if I were invisible. At least the cocktails were free.

My drummer, the talented Bobby Vandell, had previously lived in Los Angeles and was at one time a roommate of Tom Arnold's. I visited him in the spring of 1992, a month after the L.A. riots. At the time, Bobby had a weekly Sunday night gig with blues singer King Ernest at a club in South Central called the Townhouse. South Central, once considered the "Fifty-second Street of Los Angeles," had boasted one of the most vibrant blues, jazz, and rhythm and blues scenes in the country in the 1940s and '50s. Jazz pioneers Charlie Mingus and Eric Dolphy were born there, and rhythm and blues artists like Johnny Otis, Big Jay McNeely, and Amos Milburn jumped the joints along Central Avenue regularly. While rap had now become the musical currency, featuring such South Central homies as NWA and Ice-T, King Earnest held forth as a remnant of a golden time and history.

Bobby was living with a black guy named Larry Smith behind a Korean grocery store in South Central. He had met Larry on a local tennis court, admiring the way Larry smoked cigarettes while playing tennis. During the riots, Bobby was back in Minneapolis rehearsing with soul singer Alexander O'Neal, whom he'd met at the SuperAmerica at Twenty-second and Lyndale in 1978, striking up a conversation after O'Neal complimented Bobby on his afro. The night of the riots Larry had barricaded himself inside their small apartment. A group of thugs had chained the front door of the grocery store to a car and pulled the door off its hinges. After ransacking the store, they tried breaking into Bobby and Larry's apartment. Larry stood bravely behind it, hammer in one hand, cigarette in the other, and said to the hooligans on the other side of the door, "Come and get it. . . . It's HAMMER TIME!" They left without further incident.

Every Monday night we'd go to the China Club on the corner of Selma and Argyle in Hollywood, a chichi club that hosted an all-star jam. Bobby was originally introduced into this scene by Tony Braunagel, Bonnie Raitt's drummer. The house band now included Billy Preston on keyboards, Jeff "Skunk" Baxter on guitar, and Oliver Lieber, son of Mike Lieber of Lieber and Stoller fame, on drums. It had just the right amount of Hollywood glitz and rock and roll glamour. I opened the door once for Tony Curtis and a date young enough to be his granddaughter and sat next to *Soul Train*'s Don Cornelius at the bar, who was nursing a Courvoisier in a snifter. I had always signed up to play but was usually passed up by famous musicians like Lou Rawls. Finally, I got my chance.

It was way past midnight when the big bouncer who ran the jam, who I had gotten to know, told me a spot was open. Just as I was tuning my guitar he came in and said someone had just shown up, was going to sit in, and I'd be on right after him. No problem until I realized who it was—none other than Herbie Hancock, one of the greatest jazz pianists in the world. Hancock brought down the house, and I was still quaking in my boots when they announced the next act, an unknown folksinger from the Midwest. I made a snap decision and called "Jambalaya" by Hank Williams that segued into the New Orleans staple "Iko-Iko." I learned early on that you can never go wrong opening with Hank Williams or Johnny Cash. This crowd of Hollywood hipsters was a bit surprised to hear a song by the Hillbilly Shakespeare with a Nawlin's twist, but twist they did, those at the bar rattling their jewelry in time. It was a major score, and Baxter, Preston, and Lieber gave me a high-five as I left the stage.

Frank Stallone knew I was leaving town in a week and invited me out for one last blowout and go-around. We started out at the Palm, had a drink at the Troubadour, and then hit the Viper Room. We drank like Humphrey Bogart. Standing outside on the spot where unfortunately River Phoenix would die just weeks later, we plotted one last escapade. Back in his jet-black Jeep we headed up to the Hollywood Hills, in search of a friend of his, though he wouldn't tell me who. We parked on the street and approached a bungalow with a light in the window. One of the occupants answered our knock and led us into the kitchen. There with a fresh bottle of Cuervo tequila was Julian Lennon. What a striking resemblance he bore to his father. Julian cut slices of lemon and we proceeded to dive into the bottle one shot and toast at a time. Julian and Frank shared nightmare showbiz stories, and at times, closing my eyes, I heard John Lennon himself talking, so similar in tone was the voice and British accent, forever seared into our cerebral cortexes. We said good night, drove back down to Sunset Strip, and made it home just before sunrise.

I went to visit a friend in Palm Springs for two days before my return to Minneapolis. While there, Bobby Vandell called me and said I had to come back on the afternoon bus, as he had something up his sleeve. Vandell was the kind of guy who during an earthquake hearing a radio announcer say, "Call us with stories of where you were when the quake hit," would call the station and say, "I was in my bedroom, and I knew we were having a quake because the mirror on my ceiling started to shake." I couldn't pass up his offer for this next adventure.

I hopped the Greyhound and ended up at the bus station in downtown Los Angeles. This was the part of the city, so far from the beam and shimmer of Hollywood as to almost be on another planet. This was Charles Bukowski's city of angels: poor people of every color, hustlers on street corners, in a depot that had long since lost its sheen. Bobby had brought clothes for me to wear and, like the mother that he is, helped dress me in the parking lot, throwing my blue jeans and T-shirt into a paper bag. I had no idea where we were going, but it sure did feel like it might be a night worth remembering.

While we were driving to our destination, Bobby reminded me of the time I called him from a hotel in Duluth. I had met a young, beautiful, and frisky woman there at a gig, and we went out for several months. One night I was playing at the Park Inn on the Lake Superior waterfront. We were giving her friend a ride home when the friend exclaimed, "You are not going to take Paul back to the hotel and have your way with him all by yourself, are you?" My date did a U-turn on Mesaba Avenue and bee-lined it back to the hotel. The three of us ran down the corridors of our hotel, throwing off our clothes faster than you can say "three-ring circus," some of them landing on empty pizza boxes left outside the doors of other guests. The next three hours we made wild whoopee, switching positions that would have made Chinese acrobats weep with envy. I *had* to call Vandell in the morning, two young, naked, voluptuous women by my side. They grabbed the phone, both whispering in the receiver and telling him what he was missing. He told them to put me back on the phone and asked me what the hell was going on. I told him, "Bobby, this gives a whole new meaning to the term *Twin Ports!*"

Turns out, Vandell and I were going to a birthday party for a member of En Vogue, one of the most popular female singing groups of all time and riding the top of the charts. They were as beautiful in person as on television. We parked at a marina in Newport Beach. Bobby had scored entrance to the party through a caterer he had recently met. The party was on a yacht—but not just any yacht. This was John Wayne's yacht, and some say it is haunted by his ghost. With the exception of the captain, we were the only two white guys on the boat. Heading slowly out, we cruised beneath the same stars that once guided John Wayne and the *Wild Goose*, a former minesweeper, into the Pacific Ocean. Someone decided Bobby and I should lead the large party in an a capella version of "Happy Birthday." Yeah, that makes sense: have the only two white guys at the party sing a capella to one of the best-selling black female vocal groups of all time, and dozens of their closest friends. Like some twisted incarnation of the Righteous Brothers, it came off without a hitch, and we weren't thrown overboard to sleep with the fish. Two days later this flatlander was on his way back to Minneapolis and solid ground, with enough stories to fill a book.

MISSISSIPPI FAREWELL

All artists are mama's boys, or daddy's girls. My mother often told me that as a little boy I'd run around the house saying, "Mommy, I got all this music in my head and I don't know what to do." Like her father, Ernest Paul, my namesake, Mom could spin a good yarn and was never shy of exaggerating a story if it helped sell it. Nothing wrong with that. She was a wonderful singer, too. Her brother Gerald played soprano saxophone in a jazz band while in high school in Bemidji, near Lake Itasca, headwaters of the Mississippi River and home to large statues of Paul Bunyan and Babe the Blue Ox. On occasion my mom would sit in with the jazz band. As a child I loved to sit next to her in church and listen to her sing, like the precocial loon that often rides on the parent's back in its water cradle. Sitting next to my dad was a different story entirely. When he wasn't checking his watch or passing us Life Savers, he would sing in a low rumble that made Johnny Cash sound like Enrico Caruso.

Mom was also an accomplished pianist in her younger years. She wanted each of us kids to learn to play an instrument. We had an old upright piano in our dining room, and each began lessons around second grade with Mrs. Dorothea Helenius Tomes, a talented and eccentric local pianist who lived just a few blocks from our house. She wore her blonde hair pulled back in a tight bun, black cat's-eye glasses with rhinestones on the outer corners, and bright-red lipstick. Her agile fingers were long and thin and baubled with a large aquamarine or topaz ring that glinted off the keyboard as she played. We sat together on the piano bench of her baby grand as she demonstrated simple notes from music that looked to me like hieroglyphics. It messed with my brain, and I lasted for only two lessons, faking my way through both. My hands, it seemed, were more suited for fingering a fret board than for tinkling the ivories.

Weekends at our house were for *shoveling out,* Mom's term for everyone pitching in to clean, but when the work was done I could practice and play to my heart's content. She would rather hear my feet tapping time to the guitar in my bedroom above the dining room than see them running out the door with my buddies, heading for mischief.

Mom drove me to all of my early gigs and frequently took a seat in the audience. If I played within an hour of Virginia after I was on my own, she'd show up with several of her friends in tow. I would always introduce her and dedicate a song.

In 1992, Mom called me with the devastating news that she'd been diagnosed with leukemia. Sounding strong and matter-of-fact, she said she'd be coming to the University of Minnesota for more tests and to plan on the proper course of action. I hung up the phone and cried until my eyes ran out of tears. She was only sixty-two.

When she came down to her first appointment, we got together for dinner. She was always on the cusp of her next great adventure and game for new settings, so we chose an Ethiopian restaurant on the West Bank. There we ate *injera* and *doro wat* with our fingers, and over dinner we discussed her doctor's appointment and the road that lay ahead. It turned out I knew the head of the department where she'd be receiving treatments. Knowing this brought me great solace in this unchartered territory of our relationship.

A short time later, I was playing a college gig in Pocatello, Idaho. I called my folks one night and sensed something was wrong when no one answered. I learned the next morning that Mom had suffered a massive nosebleed and had been in the hospital. After we hung I up, I sat down and wrote Mom a letter on cheap hotel stationery to tell her in writing just how much I loved her, how much I appreciated everything she'd always done for me, and how her lessons will stay with me forever. We both started to realize, in spite of an outside chance for a bone marrow transplant that she probably couldn't handle, that her time on earth was finite. We were attaining the last plane of our relationship, and recognizing this, it gave us a deeper connection. Strains of early lullabies she sang to me in childhood occasionally found their way into songs I played in my professional years, softly stealing in and taking a seat in the audience, just like she'd done so many years before.

I had planned to do a farewell show in Minneapolis, cash in my chips, and move to Nashville. Music City seemed like the obvious choice. My last record was recorded there, and I knew many Minnesota musicians who had made the pilgrimage over the years and had done well.

It was around that time I had a falling out with my manager, Tom Korstad. I had booked my farewell gig at the Guthrie Theater by myself, the same theater that inspired me to jump into this racket in the first place. The details to successfully pull off something of this magnitude took two months. I had enough of a budget to put together at least a ten-piece band. I would have to teach them the songs and the arrangements while doing all of the appropriate promotion as well. I awoke every morning, a man on a mission, hypnotized by this last Minneapolis dream, driven to make it happen.

The show, titled Mississippi Farewell in an ode to the river a mile outside the doors of the theater that pumps through American's heartland down to New Orleans, sold out a week before it was going to happen. I had written a tune especially for that night called "Mississippi Farewell" with the last line in the chorus, "Will I ever come back? Well, it's too soon to tell. I am leaving tonight, Mississippi Farewell." I had obtained financing at the last minute to make sure the show got recorded and rehearsed every night for a couple of weeks.

Before I knew it, the big day arrived. I loaded up all my guitars, one amp, cowboy boots, and two suits and headed toward the Guthrie Theater, fingers crossed. At 3 P.M. snow was beginning to fall lightly.

As was their custom, when I opened shows at the Guthrie Theater, my parents drove down from Virginia and had great seats next to St. Paul Mayor Norm Coleman and his wife, Laurie. My brother came up with his family from Rochester and sat four rows up, stage left. I was playing as much for them, as anyone else in the room. My buddy Billy Alcorn was the master of ceremonies for the show. He gave me a great introduction and then announced, "Your friend and mine, Paul Metsa." Yikes!

I walked onto the thrust stage wearing the short black cowboy jacket that Bucky Baxter had given me and plugged in my '69 Telecaster "Winston" to perform for an audience for whom I could do no wrong. Most of them knew all the songs and sang along. It was sweeter than milk and honey with just enough Southern Comfort to grease the wheels.

The band—a three-piece horn section, two keyboard players, a pedal steel player, three singers, a rhythm guitarist, a drummer, and a percussionist, most of whom I had been playing with for years—was blazing. It started with a small flame, then was whipped by the wind, player to player, handing hot flares to each other in the form of solos, spreading around the stage in musical smoke signals, exploding like wildfire, great players in the flash of communion and inspired to blow the roof off the joint and burn it to the ground. The audience whooped and hollered, throwing gas on the ever-growing flame, ending with two encores. We had the after-party in the greenroom behind the Guthrie stage. My parents were there, beaming, dressed to the nines, and enjoying the moment. It was a glorious night, an evening of triumph, enchanting and recorded.

I had met Clive Gregson at First Avenue in 1985 when I opened for the Richard Thompson Band. He looked like a librarian, but as Thompson's rhythm guitar player he elevated Richard's playing to lofty heights. He met a woman from Minneapolis, married her, and moved to town in the early '90s. I had gone over to his house a few times to listen to records and play guitar. We got along famously, and I asked him if he would be interested in producing my live record. He agreed and I booked some time at Pachyderm Studios in Cannon Falls, Minnesota.

We booked four days for mixing, a few overdubs, and to record the new song "Mississippi Farewell." Clive drove back and forth every day, and I set up camp in the master bedroom and slept in the same bed that Kurt Cobain and Courtney Love used when Nirvana recorded *In Utero* there in 1993. That added to the atmosphere, though I brought my own sheets.

We worked efficiently, and Clive was a dream producer. He had a sense of humor dryer than Cary Grant's martini. We fixed a couple of guitar tracks using him on guitar, and he added some harmonies as well, singing in his high tenor punk-rock schoolboy way. We recorded "Mississippi Farewell" with two gospel singers, Mari Harris and Joyce Williams. Al Oikari, who had played with my band in 1974, came in to play solo piano. We started to record late in the evening, as the stars came out, slowly taking their place in the southern Minnesota sky. Like all best tracks, it came together quickly, and we left the studio quietly under the spell of a gentle prairie moon.

My mother had been making biweekly trips to Minneapolis for checkups and blood transfusions. Her friend Kay Dellago drove her to and from the hospital and sat with her when I couldn't. We always had dinner or lunch together, and I'd take her shopping when she had the strength and time to do so. We'd talk by phone almost daily.

She was scheduled to go into surgery the third week of May that year. She had one more blood transfusion at the hospital the week before. As a nurse she felt completely at home in a hospital. She would always strike up conversations with complete strangers, and at the hospital she got to know other patients, doctors, and nurses, and any janitor on duty. Everyone was equal in her eyes. She was also comforted that I knew Dr. Harry Jacob, the head of the department, who had assigned the best doctor he knew, Dr. Helen Enright, to her case. At her last transfusion I had taken a box of her father's photographs from his early years, many of which had typewritten explanations of the pictures on the back. We looked over them for several hours and talked about her childhood as she sweetly reminisced about her family and ours as well. She was now sixty-four.

Mom, who never liked sports or country western music, developed a love for both in her later years. She started to enjoy country music after becoming a tour guide, which she did after selling the gift shop she co-owned and operated when she retired from nursing. As a tour guide she had supervised many trips to Branson, Missouri. She decided those banjos and fiddles weren't so bad after all. She became a big Minnesota Twins fan after the World Series in 1991 (we went to Game 2 together) and especially after she got sick, listening to game broadcasts in the kitchen as she drank pots of coffee and smoked Marlboro Light 100s while writing letters and making lists of all the projects she had planned.

I drove up with my mom and dad back to Virginia to help them get the house in order before their trip back for her surgery. We listened on the radio to the Twins, who happened to be playing one of the longest games of their career. Mom spent a lot of time cooking that week. There was an older lady who was sick down the street, and Mom made sure I brought her some soup. As sick as she was, though she'd never tell us, she never forgot anyone else ailing as well.

We all met at the hospital in Minneapolis on Sunday, May 22, so she could take some final tests before the surgery on Monday. The respiratory therapist came in to do a few tests on her breathing. He asked mom if she had quit smoking. She said yes. The therapist asked her when. To which she replied, "Thursday."

We all arrived at the hospital early Monday while it was still dark. Mom was in good spirits as we gathered around her bed prior to her final preps for surgery. Looking at her face I saw the scar over her eye that she got as a young girl when she got hit with a bat playing baseball with her brother's friend. She had the same deep-set green eyes as her father, Ernest, and her grandmother Bessie, with a mysterious quality that seemed to possess knowledge of a world beyond. She smiled and reassured us that everything was going to be all right. Then she looked at me and said, "This, too, shall pass." I gave her one last long hug and kissed her forehead and told her not to worry; I planned to be back later that evening to stay by her side for the night shift.

Dr. John Najarian came to talk to all of us before I left. A large man with strong yet delicate hands, he reminded me of Minnesota football legend Bronko Nagurski. He explained to the family how the day would go. Surgery would start at 9:30 A.M. and last until around 2 P.M. He needed to repair an abdominal aneurysm and did not expect any complications. Confident and relieved, I returned to my apartment on LaSalle and got the first real sleep I had had in days, preparing for what I assumed would be a very long night as we took turns with Mom's recovery. My father called at 2:30 P.M. and said the surgery went well. I told him I would see him later that evening and went back to sleep. The phone rang again at 9:30 P.M. as I was preparing to leave for the hospital. It was my brother. Mom had passed away. I collapsed like a rag doll.

Minutes later, mustering the strength to leave, I got in my car, shirt still unbuttoned and wallet still on the stand next to the bed. I drove with one hand to the hospital, wiping away angry tears with the other. The lights along the highway blurred in a string of yellow halos. I parked somewhere, entered the building, and pushed the elevator button for the fifth floor. The door opened and I fumbled through the hallways, trying to get my bearings. A nurse appeared, looking like some sort of angel, and led me quietly to the room where my brother was waiting and my mother lay.

I couldn't handle it. I sobbed, barely able to catch my breath. Mom wasn't wearing her glasses, and I held her and tried to believe she was only sleeping, that scar above her eye even now more visible. Where was God? Didn't he know I had her red leather Bible in the drawer next to my bed, the one in which she had underlined and marked in colored highlights her favorite verses and written notes in the margins in her perfect Palmer penmanship? Was there no miracle that would awaken her from this dark and terrible dream? I don't recall how much time passed before my brother finally ushered me gently out of the room, but it felt as if my heart was releasing an invisible drop of blood in every tear that splashed behind us on the floor.

We worried most about Dad. They had met in 1949 on a blind date at the Casa De Roma in Duluth. She was a student at St. Luke's School of Nursing, daughter of a tractor salesman, he a student at the University of

Minnesota, Duluth, son of a bar owner. A trail of weekly love letters that Mom had packed away in a small black suitcase outlines their courtship and engagement from 1950 up until the time they married in September 1951, a love bound in time, through its ups and downs, that lasted more than forty years.

As funeral arrangements were being made, family and friends gathered at my parents' house. Dad, thinner now than usual, held up well and greeted everyone as they came through the door. My sister discovered in the freezer a casserole that Mom had made just prior to leaving for her surgery in Minneapolis. Dad told us that as they were packing the car to leave that day, Mom turned and patted the wall as she was going out the door and said, "Goodbye, house." She knew. And at that point we knew she'd left the casserole there, in love, to feed us one last time.

Mom's funeral was scheduled several days later at the Methodist Church in Virginia. The church was packed to standing room only. My friend Mari Harris sang "Somewhere Over the Rainbow," Mom's favorite song, the one she often sang years ago as I was falling asleep, melting any troubles like lemon drops. If only I could now look above the chimney tops and find her. Friends and family shared strong and beautiful remembrances during the funeral service. Chuck Dellago, a dear friend of my parents and a lifelong musician himself, told of the time just two years prior, in 1992, when they were all vacationing at a mutual friend's house in Florida and tuned in to Farm Aid V, broadcast on CMT on nationwide television. When I came on and sang "Slow Justice," Mom walked over to the TV, gave it a hug, and kissed my cheek through the screen. That is the kind of mother she was.

After the service we followed the hearse to Virginia's Greenwood Cemetery, past the giant floating loon on Silver Lake, symbol of the Land of the Loon and pine trees and porcupines and sky blue waters that ripple in the veins of Minnesotans. It also symbolized the arts festival by the same name that she cofounded almost twenty years before. The sun was shining and wind rustling as everyone gathered at her graveside, the same hallowed ground beneath which many of our aunts and uncles and grandmother and grandfather lay at rest. After the final prayer I took out my guitar and led the assembled in the most difficult song I ever had to sing. "I was standing by my window, on a cold and cloudy day, when I saw that hearse come rolling, for to carry my mother away. Will the circle be unbroken . . ." Many began to join hands and sing along, grief finding release in the lines of that familiar and comforting American song. I knew in my heart these words were true, as she had told me so: "There's a better home a-waiting, in the sky, Lord, in the sky."

It was a fitting tribute to one who celebrated life to the fullest and inspired all those she met. Smiles broke out beneath damp eyes, coaxing harmonies that took wing on the breezes to somewhere over a rainbow. A rich spirit pervaded. And with that we laid my mother down.

NO MONEY DOWN

It was the worst summer of my life. I was emotionally destroyed by my mother's death and felt like my soul had disappeared with hers, and in a way it had, gone up in ashes and smoke to wherever souls go. I had barely enough money to cover rent and groceries as I had spent a large chunk from the proceeds of my Mississippi Farewell show to cover the recording costs at Pachyderm Studio. I had done my Minneapolis swan song and couldn't really swim back to play any more gigs in town. Every river and road out looked dark.

I had experienced periods of depression throughout my life, blue spaces of time that would settle in, seemingly out of nowhere. I was a middle-class white kid, raised by great parents in comfortable houses, with a close extended family. So why the depression? My high school counselor suggested it could be a "seasonal disorder." It would last for a week or so, then vanish as quickly as it came. Fortunately, music provided an escape hatch through the misty gloom.

But that summer was different, darker, and deeper. As hard as I tried, I could not shake it—and there was no mother to call for advice, solace, or just to pass the time. I'd try to walk outside but the sunshine hurt, and when twilight slipped through the windows it brought all the bad spirits with it. I could barely listen to music, much less play it. I had nothing to say, and barely anyone to say it to.

I spent the summer locked in my apartment, watching little else but the O. J. Simpson saga on TV. Simpson had been one of my heroes as a kid, along with Bobby Hull, Gordie Howe, Fran Tarkenton, Harmon Killebrew, and Bronko Nagurski—one of the toughest football players of all time and a North Star State legend. Simpson's fall from grace brought another layer of sadness. Heroes don't commit murder. The world was getting smaller—my apartment was small enough—and now it was getting colder, too.

Summer gave way to fall. Winter in all of its madness was right around the corner. Thanksgiving was coming up and knowing Mom wouldn't be there was a wound unhealed. The one bright light in my life was my friend

Larry Kegan. I could count on him to pick up, and pick me up, when I called him; he offered advice like the street rabbi that he was. He told me that Jews set an empty place at the table for one year after a loved one departs this world as a way to recognize the loss and honor the person. I did that, at Thanksgiving, then Christmas, and my cousin and sister hosting both events let me do it in spite of the fact both houses were full and they probably needed the space at the table. They loved my mother, too, and understood that I was just trying to patch a hole the size of Albert Hall in my heart.

Christmas was Mom's favorite holiday. When we were kids, our little house bustled with older relatives dressed up in their fancy clothes; the living room was festive with pine boughs and ornaments, flocked snow scenes on the picture windows, angels made from *Reader's Digest* magazines, and red-and-white felt Christmas stockings that Mom's own mother had made with our names in gold glitter on the tops. Pink and pearl pillows of her grandfather's homemade taffy were tucked into tray after glass tray of artfully arranged Christmas cookies: green wreaths with cinnamon candy berries, apricot balls, sandbakkels, sweet Swedish Fattigmann crisps and fragile rosettes dipped in powdered sugar, Norwegian krumkakes pressed with ornamental designs, prune tarts, coconut/almond cookies rolled in red sugar that looked like strawberries with green frosting leaves, jelly-filled thumbprints. More would magically appear from the basement storage room whenever we ran out. One year Mom bought us matching red-and-white striped flannel pajamas from Sears Roebuck; my little brother John's even came with a nightcap. On Christmas Eve while opening presents, Dad would bring out the 8 mm movie camera and Mom would hold the Sun Gun, lighting the room in a dazzling brightness that transformed the cozy living room into someplace where elves could live. None of us realized how much Mom did, until she was gone.

There are moments in any artist's life when he or she wonders if the entire blood struggle has been worthwhile. I never called myself an artist. That was for people in black turtlenecks at dinner parties breathing rarified air, and not the smoke-filled taverns I played. I had been on an almost twenty-five-year musical and mystical journey. Like Duke Ellington referred to himself on his tax return, I called myself a musician and was proud enough of that. I was only an artist when all my work as a musical journeyman conjoined with the midnight passing of foreign stars and lifted my work to that next galaxy, the one that you could never see and could only feel. I felt none of it as the end of December approached and could barely raise my head high enough to look for whatever money I had to buy presents for a family that I could only hope still loved me.

I had one hundred bucks total to cover presents, gas money to go back and forth up north, and a couple of cups of coffee and donuts along the way. I went to gas up with the wind blowing fiercely off the Mississippi River and blinding snow in my face. On my way to pay, I somehow locked my keys inside the car. What to do next? I was just a few blocks away from my last girlfriend's house, now at home beside Blackjack Johnny, her come-lately boyfriend, and I hoped to God she wouldn't appear at the gas pump and find me here cold, lonely, and broke, confirming why she might have left me in the first place. The gas station attendant called the neighborhood locksmith, and two hours and forty bucks later I was on my way back home, limping one block at a time, like a sick animal going back to the herd. And we all know how that ends up.

I got back to the mansion, took a right up the hill to the parking lot, skidded to the top, and parked. I had a plastic bag with several presents that I bought at the Goodwill for my nephews and a blue sweater I bought for my dad on sale and was hoping would fit. The snow had turned to ice on the red stone stairway, and I walked cautiously, like old people do. Vulnerable. There was a large dark oak table in the entryway where the postman left the mail, which was neatly sorted by Babe the landlady. There were no Christmas cards or even bills, just a single letter in a tan envelope. In hand-written script the return address read: "Guthrie—New York City" and a zip code. My heart raced. I hustled up the stairs, snow falling from my jacket and boots on all three flights, opened then shut the door behind me, put the plastic bag on the kitchen table, turned on the light, and slowly opened the envelope wondering what the hell could be inside.

It was a letter from Nora Guthrie, Woody Guthrie's daughter. I read it slowly and hoped I was not dreaming. It was two pages long. The words, penned in blue ink, slanted in easy, even strokes to the right, rose from the page as if written by a sober poet. A friend of mine, Pete Ingram, had sent her one of my tapes a few months earlier, and she was responding, saying she loved the songs and asking who the hell I was. It was the kind of moment where time shifts, like tectonic plates in transform movement, pushing the clock on the wall forward, grinding past the hours that came before. Pressed between those walls of rock-hard crust, I'd been suffocating, unable to move. Melted snow seeping through my socks assured me I wasn't dreaming. Light was coming in. And oxygen. I was holding the ticket to a new and virgin dream. I was going to move to New York City and meet Nora Guthrie.

I gave notice on my apartment and cobbled together about $1,500 for the trip. My friends Tony and Mike Musial, two investors from the Mississippi Farewell recording project, offered to help pack and store my stuff. By the end of January 1995, I had my guitar, a suitcase of clothes and pictures of my family and was bound for New York City, in search of no particular dream other than to meet Nora. The frozen garden of grief of my mother's passing was slowly melting, inviting my next destination, one my mother would have applauded.

At LaGuardia airport I was picked up by Jerry Disrud, who had so kindly offered me the extra room in his apartment in Rego Park, Queens. Jerry was originally from Starbuck, Minnesota, and had moved to New York in 1973. He started out driving cab and working nights. He had developed a clientele that included working girls and others. One night he offered to forego the fare for an exchange of services. The lady of the evening wanted cash on the barrelhead. He reminded her that they were both children of the free love generation. She answered quickly and sweetly, "Jerry, the love is always free. You just have to pay for the sex." I can only guess how that ended up (he never told me). He always regretted not getting Ringo Starr's autograph, his most famous passenger. Jerry had gone to dog grooming school and now owned his own shop in Flushing, home of the 1939 World's Fair and Shea Stadium. New York City, try as it might, never changed him, and I always would refer to him as the Last Living Lumberjack in New York. Later, after a raucous and whiskey-stained gig in the Village, he would refer to me as the Pit Bull of Folk.

Woody Guthrie, Dust Bowl troubadour, was the first modern folksinger. He learned songs off the radio and records from the Carter Family and others, who in turn had learned and written songs by ear that were passed down through generations, sung in shotgun shacks and on ramshackle farms; played in living rooms around candles and gas-lit lamps; and found in mountain gospel music and shape note singing from Ireland, the British Isles, and elsewhere that connected all these first-generation Americans with the bloodlines, histories, and melodies of their ancestors. Like chinking between logs, Pete Seeger, Aunt Molly Jackson, and Lead Belly filled in the gaps of this history with songs they had picked up on that ghostly antennae wave from the past, pushing them deep for good measure. Ramblin' Jack Elliott, Bob Dylan, Ry Cooder, Taj Mahal, David Bromberg, and Norman Blake trimmed the lamps and kept them burning on this trail, backward through time, hanging them from ancient trees and at the doorstep of Doc Watson in Deep Gap, North Carolina. Their paths led younger musicians like myself back to Woody Guthrie's songs, the ever-clear amniotic fluid from which a new generation of folk, protest, and other songs would emerge.

I called Nora the moment I got to town, and she invited me to dinner the next night and told me to meet her at her office at 250 West Fifty-seventh Street. I bought a bouquet of fresh flowers from a street vendor in Midtown and arrived promptly at 5. It was the home of Woody Guthrie Publications and also the office of Harold Leventhal, Woody's and Pete Seeger's manager. Fred Hellerman, one of the original Weavers and producer of Joan Baez's first two records, had an office there as well. I took the elevator to the twelfth floor and knocked on the door. Harold's wife, Nathalie, a gorgeous woman in her seventies, answered and led me to the inner sanctum. Nathalie, a sculptor, had fashioned busts of Woody and others in copper tones, which lined the tops of metal file cabinets and reminded me where I was.

Finishing up a phone call, Nora finally walked in. If I were not trying to keep some sort of professional decorum, I would have proposed on the spot. She had long, flowing black curls around a face with Woody's nose and eyes, with the soft and striking feminine beauty of her mother. She reminded me of mine. She had a Coney Island laugh, and a smile that came easily and often. The skateboard logo on her T-shirt reflected a freedom from style that was truly her own.

She suggested a restaurant bar across the street called the Le Bar Bat. As we were standing in line waiting to get seated, I looked at the address and realized it was actually 311 West Fifty-seventh Street, the same address of John Hammond's office. I mentioned that to Nora. The owner, who was seating us, overheard us and was amazed I knew that. He seated us immediately. We had dinner, drinks, and spent the next couple of hours sharing stories and belly laughs. I had met and made a beautiful new friend.

A month later, I had hooked up with a woman from Minnesota who invited me to see *Carmina Burana* at Carnegie Hall. This epic piece, written by German composer Carl Orff, included twenty-four poems that covered the ephemeral nature of life, including vagabond songs of drinking and dancing and century-old stories of the foibles of love. It was to be performed by an orchestra and large choir. Though hard to believe, the great hall, with no steel frames and made entirely by masonry, was almost torn down in 1960. The city owes a great debt to Isaac Stern, one of the greatest violinists of the twentieth century, for leading the effort to save this hallowed structure. Sometimes it takes a musician to help even great cities see the error of their ways.

I was going to Carnegie Hall and didn't even have to practice. I borrowed Jerry's $700 cashmere coat, dressed in my double-breasted green sharkskin suit, shined my shoes twice, and met her at the hall. The concert was amazing, lifting the soul in updrafts from the Muse. Several hours and expensive martinis later, we were lip-locked at Le Bar Bat until closing time.

I walked her to her subway stop and then hopped the subway back to Queens. It was late, and this midwestern midnight cowboy just assumed that trains run twenty-four hours a day in New York City. I was absolved of that idea as my train flew past my stop at what seemed like a million miles an hour. With no idea where to get off, I rode the train to the end of the line. The wind that whipped the platform reminded me of the night at the gas station by the river close to my old girlfriend's house. I looked around at my fellow late-night travelers all waiting for the train to start back up and head, hopefully, back into Manhattan. I was dressed in a way that said, "Please rob me, I am lost." I didn't think a white guy had been in this neighborhood since Manhattan was purchased from the Indians for $24, some beads, and a few bottles of moonshine.

Forty-five minutes later, I got back on the train that was covered in rainbow graffiti from the time when Grandmaster Flash ruled the boroughs. A quartet of black guys were drinking out of a bottle in a brown paper bag and smoking reefer like it was Bob Marley's dressing room. They appeared to be homeless, riding out this arctic evening in the warmth of the train. In fear of getting mugged and rather than waiting for it to happen, I walked across the subway car and sat next to them. They looked at me suspiciously, then either sensing my fear or maybe too high to be threatening, they offered me a pull off the bottle. Either I had judged too soon, or I just got lucky. We ended up back at Times Square, and I finally made my way back to Rego Park at 7 A.M. It was the longest subway ride I ever took. I blew a kiss to the golden ground beneath the Sixty-third Street stop on Queens Boulevard, relieved to be home, another boy baptized in the cold water of the big-city night.

Nora was just starting to put the Woody Guthrie Archives together. Her mother, Marjorie, Woody's second wife, had spent her life picking up after her husband, never letting any scrap of paper, whether a typewritten song or poem, drawing or cartoon, or anything else, hit the garbage can. She was a dancer and had fallen in love with Woody after a performance they did together. Recognizing his genius and his Oklahoma red-dirt honesty, she collected it all. A student of Martha Graham, she must have danced across wooden stages, her shadows moving and swaying against violet curtains, before audiences that had never seen bodies like this in motion. Nora walked with a dancer's glide, as she was one herself. Now she was continuing her mother's work, a grown woman who had accepted this task of establishing a benchmark for her father's work.

Among the items in the burgeoning collection was an interview that described a meeting between Woody and a Brooklyn State Hospital psychiatrist. The condescending physician wrote in his notes: "He says he's a famous folksinger—says he's written over 2,000 songs." Later that afternoon, I found a notebook that Woody used in his later years. His once sure and steady sign painter hands, now racked by the debilitating muscular disease Huntington's chorea, could do nothing more than scribble erratic circles and lines across the page like the freewheeling strokes of a two-year-old child. What thoughts, songs, or images lay imprisoned in his head, and what frustration must he have had not being able to commit them to paper, and what did we lose because of it? It hit me like a bullet in the chest. I closed the notebook, said good-bye to Nora, and took a long walk in Central Park.

Punk rock, as I write this, by its own rules should be over by now. It was still alive and well in Manhattan in 1995. Not only could I never play as fast as most of those bands, to me it never had the backbeat that I loved and needed in my rock and roll, nor was I ever that angry. Don't get me wrong: the Clash ruled, Hüsker Dü and the Replacements were a true punk rock Minneapolis tag team, I loved Patti Smith and Television, and I was a big fan of Billy Zoom, the guitarist from X, among other great bands. I also loved Fishbone, the mixed L.A. punk funk band that added a little Tabasco to their eggs with ska and horns. But mostly, I loved the attitude, the look, and the hell-bent-for-leather belief that most of these bands shared. I liked to play slow songs and long guitar solos unlike these rebels who never took a pause, but I did cop a bit of their attitude. Though grunge and hard-core music was starting to supplant punk rock as we knew it, there was still a smattering of the scene left, and I'd rubbed shoulders with the spiky-haired and Mohawked true believers at St. Mark's Place in the East Village, on subways, and at the guitar stores along Forty-eighth Street in Midtown. Then, of course, there were the Ramones, the most American rock and roll band of all time.

Jerry and I lived right off Sixty-fifth and Queens Boulevard and used to go to movies at the Trylon Theater a few blocks away. The movie house was next door to Joey Ramone's mother's art studio and store, where the Ramones used to rehearse when they were getting started. Queens Boulevard was the largest boulevard in the world. You took your life in your hands if you tried to cross all twelve lanes at rush hour. I would occasionally go up to Forest Hills High School and jog (well, walk fast) around the track. That high school produced not only the Ramones, but Michael Landon ("Little Joe" Cartwright), Simon and Garfunkel, Leslie West, Art Buchwald, Jerry Springer, and Bob Keeshan (Captain freakin' Kangaroo!), as well as Peter Parker, better known in the comics as Spider Man—all of them different floors in the American funhouse of this rock and roll high school.

The Trashmen is a Minnesota band whose unlikely hit "Surfin' Bird" was an influence on the Ramones. Living in Rego Park, I had a good sense of where the Ramones came of age, why they wanted to leave, and where everybody talked in clipped sentences as the cars sped down the boulevard four on the floor, fast as 1-2-3-4. I was at the Rego Park post office on a hot July day. The air conditioner had broken down, the line was long, and the postal clerk did not speak English very well, nor did many of the customers. I was in the back of the line, next to a Jewish woman who had to be at least eighty years old. After nearly a half-hour wait, she shouts loud enough for everybody to hear, "Step it up. . . . I didn't come here to die!" The icy edge in her voice cut through the heat, straight to the funny bone. It was a New York moment. I thought about Joey Ramone, and it all seemed to make sense, somewhere between "Hey, ho, let's go," and "I wanna be sedated." Welcome to my neighborhood.

I started to get some gigs around the Village. You damn near had to pay to play, so much unlike Minneapolis, where you could actually make a living playing music. There was a handful of clubs there, but by now they were almost mausoleum-like, faded postcard pictures connected in the madrigal moments of an era when folk music mattered. It hung on barely, subsisting on foreign tourist dollars, now cashed in for the green dollars of American currency, which traded these dollars for a filmy cataract glimpse into bygone days, echoing between the clang of cash registers and the street barkers outside each club offering two-for-one discounts in hand-written Xeroxed handbills. Clubs like the Red Lion on Bleecker Street, the Back Fence, and the Sun Mountain Café—an underground club on Third Street—still had music regularly, and in spite of the fact the bloom had long since fallen off the rose, I was happy to be playing in Greenwich Village and looked forward to each and every gig.

I'd spend two or three afternoons a week at Nora's office, watching small treasures of Woody's history come through the door and then filed perfectly under the watchful eye of George Arvello, the archivist who put together the Louis Armstrong Archives at Queens College. Louis Armstrong and his wife lived in Corona, Queens, not far from our place in Rego Park. God knows I had enough free time and still wonder why I never went to visit the stoop outside their door where Armstrong serenaded the neighborhood kids when he wasn't touring. All good things in time, I guess.

Nora and I would grab lunch when we could, sometimes joined by her son Cole, a willow-wisp of a kid with jet-black hair with the Woody and Nora wave. When Nora was busy, Cole and I would go to Central Park and climb rocks, play with his metallic toy cars, and I'd hope to hell the kid wouldn't fall off a swing, slide, or rock and break his arm. He was Woody's grandson, for god's sake, and I took custody and care of him like he was John-John Kennedy.

Steve Martin was the head of the Agency Group, a musical conglomerate that booked some of the finest acts on the circuit. I had gotten to know him in 1985 on my first foray to the Big Apple, and we stayed in touch. He booked me to open two shows for Mary Black, Ireland's answer to Emmylou Harris. The Black family was a musical tribe considered to be Ireland's first family of song. I was to open for her in Troy, New York, and a few days later in Boston. I had never heard of her but soon would and would thank my lucky stars I did.

I took the train up along the Hudson River to Troy. Before grabbing the connection at Grand Central Station, I walked around outside and smoked a couple of cigarettes. I stood in the shadow of the Met Life Building. My father, after selling Allstate insurance for forty years, got laid off after a disagreement with them and started selling Met Life. He picked up the pieces, at age fifty-seven, and rebuilt 90 percent of his clientele, representing almost two thousand people who signed back up with the new company, helping him win the best independent agent in the country status, and a brand-new Winchester shotgun in the process. The lesson of Dad's perseverance and comeback would serve me well in the years to come.

Before extinguishing my last cigarette, I glimpsed a small, worn copper placard on a brick building just a few blocks down from Grand Central at Forty-fourth and Vanderbilt. It noted that American patriot Nathan Hale had been hanged at this spot. While they lowered the noose around his head, he said, "I only regret that I have but one life to give for my country." They let him write a letter to his mother before they placed him on the gallows. He was twenty-one years old. How fast history moves sometimes, and how quickly it fades away, as we forget the bravery of those who built this country, lost in our modern world and buried in history books that most students will never read. And much of the rest, symbolized by once lovely statues, now sullied by pigeons, losing their edges and corners to years of weather and neglect.

The Troy Music Hall, built in the early years of the twentieth century, hosted the likes of Rachmaninoff, Vladimir Horowitz, Yehudi Menuhin, and Arthur Rubinstein. Through their hands people felt the souls of the great composers playing music that, though sometimes centuries old, felt like it could have been written yesterday. As a musician I have always bowed to the great classical players, as I do before the gods of bebop like Charlie Parker, Dizzy Gillespie, and Thelonius Monk. Jerry Garcia once said that a musician's style is the "sum of his limitations." I knew mine. But for years I have dedicated my Sunday mornings to listening to classical music and understood what Oscar Wilde meant when he said, "After playing Chopin I feel as if I had been weeping and mourning over tragedies that were not my own." Stages like these were altars to me, and I should have known better than try to smoke in church.

The show opened with the chief of the fire department, in a red fireman's hat, welcoming everyone, then explaining how this historic hall, after years of love and renovation, had to be respected: there would be absolutely NO SMOKING. I did a forty-five-minute set. Though plagued by a constant buzz in the monitors, it went over well. Mary Black and her band came on, and I sat in the wings to watch her. She sang in a way that made me believe my true and future love may live in Ireland. She had a great telepathic band behind her. She went gently into a song of hers called "Only a Woman Knows" that segued into Bob Marley's "No Woman, No Cry." Always a mama's boy, I watched as every woman I had ever known, loved, and honored appeared in a long pastiche of balletic images winding through my skull and heart, one beat at a time, skipping none. When the song was done, I needed a cigarette.

I could have gone outside to smoke, but I didn't want to miss the rest of Mary's set. I went to the third floor and found a bathroom far away from the madding crowd, and in what I thought was an empty bathroom lit up. In my haste for my nicotine fix, I didn't see the black rubber boots next to me beyond the stall divider. I was on my second or third drag, the nicotine filling my lungs, calming me as it snaked its way into my bloodstream. In a moment like when a wife walks into the bedroom to find her husband in bed with the next-door neighbor, the door to the stall opened and out walked the fire chief. Still wearing his fire helmet and buckling his pants, he emerged and busted me on the spot. He led me to the first floor and kicked me out of the building, though my guitar and coats with house keys were still inside and backstage. I snuck in through another door, caught the rest of Mary's set, and headed back to Manhattan on the midnight train. I looked back to the lights of the city and thankfully saw no burning ring of fire.

A few days later I opened for Mary on the last night of her tour, at the Berklee School of Music Performing Arts Center. My musical quest had included being denied entrance into a music school. That I was now on the stage at the most acclaimed music school in the country was more than a small victory for me. The crowd, most of whom had Irish bloodlines, welcomed her like the queen that she was. I opened my set and told the assembled that I came from the Iron Range, the same red magnetic ground that produced Boston Celtics superstar Kevin McHale. I was in like Flynn. Mary's guitarist of fifteen years was leaving the band after this performance, and with the audience firmly behind them, they serenaded the crowd with a performance as good as I had seen in years. The Irish truly know how to say good-bye.

By now the Woody Guthrie Archives were starting to flower and blossom. I walked in one day to meet Nora and looked through the glass window of the door that was shut, into Harold Leventhal's office. I had to look twice, and when I did I saw the man himself, the Johnny Appleseed of folk music, Pete Seeger. I had become such good friends with Nora I would sometimes forget my proximity to Woody's art and music. That Pete was sitting on the plaid couch that Woody used to sleep on made meeting him even more special. Nora interrupted the meeting, introduced me briefly, and Pete signed my poster for my upcoming gig at the Sun Mountain Café. It was like getting Alexander Hamilton's signature on a fresh ten dollar bill, and a moment that I will remember like my first kiss at Southside Park.

Woody's archives were beginning to overflow with books written by and about him, in dozens of languages from around the world. Marjorie had collected almost everything he had ever written when they were together: on stationery, hand- or typewritten, and on envelopes and grocery bags. Other lost tapes, letters, and lyrics were arriving from other sources as well. By now any visitor who stopped in, by appointment, was required to wear white plastic gloves before perusing these treasure chests of American musical history.

I was sitting by the 4 × 4 white wooden desk and wearing mine when the archivist came in and asked me if I would like to look at the handwritten manuscript of "This Land Is Your Land," on yellow legal paper now protected by plastic covering, like a rare Amazon butterfly covered under glass. He gave it to me, and I held it in my hands and cradled it. For me, a vagabond folksinger from the Midwest, it was like holding the Declaration of Independence. This piece of paper, with this song, Woody's antidote to Irving Berlin's "God Bless America," had become our de facto national anthem, still sung by every schoolchild in America, by campfires, picket lines, and by Pete Seeger himself at the presidential inaugural gathering in 2008. He sang it loudly and proudly, all six verses including the line, "In the squares of the city, in the shadow of the steeple, near the relief office I see my people, and some are grumblin' and some are wonderin' if this land is still made for you and me." It was Seeger's crowning moment, sung in the long and approving shadow of the Lincoln Memorial. Leave it to Woody to write songs that get more powerful and holy with time. I now realized why I came to New York City.

A week later, I did a wonderful gig opening for former Jefferson Airplane guitarist Jorma Kaukonen at Irving Plaza, not far from the original Max's Kansas City, the celebrated rock and roll playground in the 1970s. It had been a Yiddish theater, an old union hall, and a burlesque venue, featuring burlesque queen Gypsy Rose Lee. Climbing the two flights of stairs to the old ballroom felt like you were going up to another stage in time. I imagined audiences from those times, and how they might have been dressed. After my set I went to the bar and bumped into Joey Ramone, the pride of Forest Hills. He is tall, almost like Wilt Chamberlain, dressed as you might imagine in a black leather jacket, striped shirt, tight black jeans with red tennis shoes, and dark maroon sunglasses. I bought him a white Russian, then another, and we had a sweet chat. He talked softly, his words slurred not from drink but from shyness, and I enjoyed what might have been one of the greatest New York accents I've ever heard.

I was doing Sunday nights at the Back Fence bar on Bleecker Street, open since 1945. It has a bright, old-school neon sign featuring the name of the bar on the outside, several wooden tables and chairs inside, a small bar, and a stage in the corner. It was run by a father-and-son team, both named Ernie. There were four musicians every Sunday night, and we'd each do a set and sometimes sit in with one another. One Sunday, a group of tourists came in and started to request songs you could hear on any jukebox in any sports bar in America. I soldiered on with my original tunes. Ernie Sr. came up after my set and asked me why I wouldn't do "Margaritaville" by Jimmy Buffet. I wanted to pull a Michael O'Donoghue from *Saturday Night Live* and poke knitting needles into my eyes, then ears. I thanked him for the gig and told him I did not come to Greenwich Village to play cover tunes. I bought a one-way ticket back to Minneapolis the next day.

I took the time to make the rounds and say thank-you and good-bye to everyone I got to know. Nora and I had a lovely walk with Cole through Central Park. We knew we'd see each other soon. On my very last day I went to the Coliseum Bookstore on Fifty-seventh Street where I'd spent many hours over the past year and a half. One of my dreams is to inherit a used bookstore in my old age and live out my life reading every book from aisle to aisle. There was a very handsome and distinguished gentleman in the jazz section. We were both reading books about Billie Holiday. I felt like I should know the man as his face looked very recognizable. I wanted to shake his hand but was too shy to say hello.

While reading the Billie Holiday book, I learned that her funeral was held at the St. Paul of Apostle Church right up the street in Columbus Square. I decided to check it out. The church was open, and I went in and sat inside. I imagined Lady Day being wheeled in and out of the church, now gone and never being able to sing songs of a day as sad as this. There were older women lighting small candles, and I sat there by myself in reverent silence, images of everything I loved about this city and how one could find a song or story on every corner. When I got back to Minneapolis, I grabbed a copy of the newspaper, and there was a picture of the man I was standing next to in the bookstore. He was coming to town a few days later. The great American playwright Arthur Miller would be speaking at the Walker Art Center that weekend. And that is the kind of town New York was, history dripping off buildings and walls, and rising like smoke out of manhole covers at midnight, into the air and wind, and then around the world.

SWING LOW, SWEET CHARIOT

To find true love before it even blossoms is a beautiful thing. Like rare magnets that attract without touching, souls connect and intellect catches up in its own time. My little brother Johnny was lucky like that.

John met Dianne when they were in fifth grade. Our families were neighbors. Dianne wore her brown hair in a bob, and her bright blue eyes danced beneath dark brows and long lashes. By her early twenties Dianne's naturally curly hair was shoulder length, framing her face that had matured from cute to head-turning beauty. In that time their relationship also evolved, from neighborhood playmates, to friends, to lovers. In college Dianne pursued a degree in business administration, and John honed his gifts in teaching and education. They married in 1980.

Like a mirrored image of an old photo, they began life together in a small, two-story house just across the avenue and down the street within a block from their childhood homes. They transformed the neglected, well-worn interior walls and floors with an eclectic decorative flair that would become their signature style for years to come. John worked a block away as a school janitor and bus driver, commuting to Duluth several days a week to continue his studies at UMD. By 1985, three sons had come along.

Dianne bolstered their income by setting up a day care in their home. She set up a simple accounting system of envelopes in a kitchen drawer from which she metered out cash for groceries, utilities, and even family vacations. John safely trusted her abilities. They were a dream team.

Upon finishing his degree, John accepted a teaching position in Rochester, Minnesota. It was there that their fourth son was born. Dianne set up another successful day care/night care business and decided to tackle a master's degree in education. She ran their household with efficiency and grace and kept the rest of us together as well. Part-priestess, part-counselor, full-time friend, she was mother, in a way, to all of us.

Upon finishing her master's degree, she and John set their sights on Alaska, a fresh and rugged place to raise up strong, young boys. Cousins, neighbors, and friends gathered on the day they were scheduled to leave.

It was a day without clouds, a day without fear. There they stood, with four summer-tanned and sun-bleached blond, skinny boys—Jason, Jacob, John-Paul, and Jordan—and Ike, their large German shepherd, alongside a Chevy Suburban with boat in tow and a Dodge Ram truck pulling a trailer piled high with household items. John would drive one vehicle, Dianne the other. The boys had already divided and created little traveling niches of their own, fit for playing games and sleeping on the journey, safe beneath their parents' wings. In my parting words, I urged them to look up my old friend Gary Brekke. He had moved to Alaska years before and was raising three children with his wife, Laura. Even though it is a huge state, at least they would know someone when they got up there.

They arrived on August 10, just over 3,200 miles later, in the coal mining community of Healy, Alaska, gateway to Denali National Park. It was the time of year when days were long. In less than a week they were unpacked, settled, and ready to explore.

Before John's job as assistant superintendent of schools was to begin, Dianne dashed off a few letters to family back home. In one letter to a ten-year-old niece in Maryland, she named the animals they'd seen on their journey: "Bear, moose, caribou, rams, bison, buffalo, Dall sheep, mountain goats, and deer. . . . The mountains are so beautiful. This weekend we will head south to salmon fish on the rivers. I can hardly wait. We have fished several times at night already. We are catching rainbow trout."

The oldest of the boys planned to stay in Healy to work, while the rest of the family headed out for a short camping trip near Willow. It took them along a highway that would forever change their lives.

Along the way they stopped and fished at three streams without much luck. They decided to try one more, Sheep Creek, before ending their expedition and heading to Wasilla for groceries. The air was fresh and charged with the electrons of twenty-four-hour days of sunlight. It was the sweetest time of their twenty years together, stronger now than ever, with four beautiful boys, saplings that would grow tall and strong in this wind, water, and light.

They grabbed their fishing rods and with trusty dog Ike started to make their way across the bridge. At 3:07 P.M., as they started to descend the embankment, a truck appeared out of nowhere, going much too fast. It passed into the wrong lane. In one dark and deadly moment, the driver plowed down the hill, hitting John and Ike, and catapulting Dianne into the river.

John tried to pick himself up and walk toward Dianne screaming at anyone within earshot, "My wife, my wife!" but his leg was badly broken, and he fell, landing on Ike who was not moving. In the ensuing chaos someone from the large numbers of fishermen along the river had called an ambulance. EMTs arrived and loaded John and the boys inside. The body that once held Dianne's soul now lay on the river's shore, with her spirit now in the presence of her Lord whom she loved so deeply. Ike was gone as well.

John and the boys were rushed to the emergency room in Palmer. While the boys waited outside in numbed silence, the doctors asked John if he knew anyone in Alaska. John could think of only one person, Gary Brekke—affectionately nicknamed Trickrider in our younger days—though he had no idea where Gary lived. A staff member searched the telephone directory. Miraculously, he lived only five miles from the hospital. And thankfully he happened to be home. Fifteen minutes later he was there, an old friend, no formalities required. John's immediate concern was his boys, and he asked Gary if he could take them. Without hesitation Gary kindly gathered them up and headed back to his house where his wife, Laura, was waiting.

The three Brekke kids were close in age to a couple of the boys. Gary, a bush pilot, asked the boys if they would like to go out and look at his airplane. They did. But even the best of bush pilots cannot make time fly backwards or alter the time John and Dianne decided to cross that bridge. At least for now, the boys were safe and sound with a family that wrapped their arms around them like they were their own.

John was released from the hospital a week later. He and the boys returned to Healey. Though they were virtually unknown in their new community, neighbors poured in quiet support. He opened his door to a kitchen packed full of groceries. Meals were supplied for nearly two months. One day a man he didn't know knocked on their door. He had taken up a collection at the plant where he worked and gave John an envelope that contained more than $1,500. Thank God for the kindness of strangers.

With John on Coumadin and crutches, they flew back to Minnesota for the two funerals that were planned for Dianne. Somberly our family gathered at the Minneapolis airport to meet them, a stark contrast to the hearty send-off we'd all participated in just weeks before.

The first funeral was in Rochester, Minnesota, where John and Dianne had taught in the local school system. The United Methodist Church was packed with students, family, and friends. Dianne's stepbrother Paul Richards arrived, now a leader of the acclaimed St. John's Boys' Choir in Collegeville, and former keyboard player in our early band the Positive Reaction. Though we hadn't seen each other in more than twenty years, Paul and I were asked to sing "Amazing Grace." We only had to rehearse it once—two childhood friends, related by marriage, now sharing deep sadness and loss. They transported John into the church in a wheelchair, followed by the four boys bravely by his side—the five men to whom Dianne so lovingly had dedicated her life and love. A sweet spirit permeated the gathering as many mourners that day walked forward to share stories of their connections to Dianne. Their words breathed truth to the Proverb: "Give her of the fruit of her hands; and let her own works praise her in the gates."

A second funeral was held at the United Methodist Church in our hometown of Virginia, Minnesota. Family members gathered at my father's small house on Northside, finding comfort in the close surroundings as we sidestepped slowly through the large group of cousins and aunts and uncles to countertops brimming with food brought in by neighbors and friends. As we made plans for the upcoming service, we agreed that music would again play a large part. Down in the basement my sister Jackie and I found a quiet spot in the laundry room to select a special hymn. There on Mom's old ironing board we opened a hymnal and began to search. Still stunned from the tragedy, with the image of the boys leading Dianne and the dog and John as they made their way to the river, we sought a familiar hymn fitting in respect. Suddenly there it was, "Swing Low, Sweet Chariot," with words that seemed to gleam from the page: "I looked over Jordan, and what did I see, coming for to carry me home? A band of angels coming after me, coming for to carry me home." Perfect.

Again the church was packed. Family, friends, and neighbors showered John and the boys with all the love they could muster, tears flowing where words couldn't reach. Reverend Bill Kvale, our former minister and longtime family friend, led the service. One of Dianne's cousins, a talented vocalist, shared an a capella version of "Ave Maria" that rose like incense from the altar. Our good friend Prudence Johnson, one of Dianne's favorite singers, sang "Let It Be," one of Dianne's favorite songs, a musical balm for our raw and aching hearts. Dianne's sister Barbara read Proverbs 31 in honor of the capable wife and mother whose casket lay closed before us. We closed with the song about the sweet chariot, left the church, and gathered once more around her graveside in Greenwood Cemetery, just down the row from my mother's grave where we had gathered only two short years before. Faith broke through, smiles appeared through veils of tears, and quiet praises rose in the air supplanting sorrow as we dropped rose petals onto her casket. "Where, oh death, is your victory? Where, oh death, is your sting?"

I marvel at my brother's strength. Most anyone else, after a tragedy of this magnitude, would have pulled up stakes and moved home. And though there were periods of exhaustion when he admits he just wanted to let go, he was now even more deeply committed to his boys. Still in a walking cast, he and the boys returned to Healy to finish the job he was hired to do, to a town they had yet to know.

The boys dealt with it as best they could and grieved in their own ways. One began writing poetry, another became the emotional caretaker of the family, one was quiet and introspective. The youngest would sometimes wrap up in his mom's sweatshirt and crawl under the bed with a picture of Ike. The boys wrote me letters that made me cry before I even opened the envelope. Jordan sent me a little papier-mâché Santa Claus that hangs on my tree every Christmas and safely resides in my desk the rest of the year. One day, in a way that John thought might be the ice slowly melting off the river of grief, Jordan asked, "Dad, is it okay if I stop thinking about Mom for a while?" Even little hearts find their boundaries.

John resigned his position when the school year was up and moved back to Rochester. He resumed teaching, and the boys had a chance to reconnect with some of their friends. Eventually John accepted a series of K-12 principal's positions in the small northern towns of Babbitt, followed by Orr, then Cherry, Cotton, and Cook. In 2003, he married Carol Carlson, a childhood friend of his and Dianne's, and a strong pillar of support after the accident. The ceremony was held on the sauna beach of the Metsa family cabin on Lake Vermilion. John and his handsome boys wore matching Hawaiian shirts, and Carol wore a wreath of wildflowers in her hair, all symbols of a happy, new beginning. The Reverend Bill Kvale once again officiated, a pastoral link in the spiritual journey we all had traveled.

Our family gets together every Christmas, and while I spend time with each of the boys individually throughout the year, I take special pleasure during this time watching them interact and communicate with each other in the unique unspoken language of brothers who are closer than most. Though nephews, they are as close as sons to me. In the words of Bob Marley, "He who feels it, knows it." And they do.

A couple of years ago I called Gary Brekke to wish him and his family a Merry Christmas. I told him we would never forget the gift he gave our family by stepping in at the deepest moment of need. He replied, "Paul, you may not remember this, but back when we met in Virginia, and I played with Cats for a while, I was living with my grandmother. She passed away right before my second year in junior college. My cousins inherited Grandma's house and asked me to leave, even though I still had a year left at school. It was during the final construction boom on the Iron Range, and there were no rooms left in Virginia to rent. Your father knew an old Finnish lady, Mrs. Juntanen, who had an empty second-floor duplex on Southside. My blond hair was halfway down my back when he took me to meet her, spoke to her in Finnish, and explained that I was a friend of his son and needed a place to stay. Mrs. Juntanen rented me the room, and I was able to finish junior college. I always wanted to repay your family for that kindness."

Who can figure out the ways of the world, the demon heartbreak, death that comes too early, magnetic attractions, loves won and lost, fleeting victories of family and friends, business and pleasure, art and commerce, precious moments that pass in flocks like birds soaring and swooping and floating scarf-like in twilight winds? At the end of the day, truth and love are the only things left standing. We must stay honest, healthy, and mentally strong, with the courage to give and take love with every opportunity.

How could I reply to Brekke's thank-you other than to say, "You paid us back in spades, Trickrider. You paid us back in spades."

GHOSTS OF WOODY GUTHRIE

When Nora Guthrie called in May 1996 and invited me to perform at the Tribute to Woody Guthrie at the Rock and Roll Hall of Fame in Cleveland, I was honored, thrilled, and jazzed like a beatnik on stolen Benzedrine. I spent the summer rereading *Bound for Glory, Pastures of Plenty,* and *Woody Guthrie: A Life,* and listening to all the Woody Guthrie stuff I had. In caffeine-soaked mornings and nicotine-laced afternoons listening to Muddy Waters and Robert Johnson, I was living in that holy world of vinyl records again. Occasionally I'd see it with my eyes closed—unamplified truths, dust bowl farm blackouts, teenage girls and Cadillacs—a harsh and beautiful world. Blow, wind, blow.

Arriving at the Cleveland airport on September 26, I met Country Joe McDonald and the British folkie John Wesley Harding, who were also taking part in the Guthrie tribute. A driver took us through the rainy streets of the city to the Renaissance Hotel where we were to meet Nora for dinner. We found our rooms, freshened up, and headed downstairs to the dining room. I hadn't seen Nora for several months, but she looked as beautiful as ever, long black curls around a sculpted face, dark eyes sincere and mysterious, a smile that reminded me of Mom, and a secret hug that mothers reserve for reunions of friends and loved ones.

Over dinner we all laughed and carried on, getting louder as the evening wore on. Nora and I were about to light up our after-dinner cigarettes when Country Joe asked us if we wouldn't smoke. Country Joe—the guy who led almost half a million hippies, a lot of them naked, most of them stoned, in the infamous "Fish Cheer" at Woodstock—now an avid antismoker. I looked at Nora and said, "Give me an F!" having a little fun with Joe, who took the ribbing in stride, even though he was still a little perturbed that they lost his luggage at the airport. We finished dinner, and Nora and I beat down a couple Marlboro Reds outside. Then with two hours to closing time and Nora back in her room, I thought I'd take a ramble around the city.

Having spent most of my adult life performing in nightclubs, I can move through them like an eel in a muddy river. In the drizzle of the night I headed down toward the waterfront where I was told there was a bar with a double shot of blues and booze. My ears led the way, just a whistle from the river, and I walked into Wilbert's Bar. It was small, cozy, with a classic black oak bar and tables from another era. No sooner had I paid the cover charge than I looked up at the bandstand and locked eyes with the bass player, a buddy from Minneapolis, Dapper Doug Nelson.

I grabbed the only seat open at the bar and ordered a brandy straight up for me and one for Nelson. Moments later I realized I was sitting next to Robert Lockwood Jr., blues legend, Cleveland resident and, damn, Robert Johnson's stepson. (Somewhere there is a cemetery called Songwriters' Hill with only three graves. They belong to Robert Johnson, Woody Guthrie, and Hank Williams. The wind never stops blowing and the sun shines at night. And the hill surrounding them is a diamond slope.)

That night Lockwood didn't look much older than he did in the *King Biscuit Time* radio show photos from the early forties when he was playing with Sonny Boy Williamson. He was wearing a light blue silk windbreaker with the logo of his record label on the back, the kind favored by coked-out A&R guys in the seventies. His black beret was tilted slightly to the right, and he sat with his head forward, listening intently to the band, Blues Wunderkind, and the pride of Fargo, North Dakota, Jonny Lang.

My buddy Kevin Bowe had discovered Jonny at a blues jam in Fargo, and he was now starting to make a bit of a name for himself. Still a few years shy of twenty years old, with a chiseled, young face beneath thick blond hair parted in the middle, he sang in a way that seemed older than his years. He played a blazing Telecaster guitar, and Lockwood was giving him a smoky nod of approval. Someone snapped a photo of the three of us, Jonny on my left and Robert on my right, and I was feeling bookended by the history and the future of the blues. The Woody weekend was off to a helluva start. I headed back to the hotel with a sense that something was happening that I couldn't quite put into words.

The local newspapers were filled with stories on the Woody celebration as Cleveland tipped its hat to another great musician, honored in this blue-collar port town. Disc jockey Alan Freed rocked Cleveland in the early '50s with his radio show, helping to bring the term *rock and roll* into the public consciousness. His five-act extravaganza, the Moondog Coronation Ball, first produced in 1952, is considered by some to be the first rock and roll concert. Songs of Woody Guthrie now wafted through the town, once referred to as the breakout city for rock and roll.

Two shows were scheduled. The big show on Sunday was at Severance Hall on the Case Western University campus and featured Pete Seeger, Arlo Guthrie, Ramblin' Jack Elliott, Bruce Springsteen, Ani DiFranco, the Indigo Girls, Dave Pirner, and others. It was hosted by Nora and Harold Leventhal, the manager of Woody, Pete, and Arlo. I would play with seven other performers the night before, at the eight-hundred-seat Odeon Club. Also during the weekend a play by David Lutkin called *Woody Guthrie's American Song* would be performed.

Our rehearsal started around 1 P.M. on Saturday and was one of the most stunning experiences of the weekend. Nora Guthrie, her Croatian folk-singing friend Nenad Bach, and her lovely daughter Anna Rotundi (who took notes, carried the clipboard, and made sure this bound for glory train ran on time) greeted all of us with hot coffee and rolls. One by one, performers started to arrive: Jimmy LaFave, the voice of the Oklahoma red-dirt plains, Jimmie Dale Gilmore (Sinatra in cowboy boots), Country Joe McDonald, an old-guard folkie and Woody scholar, Alejandro Escovedo, songwriter par excellence and Texas rocker with his fiddle player, John Wesley Harding, Syd Straw, a marvelous red-headed songbird, and Jorma Kaukonen, who is as close to the Hells Angels or Reverend Gary Davis as I will probably ever get.

We sat in a semicircle on chairs and couches while Nora made us run through our tunes like a sixth grade teacher getting her kids ready for a spring pageant. We exchanged ideas for songs, solos, and ensembles. LaFave, a very funny cat who sings with his eyes closed, ran through an emotional "Oklahoma Hills." Nora and I exchanged glances in a telepathic thumbs-up. We shuffled through songs from the Woody jukebox: "Roll On Columbia," "I've Got a Woman," "Going Down the Road Feeling Bad," and "I've Got to Know." Jimmie Dale Gilmore came in and told Nora he wasn't exactly sure what he was going to sing but brought to the circle his Lubbock Flatlander magic and God-given desert vibrato. Silver-haired and soft-spoken, Harold Leventhal, who'd played such an important role in this music, entered the room and sat in the corner listening with silent pleasure.

The knockdown, ten-count moment of the rehearsal for me was when Alejandro picked up his guitar. I first met him at a gig I did with his band the True Believers at the Lone Star Cafe in New York City in 1986. He showed up this afternoon feeling and looking ill. Yet when he sang the opening lines to "Deportee," joined by fiddle and on the chorus by Nora,

Anna, and another woman, any ill spirit left by way of the twelfth-story window in a magical moment when two white pigeons that had been sitting on the sill lifted their wings and flew off into the Cleveland skyline.

The rehearsal came to an end and you could feel resurrection in the air. There was a reception that evening for the performers and participants at the Rock and Roll Hall of Fame. We arrived in hotel shuttle buses after and were greeted by the recorded dulcet tones of Jimmy LaFave blasting over the sound system. Jimmy is an Oklahoma native now living in Austin, Texas, whom I'm happy to say I was able to bring to Nora's attention. The home team scores.

Two friends from Minneapolis, photographer John McCally and music attorney Dennis Pelowski, flew in that morning for the shows. As we arrived at the Odeon Club that evening, the bouncer was taping a Sold Out sign to the door. The club was packed as was the dressing room. Jorma started out wearing a sport jacket that two songs into his set was lying on the ground next to his amp, as he became the tattooed god of hellfire I remembered. Nora welcomed everyone and introduced Jimmie LaFave, who performed "Oklahoma Hills" with an authority and reverence that was to become the hallmark of the weekend. I opened my three-song set with Woody's "Vigilante Man" with John Wesley Harding on harp and Jorma on lap steel. We then did "Robots on Death Row," one of my songs, which I dedicated to one of my heroes and Woody's ramblin' buddy, Brownie McGhee, who had passed away that spring. Nora had made a point of saying that we needn't just play Woody's tunes and that everyone's original tunes were just as important a part of the evening. I ended my set with "Jack Ruby," hyperventilating, sweating, and twelve verses and two guitar-thrash solos later. Just as I felt my heart was going to burst, I hit the last chord on the downbeat and combined it (for reasons I can't recall) with the Pete Townsend leap.

To play a good gig, you've got to prioritize quickly, do your best at what needs to be done, and when it's over, take a deep breath and hope it went well. Everyone turned in lovely sets. Before the encore it was my pleasure to call Nora and Anna out to take a bow, and I asked for a round of applause for Nora's mother and Woody's second wife Marjorie. If it wasn't for Marjorie's bookkeeping skills, many of Woody's writings, songs, and drawings might have been lost for good. I thanked Nora for being instrumental in helping set up the archives for the rest of us and having enough chutzpah, grace, and intuitiveness to engineer such a wonderful weekend for both the performers and audience. The performance ended with the performers locked arm in arm, swaying east to west, leading the audience in a ragged but righteous rendition of "This Land Is Your Land."

Just before our 1 P.M. rehearsal the next day, I entered the back door to the hall to a sonorous, twisting, almost subterranean sound. The doors to the stage were locked, but the sound overflowed the empty stairwells and snaked its way around the immense three-story hall, haunting and a tad indiscernible. As I climbed the stairs it became obvious that this must be Bruce Springsteen's private sound check.

I made my way to the rehearsal hall, opened the door, and followed my ears to the sound of someone tuning a banjo. There was Pete Seeger. Now Pete Seeger should be the fifth face on Mount Rushmore, as far as I'm concerned. I took a deep breath, quietly took my guitar from the case, and walked to the corner where John Wesley Harding had joined Pete. I put my cassette player on the windowsill beside us and joined Pete and Wes on "Hobo's Lullaby." One verse later Wes and I are weaving a couple of harmonies around Pete's righteous lead. In between verses, Pete adds long and deliberate clawhammer solos, and by the look on his face I can tell he's enjoying his own playing. After a couple of verses and choruses, while Wes plays mouth harp and I keep the chords going, Pete tells the story of the song and how everybody thought Woody wrote it, when in fact it was written by a guy named Goebel Reeves. That song shows Woody's affinity for the underdog, knocks the cops, and speaks of the optimism of how things will get better in heaven. These are Woody's greatest lessons to me, to give a voice and dignity to those who deserve it but have been denied. After finishing the tale, Pete hits the last verse, we join him on the chorus, and with another leisurely stroll on the banjo he takes us out.

Ever the mentor, Pete goes on to tell us about Merle Travis, the history of fingerpicking, the origins of major musical ideas from Africa, and how by slowing down Merle's "Sixteen Tons," Tennessee Ernie Ford had himself a hit. I introduce myself and tell Pete that "Where Have All the Flowers Gone" was probably the first folk song I ever learned. He looked at me with those Pacific blue eyes and asks, "Have you ever heard it in German?" and proceeds to enunciate the lyrics in his husky sand-reed voice.

After rehearsal we broke for a press conference downstairs. On the way down I was introduced to Jimmy Longhi, a retired attorney and an old running buddy of Woody's and Cisco Houston. They convinced him to join the merchant marines with them. As the press conference came to an end, Mr. Longhi stood up and asked if he could approach the podium. In a voice choked with emotion, he told a story of how while being torpedoed by U-boats and risking death, Woody grabbed Cisco and himself and went below deck and engaged hundreds of black soldiers and sailors in a sing-along (including "The Sinking of Reuben James") that culminated with a black sailor dancing with the white captain topside. The story illuminated not Woody the songwriter but Woody the man.

Back at the stage for the sound check, Jeff Kramer tapped me on the shoulder. In tow with Kramer was the soul of New Jersey, Bruce Springsteen, who needed to learn the song. The Boss's hair was combed back in a short ponytail and he was sporting a mustache. He was a gracious gentleman with a generous smile but was all business as the clock was ticking. He needed me to teach him the encore because he hadn't had time yet to learn it. In two minutes I showed him the three chords to the song, and he took off back upstairs. I can now add guitar teacher to my admittedly short résumé that is long on gigs but short on real jobs (though it does include carpet layer, disc jockey, lawn mower, house painter, and canoe guide). Nora called us to the grand stage, we ran through the encores, and the last rehearsal was over.

For our private tour of the Rock and Roll Hall of Fame, I climbed into the first van and was joined by Mr. and Mrs. Leventhal, Jimmy Longhi, Jimmy LaFave, his friend Greg Johnson from Oklahoma City, and Pete and Toshi Seeger. I was in the middle seat next to Pete, and for the next fifteen minutes listened to a great primer on the history of folk music through the eyes of its living leader. He spoke of the work his father, Charles Seeger, had done researching European folk music and how he presented it to America, and of folk songs with "teeth." He told us how he went to Central America and South America in the 1960s, to the chagrin of the U.S. government, to sing antiwar songs loudly and proudly. He told us that he and Woody first heard the word *hootenanny* in Seattle in 1938, and how the *Daily Worker* asked Woody to write an article about folk music, which Guthrie referred to as "ear music." That article was the beginning of Woody's book *Bound for Glory*. Turning into the parking lot at the Hall of Fame, Jimmy Longhi turned to Pete, pointed to the building, and said, "Look at that architecture!" Commenting on I. M Pei's design, Pete replied, without skipping a beat, "Well, I can see he can combine a circle and a square," and then to no one in particular, "I think the 45-degree angle has been completely overdone."

After the tour, we drop off Toshi and Pete; he steps out, grabs one of the concrete chain holders that guard the entrance, and leapfrogs over it with ease. We headed back to the hotel to have dinner and get ready for the show.

The ornate Severance Hall was packed and the anticipation was palpable. Ani DiFranco opened the show with an inside-out version of "Do-Re-Mi" that sparkled with originality. She became my newest hero. The Indigo Girls were up next and were joined by Ani for a powerful three-part version of "Blackjack Davey." Billy Bragg followed with a collection of undiscovered Woody lyrics that Nora asked him to put to music, including "My Bonnie Black Bess," a beautiful song about a man and his horse. Dave Pirner, lead singer of Soul Asylum and an old friend of mine, ended the set triumphantly with a dynamite version of "Pretty Boy Floyd."

Ramblin' Jack Elliott (Woody's mirror image), in his Brooklyn cowboy staccato cadence, kicked off the second set with a stunning version of "1913 Massacre," a poignant, heartbreaking song about some company thugs in Michigan who started a fire, bolted the door, and trapped a Christmas party of union workers and their families inside, ending in several deaths. Springsteen was up next. He rattled off the title track of his new record *The Ghost of Tom Joad*, a modern reworking of the Woody classic, with laser-beam precision that burst with conviction. Joe Ely came out and joined him for a playful duet of "Oklahoma Hills." Nora sat just offstage bathed in a blue light, wearing ripped jeans and white blouse like a gypsy Madonna, holding her young son Cole by her side, proud as a mother and daughter could be. Arlo came out next and turned in a brilliant set. I watched it all from the red-light glow of the side stage monitor board, soaking in the soulful seconds of every note that was played. Heaven on earth.

All of the Saturday night performers and the musicians and actors from the Woody Guthrie play joined Sunday's ensemble for the encores. As we were about to begin, Pete Seeger came on to a standing ovation with his banjo held high and beaming. He led a sweeter-than-Tupelo-honey version of "Hobo's Lullaby." Standing between Tim Robbins, Susan Sarandon, and Nora Guthrie, I felt as if I were about to receive my spiritual diploma, in spite of the fact that I was refused entrance to the music school at the University of Minnesota so many years before. We rallied into "I've Got to Know," with everyone taking a verse, and sent it into the stratosphere. At the end, Nora took to the microphone to thank everyone for being there, and the crowd, in electric silence, watched as Harold Leventhal, tears streaming down his face, came to center stage and hugged Nora in a moment charged with emotion that I will never forget. We retreated to the greenroom, enjoyed a sumptuous fare of food and drink, and partied in Woody's honor for the man whose work had brought us all together.

I awoke to a beautiful Cleveland morning and sent some roses to Nora and Anna with a note to thank them for this once-in-a-lifetime experience we all referred to as Woody Camp. On my way to the airport I stopped by the Rock and Roll Hall of Fame. I bumped into Ramblin' Jack Elliott who was admiring John Cippolina's psychedelic flame-burst guitar and turned my tape recorder on. Amid the noise of all the displays, Jack told me a story about the time he and Woody (who he said used to keep guitar picks in his hair) took a cross-country trip from New York to California. They camped one night on a ledge of a small piece of property that Woody owned in California. When Jack awoke, Woody was gone and on his way back to New York.

I returned to Minneapolis and was back at Nye's Polonaise Room for my Wednesday night house gig. No big names, no press, no concert stage or lighting, no roadies, just a dimly lit stage in a corner bar, yet that night it felt like Carnegie Hall. I remembered something Pete Seeger told me in the van: "I'd like to remind all the young folksingers to make sure they get the audience to sing. They don't have to sing every song but let them sing something." With that, and the new blood I felt coursing through my veins as a man who if not ordained felt, at least, metaphysically knighted in the grand Guthrie tradition, I banged out the first chord and opening verse to "This Land Is Your Land," and by the end of the song the entire bar of retirees, ramblers, rounders, discount lovers, businessmen, bookies, a couple of tipsy steelworkers, a dealer and a stripper, a fallen priest, frat boys and sorority girls, the bartender, the swamper, the waitresses, and the other proud, beautiful, and anonymous Americans sang with me in a boisterous, freedom-filled, and collective last-call victory voice that echoed, at least that night, from the redwood forests to the gulf stream waters.

MARTINI GULCH

I got back to Minneapolis in the spring of 1996. I had done my time in New York having experienced as much as that town had to offer and, thanks to the generosity of friends, more than my limited means would have allowed. Over the years I had daydreamed about living in Nashville and Austin, Texas, two great American music capitals. But Minneapolis had always had its own magic, and unlike Nashville and Austin, a working musician could always make a living in town apart from the rigors of the road that have broken up more bands than girlfriends and wives put together. My bank account was empty, I missed my family, and I looked forward to moving back to Minnesota, the state where I was born and will probably die as well.

I spent the first week sleeping on my buddy Paul Mandell's couch. I then bumped into William Rogers at Kowalski's Market at Twenty-fifth and Hennepin while shopping. He and his girlfriend, Christina, one of the original waitresses at the Egg and I, had offered me the spare bedroom in their place near Lake of the Isles before I left town, in case I was ever back visiting. I asked if the room was still empty. He said it was, and the three of us got together for coffee. They offered me the room for a nominal monthly fee, with Christina's commandments: no smoking, no drinking, no sex in the house, and no guitar after 8 p.m. Beggars can't be choosers, and I moved in the next day. While it was as close as I will ever get to monastic living, I appreciated their kindness and spent most of the winter on the porch with Gracie the dog, sneaking cigarettes. The smoke would trail out the screened window and wind down the avenue, take a right, and vanish on its way to the lake.

It was now time to start working on my second comeback. I got a weekly gig at Sawatdee, a Thai restaurant downtown, and played unamplified in the window next to a stuffed elephant, a fake cactus, and lots of straw that surrounded knickknacks from Thailand. Nobody said a second comeback would be easier than the first. Guitarist Preston Reed advised me, "Never let the music business break your heart." I was not going to let that happen now, and I was enough of an existentialist to enjoy the absurdity of it all. Humility came this time cloaked in a gig as a storefront musical mannequin with coconut shrimp and fresh spring rolls in Styrofoam boxes to go.

In May, I ran into Tony Tieberg at Lyon's Pub in downtown Minneapolis. We were buddies, not great friends, but both from the Iron Range. His mother, Edna, was a student of my father's when he taught high school in Mt. Iron (pronounced Mount Ny-ern by most Rangers). Tony was recently divorced and living in a two-bedroom house in Northeast Minneapolis, now an empty nest without his young daughter, Frances, and his wife. I asked him if he would consider renting me the spare bedroom. You would have thought he had just won the Powerball by the way he said yes.

I gave notice to William and Christina and told Tony I would be there on the first day of June. I moved in with a suitcase of clothes, several guitars, four boxes of papers and pictures, and a twelve-pack of Budweiser as a gift for my new roommate. Having trained as a chef, Tony was an amazing cook. My first night there, after a dinner of T-bone steaks, bacon-wrapped shrimp, and baked potatoes, we cracked open the beer, sat on the beat-up couch, cranked tunes on the boom box, and smoked cigarettes like prisoners waiting for the electric chair in their last minutes on death row. I was home. We were roommates for the next seven years.

I was looking for new places to play, places I had never played before. Like I had done twenty years earlier when I first moved to town, I made the rounds, tapes and promo pack in hand. Nye's Polonaise Room was an old-school supper club and bar a block from the Mississippi River on East Hennepin Avenue, anchoring the gateway to Northeast Minneapolis. It was less than a mile from my new house. This neighborhood was founded by Polish and Russian immigrants at the turn of the century who worked at the lumber mills, grain elevators, and the Grain Belt Brewery, a massive brick building whose shadow reached to the river and across to the other side. For years workers could drink beer out of spigots that dotted the walls while at work. Some of my neighbors spoke either Russian or Polish as their native tongue, and while you could not see Russia from my back door, you could sometimes hear it.

I met the owner of Nye's, Steve "Andy" Anderle, and Danny Bell, the manager-maître d' for lunch. I told them I was brave enough to be the first act-sans-accordion on the saloon side and was excited to play this place that could easily have been nicked from a David Lynch movie set. I asked for $150 a night, two martinis, and their notorious prime rib sandwich. Andy and Danny had both seen me over the years and welcomed the chance to help move the place toward the new millennium with the addition of a little folk and blues to their musical menu. It was a short conversation, coronated by a shot of Danny's favorite liqueur, Rumple Minze. He said, "Metsa, we only have one rule here. You can't get drunker than the customers." The deal was on, punctuated by a brandy bullet point, and I was to start the following week.

Built in the 1880s, Nye's was originally a horse stable. It became a workingman's bar after prohibition, and Al Nye bought the joint in the 1940s while Harry Truman was president. The workingmen still came and were sometimes joined in the morning by a priest who'd occasionally whiskey-up his coffee cup before heading to work at the Catholic church a few doors up the street to take confession.

Al was a handsome guy, built like a longshoreman. His portrait graces the entryway to the front door, and his picture is still handed out on plastic key chains to lucky customers. As a boss he was well liked, a leader who inspired loyalty and dedication. Many of the bartenders and waitresses had been working there for years. While Al ran the bar with an iron fist, he kept a small baseball bat behind the bar just in case, which is still there as both a talisman and an enforcer. One day a man walked in, already inebriated, and Al asked him to leave. He did, only to return a couple of hours later. People go to bars to drink, tell tales, and relax. This barfly was starting to bother the customers. Another bartender asked Al if he wanted him to take care of it, and Al said, "NO. This one is mine." He followed the unfortunate drunk back out to Hennepin Avenue, and as the story goes: Al grabbed the bat, hit a single to his legs, a double to his torso, a triple to his shoulders, and for good measure, a love-tap home run to his head. The guy never returned.

In 1964, after many years of running a successful watering hole, Al expanded and bought the building next door and built a supper club. It was a swank place that featured gold-speckled vinyl booths, red carpet, and dark-stained oak—a touch of Vegas on Hennepin. It featured the Sinatra booth, a horseshoe-shaped affair where usually sat the captains of industry, politicians, and other VIPs. Their specialty martinis would have made Winston Churchill weak in the knees, Liberace flirt with women, and Florence Nightingale drop her uniform and head straight for the strippers' pole.

The place was bipolar in a way only Nordeast could be—on one side a ritzy restaurant and piano bar, and on the other, through two swinging doors beneath two accordions, one red and one yellow, a dimmer lounge, more casual and forgiving, that had featured a polka band long before the guys in Lawrence Welk's band were dyeing their hair. Blue collar or mink, it was the kind of place where every night felt like some sort of holiday.

F. Scott Fitzgerald called alcohol the "writer's vice," and bars and saloons have contributed in no small way to the flow of ink from writers' pens, stories brimming like low-ball glasses filled with brandy to the rim. I remember nights at the 400 Bar when a black man with a scruffy graying goatee, wearing a rumpled suit coat, sweater over a white shirt with a tie loosened at the neck, would stand at the bar, smoking an endless stream of Camel straights, and write with a pen in a small notebook, lost in the world of ideas. I would find out later it was Pulitzer Prize–winning playwright August Wilson, who was at the time also working as a part-time cook for Little Brothers–Friends of the Elderly.

The Polonaise Room had more stories than the Pillsbury Doughboy had giggles. Lou Snyder, with her blonde bouffant and pearly white teeth, after forty years still commands her seat at the curved piano bar beneath the austere painting of Chopin, keeping in line, like Margaret Thatcher, the tipsy wannabe Sinatras who straddle up. For years it was surmised that Lou must be a polio survivor from the way she walked on crutches between sets. In actuality, she had been shot in the back by her mentally unbalanced father when she tried to run away from the farm as a young girl. We did not know that until we read an article about her in the newspaper, in which she still proclaimed her love, raining down forgiveness for him, and reminded all of us of the power of love, forgiveness, and family. She is both a grand entertainer and a saint.

The polka band on the other side was equally storied, led by accordion player Ruth Adams and, for years behind her on drums, Al Ophus, a drummer nearing his nineties with gray hair styled like George Burns and a white shirt with skinny black tie. On breaks, Al would sell nylons out of the trunk of his car to beautiful women at the bar, asking to see their legs in order to get the correct size. The stage was small, three feet off the floor, surrounded by a metal bar that men would bump against,

pushed by dancers who were dancing in three-quarter time and party-
ing like it was 1949, on their way to the restroom. They would witness
the Queen of the Accordion, leading the "world's most dangerous polka
band" from her chair on stage, pumping up the volume on the polkas,
sometimes with her eyes closed as if she were saying, "I could do this in
my sleep"—and sometimes she was.

The bartenders were the best in town, in pressed white shirts and
black slacks. Phil, the day bartender, knew more jokes than Henny Youngman and was like the uncle you looked forward to spending time with
over the holidays. Mark worked afternoons with a deliberate step, and I
remembered him from his days slinging ruckus juice at the Five Corners
Bar on the West Bank. Corky, who would refer to my newly found taste
for martinis—straight-up, dry, one olive—as "strumming sauce," used to
own Cork's, a disco downtown in the Foshay Tower, the first skyscraper
in Minneapolis and where John Philips Sousa played the opening. Mikey,
still fit as a fiddle from his days as a high school gymnast, sporting a
Hercule Poirot mustache, would share his vision of how Neil Diamond's
Brother Love's Travelin' Show would make a powerful Broadway show.
Mikey would be happy to know that a couple of years ago someone bought
the rights to the show, and it is in production headed for Broadway.

My friend Doris was a spitfire. At eighty years old, with jet-black
hair, and five feet tall and about a hundred pounds soaking wet, she was
still working the floor as a waitress. On her nights off, on her way back
from the casino, she'd stop in and drink brandy cokes and after several
would grab the microphone and do a version of "I'm Gonna Move to the
Outskirts of Town." When she got to the line "I don't need no iceman,
I'm gonna get me a Frigidaire," she was just enough off pitch to wake the
bats in the basement and shatter the glass on the submarine window that
faces the avenue, all with a hip bump that recalled her days as a stripper
sixty years ago. She'd bring down the house. She told a great story of the
time she was at the Minnesota State Fair and ran into a nephew who had
a prized hog and needed money. She lent him the cash, then called a cab,
which fortunately had wing doors, and with the pig as collateral hopped
in the cab and told the surprised cabbie to take her and her "husband"
home. The driver asked no questions.

Nye's was one of the last union shops in town. All the employees were
union members and received union wages and benefits. Because of that
it was a favorite watering hole for DFL politicians, cops, and firefighters

who would stop in after their shifts for a cold one. The customers were as much a part of the experience as the bar itself. The regulars, the lifeblood of any saloon, would be at their usual stations both when I left and when I returned, as if they never left the place. It was a Edward Hopper gallery of nighthawks, business men and women, working folk, people from the neighborhood, professors, pupils, politicians, priests and passersby, and out-of-town tourists out for a night on the town, with family and friends, to show off this unique slice of Minneapolis night life. On a good night, it was as good as any saloon could get, fueled by strong drink and food that made you loosen your belt buckle, shared with friends and strangers within the walls of a place from the past that kept its secrets.

Sundays were the slowest of the three nights that I played there. I had developed a regular Sunday clientele that included many other industry workers who drank large and tipped big. Others were not so generous. There was a rooming house upstairs where one of our ninety-year-old patrons had lived since Eisenhower was in office. He would drop in every Sunday night just before last call wearing a hat, plaid jacket, shirt and tie on top and boxer shorts and old scuffed wing tips with long black socks below. He always complained that I played too loud, and the bartenders would always pour him a glass of Christian Brothers brandy, and he'd head back upstairs. One night, he flipped me the bird before he left.

Dan and Dean Oberpriller were identical twins and almost sixty years old when I met them. They have been compared to the identical twins in the David Cronenberg movie *Dead Ringers*. 'Nuff said. They must have been chained together in the crib and stayed connected ever since, as you never saw one without the other. They'd anchor the end of either bar, remnants of a time when the three-martini lunch was still a tax write-off. They took a shine to me, and it was impossible to buy a drink when beside them. Sitting between them was an exercise in patience, as they both spoke at the same time, arguing with each other in stereo. Between these twin bookends was an encyclopedic knowledge of country music, and I'd often invite them to sing along with me. While not exactly Sam and Dave, Dan and Dean would serenade both sides of the bar with songs that deserved to be sung, resurrected from the jukeboxes of memory.

There was a buzzer under the bar, the Batline, which would go immediately to the police station in case the bar needed immediate help from the authorities. It was only used once in the five years I worked there.

On that particular Sunday night we started out with a handful of patrons. A trio of two construction workers and one balding hippie uncle with a ponytail were just starting their evening playing dice and drinking beer. They were nice enough and dropped dollar bills in the tip jar as they requested songs. The next dance was one I'd seen a hundred times before: they were getting mildly buzzed when they switched to shots of Jägermeister, the licorice-tasting liqueur stewed in a mixture of anise, poppy seeds, saffron, ginger, and water that could make Mahatma Gandhi morph into Jack the Ripper. Trouble was brewing.

A woman walked up to the bar, who for some reason rattled the nerves of the now-drunk three stooges who started to make fun of her. What they didn't know was that she happened to be an old girlfriend of mine. A line was crossed—nobody makes fun of anybody on my gig, or anywhere else. I nodded at Danny Richardson, the bartender, and we were both ready to give these bastards the bum's rush out to Hennepin Avenue. We got as far as the door, next to the pull-tab stand, when the toughest one of the bunch threw a punch at Danny, just over my head, and I exploded. In a rare display of temper that surprised even me I grabbed him around the neck and pulled him outside. In a move I learned by watching my hometown friend Jack Carlson play hockey as an enforcer for various NHL teams, I pulled his jacket over his head, headlocked him with my left arm, and landed a half a dozen punches to his face. I pushed him onto snow-covered Hennepin Avenue and fell on top of him, landing a couple more punches on our way down. We were in the middle of the street, cars slowing to avoid us. Danny went back inside as the remaining two stooges picked their buddy up off the street. Danny walked over the thousands of pull-tabs on the floor that had spilled when the stand was knocked over and pressed the black button beneath the bar that called all cops. They were there in minutes. After they rounded up the suspects, I went back inside and realized the fingers on my right hand were swollen and bleeding. Danny told me I could quit if I wanted. Why stop now? We shared a bump of Jägermeister in their honor. I said hello to my old girlfriend and got back on the stage to play—what else?—"Where Have All the Flowers Gone," a song I hadn't played in years. It was the last fight I would ever have.

I was able to help my roommate Tony land a job at Nye's as a chef. It was a union job, starting at $18 an hour with benefits. He worked his magic over the stove and got nothing but compliments his first few weeks on the job. Unfortunately, at Nye's the produce cooler was in the basement next to the imported beer cooler. One day, after Tony's sixth week on the job, Andy came upstairs with two six-gallon pickle pails full of empty imported beer bottles. "Tieberg, do you know anything about this?" he asked. With the slick brilliance of any honest thief who needs to cover his tracks, Tony replied, "Come on, boss, you know I drink Budweiser!" Andy gave him a second chance and let him work there for two more years.

Saloons are the home of second chances. Everyone, at some time, has been large and in charge, and bars are not a bad place to lick your wounds, sit quietly by yourself, the mayhem and music around you, and revisit the choreography of your personal fall, while building some ladder, if not to the stars, at least back to solid ground. Sure, there are the young bucks and lucky ladies on their first night out on the town who can wish for the world if they want it and may get it. But most of my favorite people I have met in such establishments have walked more than a few miles in someone else's moccasins and will humbly shake your hand, knowing you both have scars and that we all have more in common than we are led to believe. At its best they represent democracy in the process of reinventing itself, the shining light of America's greatest truth.

Occasionally, the bar would be visited by celebrities in town who had heard through the grapevine that this was not a bad place to have one more cocktail before retiring. Ani DiFranco stopped by one night and joined me onstage for a version of Woody Guthrie's "Ramblin' Round Your City." Actors and actresses stopped by as well. Jack Nicholson and Sean Penn stopped by to scout the location for their movie *The Pledge* and enjoyed a plate of Polish appetizers. One night my old buddy from Folk City, Pat DiNizio, dropped by after a Smithereens' gig in town, got onstage, and did a medley of Who tunes on the tiny stage. Pete Townsend in the air, echoing across Northeast Minneapolis. It was that kind of place, and after those songs you could see for miles and miles.

I had some gigs during that time that remain with me, invisible tattoos on my heart and mind, that unlike those on a sailor's arm actually get brighter with years. One was with Gordon Lightfoot, and the other with John Hartford, two musicians who shone like the Northern Lights, the same lights that guided me here in the first place.

I loved Bob Dylan but adored, if not worshipped, Gordon Lightfoot. My sister Kathy had his record *Lightfoot!* that featured songs like "Rich

Man's Spiritual," "Early Morning Rain," and "The First Time Ever I Saw Your Face," maybe the greatest love song ever written, by Ewan MacColl for his wife, Peggy Seeger, Pete's half-sister. On the cover he wore a blue shirt with a vest, jeans, and cowboy boots that looked like the suit of self-respecting folksingers everywhere. Roberta Flack would later bring a version of this romantic ode to the public in 1972. He was from Canada, seemingly somewhere close to the North Pole. His vibrato seemed whipped by a once-in-a-lifetime wind. His backing band, an acoustic guitar and upright bass, served up songs that flew like some glorious flag of folk music above my young head, and I would look up and salute them for years. I believe it was probably the blueprint for Dylan's record *John Wesley Harding*, though I did not know that at the time.

Lightfoot was playing in Superior, Wisconsin, the port that the iron ore ship *Edmund Fitzgerald* sailed from on its last voyage when the gales of November came early. Amazingly, he had never played there. I called my old friend Tracy Lundeen who was putting on this show at Connor's Point, a park in the shadow of the grain elevators and rusting ships now dry-docked. Lightfoot never used opening acts, and I was surprised when Lundeen called me and booked me for the show.

I arrived at the gig early. This was a big deal for me. It was not only the first big gig I had had since New York, but the geographic halfway point between where I came from and where I ended up. There is a point that is invisible to those who only seek fame or fortune in the music business, beyond the glory and the groupies, the drugs and the damned, beyond the yonder wall that beckons us but never answers when we call and ask for everything, the place where, after all, the rest of us are supposed to be. And there I was.

I played five songs, and my set came just under a half-hour, my allotted time. My ex-girlfriend's parents were there, and I took a seat beside them waiting for one of my first heroes to take the stage. From our vantage point we watched the lights of Duluth, just beyond us to the north, slowly light up. A light fog drifted in from the bay just as the dusk dropped, connecting it all like an altar boy walking on terrazzo tiles of an old church swinging copper bells of incense while the priest is in the sanctuary putting on his robe.

Gordon Lightfoot played several songs, the sound starting to settle and his band easing into a powerful groove. He started to play the opening chords to "The *Edmund Fitzgerald*" as a fog horn somewhere in the distance, as deep as Lake Superior, rang forth like a distant ghost ship calling the service to order. A flock of white seagulls, almost in formation, flew over as if representing the twenty-nine sailors who went down, two wings for each of them. It seemed like a sacred prayer. And like audience members at all great performances, shared only by those in attendance who took the time to witness this powerful meditation as song, we were rewarded with a moment we'll all remember.

The other great show cherished in both memory and heart was in St. Cloud at a place called Pirate's Cove on the banks of the Mississippi River, where I was opening for John Hartford. He was not only a songwriter ("Gentle on My Mind") but also a multi-instrumentalist. And besides representing a catalog of some of the finest folk and country songs of the past century, he also had his steamboat captain's license.

When we got to St. Cloud, I realized in my hurry I had forgotten to pack my stage clothes. Fortunately, there was a garage sale across the street from the club, held by the man and his wife who were the previous owners of Pirate's Cove. When I put on the light-green plaid suit coat before I went on, I was happy to find two free drink tickets for Pirate's Cove in the pocket.

The music room in the club was on a lower level, and the stage surrounded by Christmas lights reminded me of stages in the '30s and '40s and would be a great backdrop for Hartford's set. I inserted an old ragtime tune "Whinin' Boy Blues" by Jelly Roll Morton and "Digga-Digga Do" by Duke Ellington into my set, which I thought Hartford, now sitting at the bar in a bowler hat, white shirt buttoned at the neck, and black vest, would enjoy. I always took literally the meaning of *warm-up act* and wanted to warm up the audience for this great son of St. Louis. The crowd was gracious, my set well received, and before John went on stage he shook my hand and said, "Keep up the great work." To be complimented by a great musician is a beautiful thing.

Hartford took the stage with an upright bass, acoustic guitar player, and banjo player behind him. He was rail thin and wore half-glasses beneath that dapper bowler hat. He played banjo and fiddle and during one song stomped his foot like a buckdancer, while playing the fiddle. He then played banjo and sang the most stunning version of "Lorena," a haunting lament of lost love written before the Civil War but sung by soldiers in that war, remembering the wives and lovers they had left behind. Hartford noted that soldiers on both sides would sing it together, across barricades the night before battles, and surmised that the tune helped bring an end to the war. Once again, I was reminded of the power of song.

We hung out with the band after the show and had a little picking party upstairs. Charlie Roth, a St. Cloud native who had booked the show, led the charge, and we were soon joined by the guitar-playing bus driver. The band told us that John was suffering from cancer. They had a few more shows on the tour, and Hartford wanted to stop at the Ringling Brothers Circus Museum in Baraboo, Wisconsin (where it was founded) to enjoy more of the roots of Americana of which he was such a shining example. It was his last tour, and the master would die but a year later.

The following summer I joined an excursion with the Audubon Society, two houseboats, and floated down the Mississippi River to Davenport, Iowa. We did a series of gigs: on the houseboat while navigating the locks, and on the banks of the river under tents and in parks. You don't realize how large the river is until you've traveled on it. When you enter Lake Pepin, the birthplace of water skiing, you start to see the expanse of what is one of the largest river systems in the world. We met river groups along the way, and in small motorboats we explored the almost prehistoric backwaters. We passed the majestic bluffs of Red Wing, and down into Iowa past huge Indian burial mounds, eagles flying above as if to protect them. And while it was not hard to envision Mark Twain, with his wild flock of white hair, bushy mustache, and white suit farther down the river, the man I most recalled was riverboat captain John Hartford.

Josh Horowitz is the director of the Stop Handgun Violence Coalition in Washington, D.C. I had met him at a Bob Dylan concert at Wolf Trap Amphitheater in 1990. In 1999, he called and invited me to play as their guest at the Million Mom March in D.C., on Mother's Day, 2000, as they were one of the sponsors of the event. I got there the previous afternoon, and we took the subway into downtown. We got off the train, walked upstairs, turned a corner, and ran into James Brady, Ronald Reagan's press secretary who was wounded in the assassination attempt, being pushed in a wheelchair by his lovely wife. The timing of that gave me pause.

The next day the Mall was packed, and the organizers said there were more than 750,000 people in attendance. I played before Ann Wilson from the band Heart on the second stage. After the rally, Josh and I went to the Monocle Bar, between the Capitol and Union Station, by the rear entrances of the Hart and Dirksen Senate buildings. While we were there, Henry Hyde and Kay Bailey Hutchinson were dining below the pictures of everyone from Ronald Reagan to Steve McQueen. The bartender, a tall elderly gentleman who looked like Robert E. Lee, and had served everyone from JFK to Miss Universe, served us several of the finest martinis I had ever had. I imagined it was from there that in 1974, Arkansas State Representative Wilbur Mills had left, after several of the "general's" concoctions, got pulled over for drunk driving, and his date, Argentinean stripper Fanne Foxe, jumped into the Tidal Basin.

Not long after I started playing at Nye's, I made my way to Mayslack's Bar, on the corner of Fourteenth Avenue and Fourth Street. Northeast Minneapolis is known for its equal number of churches and bars, and Mayslack's had been there since professional wrestler and Pole Stan Mayslack opened it in 1955. Mayslack's served a garlic-flavored roast beef sandwich and on Tuesdays at lunch you would see a line form around the block for a chance to get served by Stan himself, berating customers if they did not hold their plates up with two hands as he loaded them with heaping helpings of this house specialty. It has been the heart and soul of the Polish community for years.

The owner now was Jeff Moritko, a Northeast boy, graduate of Edison High School, in the neighborhood where Terry Gilliam of Monty Python fame lived for awhile. Moritko had been an offensive lineman for the Minnesota Golden Gophers and at nearly three hundred pounds had a commanding presence. He could also glide across a dance floor with ease, a Polish Jackie Gleason. He used to be a bouncer at Bootlegger Sam's in Dinkytown where Cats Under the Stars played and knew me from there. He would hire a polka band every Sunday afternoon that would serenade older listeners and dancers from the neighborhood. Much like the civil defense foghorn that blew once a month in Virginia, I'd hear a fire truck go by my house with the same regularity on its way to 'Slax to resuscitate one of the dancers, who would usually be back the following Sunday to start all over again.

Jeff booked me to play at Mayslack's, and it was the first time since before I had a driver's license that I could walk to a gig. I threw my guitar over my shoulder and, for the hell of it, wanted to count my steps from my back door to the red front metal door at the bar. I counted 237 steps. On my way home, after three sets and twice as many cocktails, I counted my way back and by the time I had hit the 237th step, I was still two blocks away from home.

Jeff, like Nye's, wanted to add other types of music besides his weekly polka gig. I helped him find bands, along with John Eric Theide, a former rugby player and pianist who lived in Stan's old apartment above the bar and was spooked by the doors and cupboards slamming in the middle of the night, perhaps by Stan's ghost who was hesitant to leave the neighborhood. It became one of the hot new music clubs in town and helped spawn the now-active arts community in Nordeast. Stan, a man of few words, is remembered for many things, but his final farewell to the crowd that had gathered to celebrate him the last day he owned the bar, and before he went back upstairs, was heartfelt and concise: "I love you fuckers."

I hosted two different gigs. One was an open stage and the other was Chicks Rule, a night featuring all female musicians. I had heard a great young blues guitar player named Charlie Parr, from Duluth, Minnesota, and would offer him $20 to drive down for the shows. He was stunningly good. Charlie has now gone on to a great career and now tours the United Kingdom, Europe, and Australia. I also booked some of Molly Maher's first gigs at the club, and she is now regarded as the Lucinda Williams of Minneapolis, a complete sweetheart. During one of her first radio interviews, after the release of her first record, she was still doing Chicks Rule. While she wanted to say that in her eyes I had done more for female musicians at that time in Minneapolis, she said—while my girlfriend was listening—"Paul Metsa has done more for women in this town than any one musician." While I was honored and delighted to hear that, my girlfriend went through the roof.

One day I went down for lunch at Mayslack's and found Jeff's twelve-year-old son Adam was wearing a white apron and waiting on tables. He was the spitting image of his dad: full head of blond hair, large strong hands, built like an emerging offensive lineman. Jeff's father had also stopped by that day for lunch. Later that evening Jeff's mother called him and sounded concerned. She peppered Jeff with questions: "Is everything okay?" "Yes, Mom." "You're sure?" "Yes, Mom." "Do you need money?" "No, Mom." "Well, if you do, all you have to do is ask." "Why are you asking?" Jeff asked. She replied, "Well, your dad was down at the bar today and saw Adam working." Jeff chuckled and gently explained, "It was Take Your Kids to Work day, Mom."

Sherwin Linton is the Midwest's answer to Johnny Cash. A native of South Dakota, he had been playing rockabilly and country music since 1955 as a teenager with his band the Rockateers. I was playing a few gigs at Bunker's Bar in downtown Minneapolis as Paul Metsa and the Naughty Pines, and we shared a bass player named Steve Murray. He invited Sherwin, now sixty years old, to sit in one night. I had heard his name for years, but as both of us played on the same nights, we never had a chance to meet each other. He showed up in a blue windbreaker, jeans, and cowboy boots and joined us onstage for the Elvis Presley version of "Good Rockin' Tonight." I was knocked out: Sherwin was the real deal.

He had done more than ten thousand gigs, was signed to Acuff-Rose Publishing, recommend by Roy Acuff himself. He had shared the stage with everyone from Johnny Cash, Carl Perkins, Waylon Jennings, to Wanda Jackson and was one of the first guys in Minnesota to record a Bob Dylan song, "Girl from the North Country," in 1964. He sings in a luscious baritone, knows thousands of songs, and has delightful stories from over a half-century of performing. I got Sherwin a steady gig at Mayslack's where he entranced and became revered by a younger generation. While he credits and thanks me for helping kick-start his career back in the city, the pleasure was all mine.

Kieffer's Clothing Store was located on Hennepin Avenue and Sixth Street. It was a store frequented by musicians, blacks, and other high-fashion aficionados, much like Lansky's Clothing Store in Memphis where a young Elvis Presley shopped. Sherwin and his band, now called the Cotton Kings, were doing a show with Roy Acuff in 1965. Sherwin's bass player was changing into his stage clothes and Acuff noticed him wearing a pair of blindingly iridescent, colored paisley briefs. Roy asked, "Them's men's underwear?" The bass player said yes. Roy replied, "Really! Men's underwear?" The bass player answered, "Yup." Roy says, "Damn, I'm going to have to get me a pair!"

Northeast Minneapolis was a lot like the Iron Range. It was solidly working class, the neighborhoods were safe, and at night people liked to frequent the bars and restaurants, enjoying themselves with a certain abandon that reminded me of home. I liked to take my out-of-town friends to Mayslack's and Nye's, show them where I was working, and have them taste the gastronomic delights of Nordeast while downing beverages that were never in short supply at either.

Hubert Sumlin, Howlin' Wolf's guitarist, one of the nicest people I had ever met in the music business, was a direct link to the ground zero of the blues. Howlin' Wolf had learned his stuff directly from Charley

Patton, the Father of the Delta Blues. Patton may have had some Indian blood that makes the origins of the blues even more unique and powerful. Hubert had snuck out of his house as a young kid and while watching Wolf from a window standing atop empty wooden pop bottle containers, fell through the window and right into Wolf's lap. Howlin' Wolf brought him back home that night and would years later invite Hubert back to Chicago to play with him. Hubert referred to Chester Burnett, a.k.a. Howlin' Wolf, as his daddy.

I booked Hubert several times at Famous Dave's and would always take him to Nye's for his favorite, the broiled walleye. He loved it. We'd sit for a couple of hours and my heart would beat faster as he shared stories of Wolf, Muddy Waters, and others. Once, I took him back to my house, where he showed me the original licks to "Smokestack Lightning," one of the most powerful and most evocative of all blues songs. He enjoyed being around my dog, Blackie, and was kind enough to record an outgoing message on my answering machine. I love and adore the man.

I'd also take friends like Booka and Edythe Michel, in town from Austin, Texas, for dinner at Nye's. Booka, originally from Grand Rapids, Minnesota, was a percussionist, for folks like Townes Van Zandt, Butch Hancock, and Ponty Bone, who had started a label called Loudhouse Records in 2000. I told him about a cassette I had stumbled onto in a drawer that I had recorded as a demo in 1990. He heard it, liked it, and offered to put it out on his label. "Texas in the Twilight" came out in 2005 and got great reviews, making it to the Top Twenty on three European Americana charts. The Michels are now producing films, the most recent one called *Baghdad Texas.* They always enjoyed their visits to Nye's.

I loved our duplex in Northeast Minneapolis. We lived downstairs, had a sweet little backyard, garage, and a garden with a swath of Concord grape vines that every two years produced a two-case batch of Blackie's Burgundy, including a label featuring a photo of Blackie, the king of all dogs. Tieberg and I were an unlikely pair but somehow enjoyed living together. Tony would spend an amazing amount of time on the couch watching the movie *Slap Shot,* the cult film about a minor league hockey team that featured Paul Newman and Jeff and Steve Carlson from my hometown. Many mornings as a kid I would watch the Carlson brothers practice during the season at the Miners Memorial Building and was especially interested in following Jack Carlson when he was drafted to the Minnesota North Stars and went on to other teams. For Tony, it reminded him of home, though I am not sure that justified his viewing it, according to his count, more than 250 times.

Our landlord had been pestering me to buy the house since 1997. Though my dad was in real estate, I considered myself more of a rolling stone and thought it might tie me down. Steve Baker, my first buddy in Minneapolis, ran the numbers for me, I secured financing through ACORN, got some of the down payment from the Michels, and secured the house in 1999 with that and, thankfully, my three years of paystubs from Nye's. It was one of the smartest things I have ever done, through really no fault of my own. At night, Blackie and I will sit on the back porch, watch the moon rise over the buildings downtown, and off to our right the copper steeples of the Russian Orthodox church two blocks away. On a summer night sitting side by side, as we survey our surroundings that include a little memorial garden for my mother in what was once a fish smoker, now filled with black dirt, plants, and flowers, in our little Mark Twain backyard, and can smell the grapes wafting over from the trellis, I hold him tightly, this stop long down the journey on the blue guitar highway, and am happy for the simple life we lead. I call it the House That Nye's Built.

In 2006, I went down to see Molly Maher play at Lee's Liquor Lounge, a little roadhouse on the outskirts of downtown Minneapolis. Louie, the owner, was in the army with Elvis and has an Elvis decanter selection, behind glass, that would not be out of place at Graceland. On the break, Molly showed me the article recently published in *Esquire* magazine naming Nye's as the Best Bar in America. Fantastic.

On my way home, I had to stop in to Nye's and congratulate the bartenders, wait staff, and the regulars that of course included, as described in the article, the "bickering" Oberpriller twins at the bar enjoying their usual glasses of B&B, an inspiring blend of Benedictine liqueur and French Cognac. Lou Snyder was in her second set at the piano bar, and Ruth Adams's polka serenade would lilt through the swinging doors while Bruce the swamper was running several cases of beer up and down the stairs. At the piano bar a half-dozen people sat on high back stools, and bespectacled Professor Craig Hergert was doing a comical send-up of "Sweet Caroline." Bouncer Pete had met me at the door, smoking his first of many Marlboro Lights of this warm October evening, opening the door as couples entered after a romantic stroll by the river. I walked up to Dan and Dean, who were of course arguing about what the article got wrong, and I realized our secret was out.

WHITE BOYS LOST IN THE BLUES

I was on break at my regular gig at Nye's Polonaise Room when the bartender handed me the phone. The bar was packed with the usual regulars making the usual noise that always got progressively louder as the clock moved toward last call. It was a fellow by the name of Bob Wilson. He was a harmonica player and said, with summer approaching, he had a gig at an outdoor patio on the banks of the Mississippi lined up at a place called Gabby's Saloon and was looking for a guitar slinger. It happened to be in my neighborhood. I had never heard him, or of him, but I was always on the lookout for new places to play, and this sounded interesting, and nothing beats playing music outside in the summertime. I gave him my address and told him to swing by my house in a couple of days and we could kick it around.

I was out doing errands that day, and I arrived forty-five minutes late. My roommate Tony and he were on their second beer. Tony was a truly lovely soul, drank more than Dean Martin on vacation, but made new friends easily. He had pulled out a shoebox of old photos from his childhood, deer hunting pictures, photos of his mom and dad, and dozens of his daughter, Frances, whom he adored and only saw a couple of times a month. Bob was in a two-piece suit, wearing shoes that suggested he had a well-paying day gig, and was casually taking in this photo display with good humor. He had a briefcase full of harmonicas and a cheap guitar in an even cheaper case. We shook hands, and I invited him downstairs to my studio, which Tony always referred to as the "st-st-st-studio," thank you, Phil Collins.

I was assuming that this gig would entail my playing one set and he the other. He had called me out of the blue on a whim. After asking his wife who she thought might be able to play with him, she said "Paul Metsa." Bob asked, "Is he even still alive?" I guess my reputation had preceded me. He tracked me down through an ad in *City Pages* and, with nothing to lose, made the call. So here we were, in my cramped and musty basement, the light barely bleeding in from two dusty windows. I asked him what the guitar was for, and he said, "Well, I thought I could back you up on a few numbers." Really? Let's hear you play it. I could tell by the way he was getting the guitar out of the case that he sucked. But I gave him the benefit of the doubt and asked him to play something. He fingered a G chord, and before his right hand strummed three out of the six strings, I stopped him in his tracks, and said, "We won't be needing that." It might have sounded arrogant, and perhaps it was, but the one thing I knew how to do after three decades of doing it was play the guitar.

I asked him to take out a harp and play something. He reached into his Brooks Brothers briefcase, took a harp out, and started to wail. He was really good. I dug into my Sonny Terry and Brownie McGhee repertoire, many of the tunes I hadn't played since Metsa and O'Keefe in the '70s, and he followed me like the tail on a cat. I got a big kick out of that. We played for about a half-hour, and I asked him when the gig started. He answered, "Well, I was hoping we could rehearse." I had already rehearsed this stuff with O'Keefe years ago and explained to him that it is really impossible to rehearse the blues—or rock and roll, for that matter. You either know the tunes or you don't. I relented and we set up a rehearsal for the following week, the gig starting a week after that. Turns out, he was a personal injury attorney during the day, a father of three lovely daughters, and his wife's father and mother were from Chisholm, about fifteen miles from my hometown of Virginia. This all made a certain sense to me. He also had impeccable manners, unlike many musicians I knew who weren't half as good as he. I would find out he was also a hell of a singer. It was the beginning of a musical partnership that has endured, on a weekly basis, to this day.

We developed a soulful simpatico, and besides his musical talents, he was a Grade A promoter. We spent two years of summer Friday nights on Gabby's deck, populated by Bob's suburban friends, inner city clients, and new fans, many of whom had never heard of me and started to envision me as a "blues guy." It gave me a certain anonymity and was the first time in years I didn't have to lead the charge or band with my original tunes. I let Bob do some of the heavy lifting and could concentrate on just playing guitar, doing the original Metsa tune when requested. And like we'd say, "We are happy to do requests, as long as they are written on the back of a twenty dollar bill, and if we don't know it, we'll send you ten back." Not only was it fun, but Bob and I became great friends, and there is never anything wrong with that.

In 1999, I got a call from the Minnesota Department of Tourism. They were taking a dozen folks from the office to participate in a tourism conference in Reykjavik, Iceland, and asked if I would like to come along, as the Minnesota musical ambassador, and headline Minnesota Night on the final night of the conference. There was no reason to say no. The money was great, enough to afford taking my new harp player along if they could pop for an extra plane ticket. They thought it was a great idea, and I immediately got Bob on the phone. He was ecstatic. All he had to do was call his wife and clear it with the boss.

Someone once described Iceland as "three hundred thousand alcoholics clinging to a rock." It is also known for its beautiful women and wild party scene. For Bob, it was a no-brainer: an all-you-can-drink trip to Reykjavik with Metsa to party with Swedish travel agents? Absolutely! For Bob's wife, the only woman whom he had ever been with, his high school girlfriend, and now wife of twenty years, this was also a no-brainer: no way in hell! I would have suggested a better setup for Bob when presenting the idea to his wife. I would have tendered something like, "An exchange of artistic impressions to enhance cross-cultural promotion and development of tourism." In his enthusiasm, and perhaps being the only lawyer I knew incapable of lying, it came off a lot less high-handed than that.

The line was drawn in the ice. Bob said he was going, and his wife Lesa, who is tough but also very generous, said he wasn't. They agreed to resolve the matter with an old-school vote at Christmas. In spite of his abilities as a high-buck personal injury attorney, he did not negotiate a neutral playing field for this battle. The vote would be decided by his Serbian in-laws on Serbian Christmas in the Quonset hut on his wife's family farm up on the Iron Range. Serbians can turn a candle into a four-alarm fire at the flip of a switch. It bears remembering that a Serbian terrorist group that assassinated Archduke Franz Ferdinand in 1914 lit the fuse that became World War I. Somehow, Bob pulled off a come-from-behind upset of the decade, the likes of which have not been seen since O. J. Simpson was declared innocent. I am told the vote was nearly unanimous, with the two no votes coming from his wife and her sister.

We were to be there for four days, arriving early Thursday morning, our show not being until Saturday night. After a little research, I found out that we'd be enjoying four hours of daylight during our stay. I also found out that Iceland is known as having the best lobster in the world. I had given up a twenty-five-year love affair with Southern Comfort whiskey and was easing into middle age with a lust for the perfect martini (straight up, very dry, one olive). Bob had never had one. I promised him a lobster dinner and his first martini after we hit the barren Icelandic shore.

Over the past couple of years we tried in vain to come up with a new name for him. Bob Wilson is a great name if you are an accountant, ninth grade geography teacher, or insurance salesman, but a truly lousy name for a blues harp player. This would soon be solved. Bob got on the Internet and found a couple of clubs where we could play on our nights off. We got a hold of a club owner named Thordur who ran a club called Fodetinn. He set up a conference call among the three of us. Bob pretended to be an agent representing me and my "legendary" harp player, "Sonny Earl." Sonny is a well-established name for a couple of great harp players (Sonny Boy Williamson and Sonny Terry), and Earl came from Bob's uncle who bought him his first harmonica. It rolled off the tongue, was easy to remember, and had a nice ring to it. The call was a little bit like the Abbott and Costello routine "Who's on first." It got a tad convoluted, as I kept forgetting if I was talking about or to Sonny or Bob. Thankfully, Thordur's English wasn't the best, and we picked up his club for Thursday night. We also scored a Friday nightclub gig, a radio show, and an appearance on the local public television station.

We arrived at the Minneapolis–St. Paul airport at 7 P.M. Wednesday night. We met the group from the department of tourism and were surprised and delighted that we not only had first class seats but also passes into the Northwest World Club, which we would find out had liquor dispensers not unlike the soft drink dispensers at McDonald's, all free. Yeah, baby! I ended up behind my friend Senator Norm Coleman, who was on his way to Florida. I had on a black motorcycle jacket, cowboy boots, and a guitar in a gig bag. When I walked through the scanner, it lit up, buzzers and lights, like a slot machine in some cheap Las Vegas casino. Someone came up and asked Coleman what he was up to. He drolly replied, "Just trying to help Metsa get through security." Thanks, Senator. Once through, Sonny and I headed straight to the World Club.

We hung around there like sailors on shore leave. Sonny had not been free to travel without his wife since before they married, so he took more than good advantage to sample a variety of the adult beverages at our fingertips. Speaking of booze, I had talked to a couple of my musician buddies who had played Iceland, and they warned me about a liquor called Brennivin, what we would come to find out was the National Turpentine of Iceland, disguised as booze, and what natives fondly called Black Death. It was the first thing we ordered once on the plane. You could peel the paint off your garage with this shit. But being good ambassadors, we soldiered on, gagging on every sip and smiling like Pee Wee Herman before the incident at the movie theater in Florida.

Sitting next to us was a professional photographer from Iceland, on his way back home from photographing the recent Rolling Stones U.S. tour. We toasted Keith Richards, with Brennivin of course, thirty thousand feet over Greenland and invited him to the show on Saturday. We arrived in Reykjavik at 6 A.M., and Sonny made a quick calculation of the exchange rate, dollars to krónur on a small notepad, and we were off to the hotel. We went to bed in darkness and woke up six hours later still in darkness, although it was only early afternoon.

After dinner, we took a cab to the club. It was housed in a building that was built in the late 1700s. It is where several Christian missionaries would wait out the winter, before foraging out into this cratered moonscape of an island, to try and save the souls who were not in hiding from the previous couple of centuries of Viking marauders. Many of them went insane before the spring thaw from the simple desperation that was the Icelandic winter. You could almost feel the ghosts of some of them floating throughout. Bartender, two more Brennivin, please.

The crowd was very welcoming. There was a group of young guys, in their midtwenties, who sat near the stage and were paying very close attention to us. Most people their age, like those in the States, were more interested in deejays than live musicians, and Iceland had developed a very progressive pop and electronic music scene, Björk and Sigur Rós being but two great examples of that. They were all young blues musicians, and we buddied up to them, and they invited us to a jam session after the gig. We piled into an old van and headed to their place. On our way there, the harmonica player had to run into his apartment to grab something to drink. He came out carrying a Pepsi bottle full of clear liquid. I assumed that it was actually Pepsi, being sold here as a clear liquid. Come to find out, it was Icelandic moonshine, made from boiling potatoes on the stove for most of the day, and god knows what else. This brew could blow a hole through the top of your head, make flames shoot out your ears, and rip through your stomach like broken glass and razor blades. I took one gulp and had to go outside and stand in front of this rundown government housing project and catch my breath, the stars seemingly close enough to hit them with a canoe paddle. Sonny and I played with them until about 4 A.M. and cabbed back to the hotel, satisfied to know how much guys like Muddy Waters and Howlin' Wolf were respected in this land of fire and ice.

Sonny and I had our dinner date at 7 P.M. that evening, and a gig later at a club downtown at 10 P.M. I had promised him his first martini and lobster dinner, and he was waiting to collect. I had made a reservation at an opulent and exclusive restaurant, candle lit, with whispering waiters in pressed white shirts, bowties, and pressed pants. I asked our waiter to put two martini glasses on ice, while I gave Sonny my *CliffsNotes* version of the history of the drink that runs through the history of American luxurious boozing. The martinis arrived as I was about to start my dissertation. We toasted our trip, Sonny took his first sip, his eyes sparkled like a poker player who was just dealt a full house. In twenty minutes or so I tried to give Sonny a little bit of background on Dorothy Parker's favorite cocktail: it was invented by a bartender named Martinez in San Francisco; FDR's motto was four martinis and a treaty; and the perfect martini should conjure images of Greta Garbo skinny-dipping in an arctic lake. Midway through Sonny asked, "How the hell do you know this much about the martini?" I told him, somewhat incredulously, "What do you think I do all day?" There was a short pause, before we realized how ridiculous that sounded. We started to chuckle, then belly laugh, like schoolgirls in church, and shortly were completely howling (the 'tini's had also just started to kick in), as our fellow diners looked upon us in disgust from their dimly lit tables, and the head waiter started directly toward our table. We excused ourselves, stepped outside, nearly fell into the snow bank, took another ten minutes before we could compose ourselves and act like adults, and went inside to our dual orders of lobster. Indeed, they were the best we had ever tasted.

We were scheduled to do a set at around 10 P.M. As we were walking to the stage, Sonny kept getting almost knocked over by this fellow. We both thought he was trying to pick a fight. What we came to find out was he was completely wasted, and he was one of the more sober people in the club. One woman, immaculately dressed in black with a white pearl necklace and in her late fifties, came up to the bandstand, stared at us, and immediately fell face first into the drum set; unfortunately, we did not have time to catch her. She put herself together, got right back on the dance floor, and blended back into the pack, all of whom acting and drinking like runaways from the treatment center and now on their first bender, holy-rolling booze hounds on the dance floor of the damned.

The street scene, when we left the club, was no less incredible. People were emptying out into the street from the various clubs and restaurants, each one drunker than the next. They walked arm in arm, picking up wasted strangers as they went, in some kind of booze-fueled conga line on their way to the cab line, which seemed to stretch to the coast.

Iceland is also known as having the deepest strands of DNA anywhere in the world. Scientists come from all over the world to study it. Sonny and I stopped by an outdoor food wagon for a bite to eat. The young woman behind the counter looked beautiful and almost from another time. Her skin was an alabaster-olive mix, and her eyes a shade of blue I had never seen, like a mixture of blue from a Hubble telescope shot from outer space, hypnotic and wolf like, a descendant from a Viking bloodline, now long since disappeared from the continent and earth. The kind of beauty that ancient poets wrote about and for whom wars were started and won. Absolutely breathtaking.

Our big show was Saturday night. I needed to spend the day at the local music store, rent a PA system, and get it back to the hotel to get set up and sound checked. Sonny had been invited by a group of Irish travel agents whom he had befriended in the hotel to visit the Blue Lagoon, the geothermal silica and sulfur waters with the lava foundation, whose steaming waters were a major tourist attraction. While "Irish travel agents" should have rung some bell of caution with me, I sent Sonny off that morning to enjoy himself.

The dinner was at 8 P.M., and our show was at 9 P.M. I called Sonny's room at 7 P.M. to check in and to tell him I'd meet him downstairs to get plugged in before the guests started to arrive. I called in five-minute intervals and got no answer each time. I headed down to his room and saw the door slightly ajar. Inside, cross-legged on the bed in his cotton pajamas, head titled to the side, eyes closed, smiling, he was completely fucking smashed. I called the front desk, ordered two pots of coffee, and tried to take off his PJs and hold him upright so I could dress him in his suit. I was able to get off his top, wrapped him in a shirt and tie, and had to put his pants on over his pajama bottoms. I struggled with his wing tips (he had his new blues name but was still wearing shoes that belonged on a stockbroker), tied them, and led him gingerly downstairs to the ballroom. Fortunately, he neither passed out nor threw up at the table, and I prayed to the gods of fire and ice that he would be able to play. After a dinner of wild rice soup and walleye (this was Minnesota night, after all) we were introduced. We started "Stranger Blues," an Elmore James tune done Brownie and Sonny style, and a song I had opened with, for both my and our shows for years. He started to chug on the harp, eyes still closed, and miraculously came through, and we received two encores. The photographer we had met on the plane came down to the gig and shot some photos. The next day on the front page of the variety section of the newspaper was a big picture of us. I was leaning into the camera, and he caught Sonny at the exact moment he sobered up, opened his eyes like a deer in the headlights, and realized he was playing in front of two hundred people. It was an absolutely priceless shot and one that I would have loved to hear him explain to his lovely wife, Lesa.

We got on the plane the next day to head back to Minneapolis. By now, we were drinking Brennivin like it was chocolate milk. We'd order two per pass, one to drink, and one minibottle to take home as a souvenir. As we were about to land, we asked the flight attendant for one more round. She smiled that beautiful Icelandic smile and said, "You drank it all." Iceland, at last count: three hundred thousand *and two* alcoholics clinging to a rock.

FROM RUSSIA WITH LOVE

I have met some of my best buddies bellying up to the bar. God may have created Sunday as a day of rest, but he designed Friday and Saturday, the fifth and sixth days, to stop by the saloon to blow off a little steam after a hard week of work.

I met Eric at Eli's Bar in the early '90s. My friend Fast Eddie and his girlfriend Laurie bought the place a few years earlier. Eddie was my buddy from the McCready's Bar gang of the mid-1980s that included writer David Carr and comedian Tom Arnold. Eddie bartended at McCready's but spent more time on the other side of the bar. I could never afford to gamble; Eddie couldn't afford not to. Eddie was a poet by accident, a barroom philosopher through training. I walked into McCready's one night around 11. A half-dozen wishers and dreamers were sitting at the bar watching *Monday Night Football*. I asked Eddie how his bets were going. "Well, I lost five grand on the Cowboys yesterday but won three grand on the Vikings tonight. I feel like a winner," he said matter-of-factly. It was that kind of attitude that got Eddie and the rest of us through. On another night, in the back room after closing time he told me, "You know, Paul, one of these days I am going to own my own joint." Eli's Bar was that joint and, once again, proved there is no reason to dream small.

Eli's was at Twelfth and Hennepin, the main drag in Minneapolis before it empties southward into the upper-crust Kenwood neighborhood. My friend Jimmy Wrayge, an abstract expressionist painter and also one of the McCready's Gang, was the bartender and mixologist supreme. He was also a rock-solid intuitive DJ who sound-tracked the nights with a celestial mix of Dylan, Cash, Ornette, Zappa, Miles, and others in the bar. On any given night, members of the Jayhawks and Soul Asylum hung out, and whoever may have slipped in after their performances at First Avenue. And occasionally, while the regulars would be leaving, the after-hours party there would have just begun.

Eric, who also lived in a condo upstairs, was one of the regular VIPs in the joint. He was well mannered, a big guy with red rosy cheeks, who tipped liked Joe Namath and was a supremely gifted entrepreneur. While visiting his brother in Moscow, he found a place that made hockey pucks for a penny a piece. He bought thousands, loaded them in 55-gallon drums, and shipped and sold them back in the United States for a handsome profit. After that, he switched to exporting expensive cars selling them to the Russian elite. He eventually married a woman from Moscow and would spend equal time operating out of both countries.

He bought me more martinis than I ever bought him, and our political discussions resembled Hubert Humphrey arm-wrestling Barry Goldwater. Eric was a libertarian-leaning Republican and would always take me to task for the chorus of my song "Slow Justice," which goes, "If the rich man owns the land, why must the poor man pay the taxes?" His three-martini response was, "I have never seen a poor man pay the taxes." A mutual love for Bob Dylan and Frank Sinatra bonded us. Be it "Desolation Row" or "Strangers in the Night" turned up louder as the night was beginning to end, we would end up toasting both of them and each other.

One night he said, "Metsa, if you ever need some money, and not to fix your car, pay your bar tab, or buy another guitar, call me." He meant it, and we shook hands, like our fathers did with their bankers when they signed their first mortgage.

I started to pick up a good head of steam by the end of 1993. My record *Whistling Past the Graveyard* had gotten airplay all over the country. It had received glowing reviews in the local papers (with the exception of the local weekly *City Pages,* which compared it to music for a Bud Light commercial) and had been reviewed next to Neil Young and Elvis Costello in *Billboard* magazine. The *Austin Chronicle* said, "This record should place Metsa next to the Springsteens and Mellencamps of the world." One tune from it, "Jack Ruby," was in steady rotation on Cities 97, the top-rated triple-A station in the Twin Cities.

I decided that it was time to bust a move and relocate to Nashville, from the batter's box in Minneapolis to home plate in Music City. I had developed a great relationship with Bucky Baxter, Garry Tallent, and others there. A half-dozen other Minneapolis musicians had moved there over the years and had done well. I had played every gin joint, house party, rock club, and coffeehouse in town, and through independent promoter Sue McLean, my good friend, booked the vaunted Guthrie Theater for my swan song, a show we dubbed Mississippi Farewell. A few days before the gig, Sue called and told me it was sold out. Two nights before the show it dawned on me that I should record this once in a lifetime experience. I made several phone calls and found a company that could do it for $2,500, two grand more than I had in my savings account. I remembered Eric's offer.

I entered the bar just before last call, and there he was with an empty seat next to him. I threw down a twenty and ordered two double martinis, one for each of us. I told him about my show, that it had sold out, and that I really wanted to record the concert. I told him I needed $2,500 to tape it, and if he was interested in backing that, it would come with two front-row seats. Eric reached into his pocket, pulled out a tattered blue checkbook, and wrote out a check. I thanked him and told him that I would pay him back in whatever way I could. The concert was a major success, was recorded, and released in fall 1994 as *Mississippi Farewell.*

I had another friend named Jack Smith, a radio guy who ended up in Moscow after helping *Spin* magazine set up its European radio network. I couldn't wait to introduce Jack and Eric to each other when those two Minnesota boys were back in town at the same time.

At 4 A.M., Central time, I got a phone call from Moscow. Two guys sitting next to each other in an empty Moscow bar had started to chat. It turns out they are both Americans, both from Minneapolis. One asks, "Do you know Paul Metsa?" The other replies, "Who is asking?" The first says, "I am Jack. You must be Eric."

Eric's wife convinced him they should move from Moscow to Siberia to be closer to her parents in Novosibirsk. Once there, Eric started a variety of businesses. He called me one night and invited me to play at his new nightclub. He had started with a couple of pizza joints, and built a jazz/blues club beneath one of them called the New York Times, offering music seven nights a week. He offered me a plane ticket, $500, and a place to stay. I always used to dream about traveling around the world with my guitar, and while these dreams never included Siberia, I gladly accepted the offer.

The $500 down payment arrived the next day via Western Union, with the phone number of his mother in Minneapolis, who wanted me to take a "couple" of Christmas presents to her three grandchildren. She brought them to me—toys, DVDs, candy—in a brown gunnysack with the head of a Barbie doll peeking out over the slim rope that tied the bag, which weighed almost seventy pounds. I packed a small suitcase, my guitar, passport, and the bag of toys, with twinges of apprehension mixed with eager anticipation for a journey that would take me halfway around the world.

A seven-hour layover followed my four-hour flight from Minneapolis to JFK. I stood in one corner of the airport, guarding Barbie dolls, my guitars, and suitcase and using the restroom sparingly. Seeing Moscow on the list of departing flights conjured up images of crawling under our grade school desks for routine drills in preparation for a possible nuclear attack. One wrong move and I could see the ghost of Solzhenitsyn in some frozen gulag subsisting on dry bread and stone soup.

The long overseas flight challenged my comfort threshold, but I arrived there in due time. Eric had arranged for a car and driver to meet and drive me to another airport for the plane that would take me to Siberia. He spoke no English but drove skillfully on pothole-covered road, swerving around broken-down cars on the freeway and going much faster than I would have liked. Fortunately, we arrived without incident at the next airport. With no signs in English, and Russian words longer than my right arm, all I could do was walk up to people who looked like they worked for the airport, and one by one, they would point around corners, and I eventually found my flight.

My seat was in the back of the plane in the smokers' section. On this final flight to Novosibirsk, I was dog-tired but too overwhelmed by the experience to sleep. Only one passenger was still awake at this ungodly hour, a Russian gentleman who appeared to be around seventy, dressed in a poor man's clothes, tapping his foot, bopping his bald head, and listening to modern headphones. West meets East.

The seat next to him was empty. I sat down, and he offered me a pull off what seemed to be moonshine in an unmarked pint bottle. Small talk revealed that the only thing we had in common was insomnia. He looked old enough to be my grandfather but was dancing in his seat like a teenager. I was filled with trepidation playing for a foreign audience in a country I grew up fearing, and felt blush with fatigue.

After a few more pulls off the bottle, he offered me his headphones. I accepted. I put the headphones on and was stunned and delighted to hear America's favorite baritone sing, "I shot a man in Reno, just to watch him die." Johnny Cash and "Folsom Prison Blues" as a universal language. I shook his hand, smiled, returned the headphones, relaxed, and fell soundly asleep through most of the six-hour flight.

I awoke now halfway around the world, having passed through twelve time zones, enough to give even Superman a kryptonite headache. Eric was there to meet me when I got off the plane and asked me if I wanted to go to his home to sleep or to the club to hear that night's blues band. Like Warren Zevon said, "I'll sleep when I'm dead," and with that we were off to this Russian rodeo of rhythm and blues.

The club was sardine-packed even for a Monday night. Several large posters of me hung on the club walls, the joint was jumping, and we headed immediately to the bar. We ordered a couple of Heinekens and, as we had done so many times in Minneapolis, bellied up.

The band was really good. A quintet of five young cats in their twenties played and sang a choice selection of Chicago Blues: Muddy Waters, Howlin' Wolf, and Jimmy Reed. Although exhausted, my trepidation was turning into excitement through the healing and rejuvenating power of music, refreshing as a cold cup of water from the spring of Ponce de León.

I introduced myself to the band on the break and was astounded to find out that none of them spoke English, these boys who sang American songs so well. They were true young blues' disciples and took the music and themselves very seriously. It showed. I borrowed an electric guitar and sat in for the rest of the night. We had a ball. The crowd was soulful, respectful, the dance floor packed, and shots of vodka appeared with assembly-line regularity, a theme that would recur throughout the week. We did a couple of encores, as the audience of working men and women, supermodels, ex-KGB agents, and a smattering of American tourists filed out. Afterwards, Eric and I climbed into his car and headed to his house.

We arrived at the house he had built for his family of five. It was good to see his lovely wife, Anna, and their three cute kids, all jabbering away in Russian and doing gymnastic moves around the house, and having fun with their new presents from Grandma. Barbie had survived the trip.

We had a small press conference at the club the next day to announce my arrival. There were three reporters, one from a Russian version of MTV, all women. It was noon. They brought out a large teapot and four small glasses. What I thought was going to be a batch of Earl Grey turned out to be straight vodka. The interview lasted a little more than an hour. The women, who I tried to match cup for cup, all went back to work. I, however, was chin on chest and needed a long nap to sober up before my debut that evening.

I performed pretty much the same couple of sets every night, two solo and one with the young blues band. It was a riot and damn good time. I'd always save my Johnny Cash medley ("Folsom Prison," "Big River," "Rock Island Line") for the end, and the non-English speaking crowd sang along in a full-throated Siberian yell, arms around each other, all on their feet, swaying side by side to those well-known melodies that reached across all boundaries, political and geographic, in one big beating universal heart. Berlin Wall, be damned.

We spent our days sightseeing when Eric wasn't doing business with his three pizza joints, one nightclub, two bakeries, and a woodshop that the state had just given him to run. He had come a long way from one-cent hockey pucks.

Novosibirsk is the sister city of St. Paul, Minnesota. With a population of about three million people, it is a center for several universities specializing in scientific research. The countryside looks very much like northern Minnesota with birch and pine trees, and freshwater lakes and rivers. Fishermen sell their catch from their bicycles on the sides of the river. As we'd drive from the city to the suburbs to the country, however, seeing the amount of poverty was unsettling. There were small conclaves of log dwellings with tin roofs with the occasional dog running on top of them that reminded me of American scenes from the Depression and Dust Bowl days. Chickens and pigs ran around in yards, and men in flannel shirts carried water and chopped wood. Cars and trucks, some running that had never been washed and some that weren't rusting, were strewn alongside the road. Lots of people rode old bicycles.

Eric's company sponsored an orphanage, and they brought me out to play for the kids, about three dozen, ages five to twelve, who lived there. The building that housed them was built in the '30s and still had the original wallpaper. There were old wooden dinner tables, metal beds, a kitchen that smelled like potatoes cooking, and a menacing security guard. Most of the children had been abandoned by parents with drug and alcohol problems. They all seemed rather small, but still, in spite of their surroundings, if you put them side by side they would spell the word *innocence.* I sat on a chair, and they formed a little half-moon circle around me, eyes beaming with light and kindness. I let them all strum my guitar, one by one, amazed by their tiny hands making sounds as their fingernails glided across the strings. I made up a little instrumental that sounded like a railroad train and, as the train picked up speed, had them all move their arms to pull the train whistle, yelling "Choo-choo" in unison. I wished I could have rounded them up and taken them all home with me. It was a place that was very hard to leave, and I can remember several of them in the window, behind a metal screen, waving to me as I left. It was impossible to hold back a few tears.

Russia is a land of the very rich and the very poor. Back in the city, beautiful people in fancy cars and expensive clothes would have fit in well on the Upper East Side of Manhattan. In between were beat-up coldwater flats, and ragged drunks and drug addicts in the alleys and on the stoops of boarded-up shops and tenement houses. The juxtaposition was striking. We toured the war memorial for all the dead Siberian soldiers lost in the past century's wars, and you could sense the strength of their national pride.

We made a final stop that day at the train that brought Lenin to Siberia. I climbed on top, with my guitar, and got a photo next to the thick red star on top, to remind myself how far I have traveled since I took that first guitar lesson at Beddow's Music in Virginia almost forty years before. The rest of the week's gigs went exceptionally well, and I made friends with three beautiful women, all named Natasha. The first wanted to see a picture of my house, I think to gauge my net worth; the second wanted to get her green card; and the third was just looking to have some fun. We did.

You realize how much we take for granted in America, simple things, like well-maintained roads or amply stocked grocery stores. We got pulled over once by a traffic cop, dressed in a full-length green wool army coat, with a submachine gun around one arm. Eric thankfully had all his papers in order. The grocery store shelves were about a quarter full, with very little fresh fruit and scant supplies of milk, eggs, or other dairy products. While Eric took me out to a five-star restaurant one night, I spent most of my lunches and dinners at the club eating pizza.

Saturday night at the club was a complete blowout. It featured another good young blues band, and a jazz band made up of expertly trained classical musicians. We had great time playing "Take the A Train," "Honeysuckle Rose," "Take Five," and others. To say music is the universal language sounds trite, but it is true. It felt like we had known each other for years, like closing time at any bar on the West Bank. More guitars and fewer guns in this world would do us all a lot of good.

We returned to Eric's house in time for me to pack my bags, including a couple of bottles of good Russian vodka, a cool wool jacket, and knick-knacks for friends and family. My flight was at 7 A.M. Eric and I shook hands, he gave me an envelope to open on the plane, and we said our good-byes.

As the plane ascended into the cold Siberian air, I opened the envelope. It contained $200 in American bills and a note from Eric that said my debt to him was paid in full. I closed my eyes, visions of the week reeling through my head. I remembered the old man with the headphones on the previous flight. Leaning back to sleep, images blurred with the headphone strains of Johnny Cash in my brain: "I bet there's rich folks eating in a fancy dining car, they're probably drinkin' coffee and smoking big cigars." From the Mississippi River to the streams of Novosibirsk, the music rolls on.

KEY TO THE HIGHWAY

In June 2001, I was playing at a blues festival at Ironworld, on the border of Chisholm and Hibbing, that included a library of artifacts and old newspapers where one could research the history of the Iron Range, and an amphitheater that featured musical events and everyone from Tony Bennett to Waylon Jennings. The most popular yearly event at Ironworld was Polka Days. I was approached by one of the promoters whose main gig was booking Famous Dave's Barbeque and Blues, a club in Minneapolis that featured blues seven nights a week. He asked me if I would like to do the weekly Sunday brunch gig for a month while their regular musician, a piano player, finished a month in dry dock. As a lapsed Methodist, I only attended church on Christmas and Easter and had most of the rest of my Sundays available. I took the gig.

It started at ten and went until two in the afternoon. At first, I sang my original tunes with a smattering of blues cover songs. I realized, about an hour into it, that people were more interested in enjoying their eggs, sausages, pancakes, and Bloody Marys than they were in paying attention to whoever was making a racket on the stage, much less whether they sang or not. I was fine with that. Only those in church choir sang that well in the morning, and I had long been kicked out of mine for singing too loud.

I had twenty-five to thirty instrumentals in my quiver and enjoyed playing tunes by Fats Waller, Leo Kottke, John Fahey, Duke Ellington, and others. I realized I could also work on my guitar chops and play extended versions of blues variations and song ideas, essentially getting paid to practice. On the breaks I would read the *New York Times*, drink coffee, eat breakfast, plan my midafternoon middle-aged rocker's nap, and decide which movie I was going to attend in the evening. The piano player got out of treatment a month later, immediately fell off the wagon, and the gig was mine.

After a couple of months, and dozens of favorable comments from what I thought was an inattentive audience, I was asked if I could do the 6–8 P.M. happy hour on Saturday as well. I told them I would happily forgo watching *Cops* and could do the gig, as long as I could make whatever show I had in the evening. The summer was coming to a close, both gigs were going well, and I told them I'd be happy to bring my harmonica player, Sonny Earl, in for a Friday happy hour as our weekly Friday patio gig in Northeast Minneapolis, where I called myself the "Daddy-o of the Patio," was coming to an end. They happily obliged. I was now making six bills a week, eating three meals a week for free, and had an unlimited supply of free drinks, depending on who was bartending.

I was paying $300 a month in rent and was driving a series of cars loaned to me by a good friend in my hometown whose dad got started in the bar business by bartending for my granddad at the Roosevelt Bar in Virginia. Iron Rangers have always had a way of taking care of their own, although not always while they were on the range but after, when they had all left and ended up somewhere else, much like a father who could never tell his kids he loved them until they left the nest.

One day in August 2001, I walked into Famous Dave's in the middle of the afternoon to pick up my amp to take to the repair shop. The managers were bitching about the booking agent, the guy who gave me the gig. I told them, "I could book this place." I had been booking myself for years, had booked a handful of other clubs, and knew enough about it to make that claim. A week later I was hired. I had seen one of my predecessor's checks for $840. I didn't know if this was a monthly salary, biweekly, or—OMG—weekly. It was weekly. I was now making almost $1,400 a week. Jackpot, seven come eleven, and then and when, dig my grave with the ace of spades.

A week later I had my first meeting with the corporate, front-line, muckety-mucks, as I would fondly soon refer to them. We went over every detail: the price point of French fries, Coke or Pepsi, other nap-inducing items, and the acts I had booked for the fall. I was copiously taking notes on the palm of my hand with a Bic pen. The vice president of operations, who knew my story from back in the day, looked at me and said while rolling his eyes, "You have got to be fucking kidding me!" I had a yellow legal pad by the next meeting.

Famous Dave's Barbeque and Blues had opened in 1994. Seven years later, the bloom was off the rose, and it needed reinvention. I could be the mother of that. None of the great local blues acts in towns would have anything to do with them. The bands got treated very poorly, and none of them would pay any attention to the six-foot sign in the dressing room explaining the management's rules for the bands, one of which was "No more than two slow songs in a set." Any working band worth its salt can read a dance floor, and trust me, if they want to keep working, all of them want to jump the joint. My first official act as music director was to walk that sign out to the garbage can, break it in half, and lay it to rest among the naked ribs of pigs and cows that have long since gone to meet their maker.

I called the best acts in town, most of them friends of mine, to tell them there was a new sheriff in town. The club was located in the southernmost space in a shopping mall in Uptown Minneapolis. Yeah, the same Uptown that Prince named his first record after, but a shopping mall nonetheless. For the guys I was courting, playing a club that treated musicians like prisoners on an Alcatraz smoke break, in a mall in a pop-culture neighborhood, was a tough sell. I invited to buy them lunch and kick the gong around.

The first guy I invited to lunch was Curtiss A. He is not a blues act, but a man I considered, and still do, to be the greatest rock singer in the world. He had been dubbed the Dean of Scream by the rock cognoscenti and is the Godfather of the punk rock scene in Minneapolis. He had done almost a decade's worth of gigs at the Uptown Bar, which was located right across the street from Famous Dave's. By reviving his weekly gig at Dave's, I thought would be a great way of bringing that mojo back into the neighborhood, when his explosive Wednesday house gigs seemed like Uptown was the rock and roll center of the universe.

Curtiss was quoted as saying in an article about the recent demolition of the Uptown Bar, "I slept with every waitress in the place except Courtney Love." He is that kind of guy, and it was that kind of club. A tad eccentric, he has taped every broadcast of *Jeopardy* since 1982. His bedroom is designed to include thousands of small plastic army men in battle formations, other action figures like Batman and Superman in various poses, and various posters from the thousands of gigs he has done with his various bands. I had told my bosses when I got the music director gig, "There is no way in hell we can be successful with blues seven nights a week. They can't even pull that off in Chicago or Memphis." My goal was to feature the cream of the crop of blues and rhythm and blues on the weekend, and let the club breathe and evolve with great and swinging music from a variety of styles the rest of the week.

Curtiss worked at Comic Book College two blocks south of Famous

Dave's. He showed up at the club for a noon lunch meeting with a small brown paper bag of new comic books, and a sleeveless T-shirt in which he immediately flexed to show me what good shape he was in. We sat down with the new GM, who, like most of the managers who came through the club, came from the corporate paradises that were the Holiday Inn, Olive Garden, and the Old Country Buffet. The GM told us that he just came back from Memphis, where Famous Dave's had opened a club, and said, "Yeah, I just saw Ike Turner in concert." Without skipping a beat, Curtiss said, "That really pisses me off!!" I asked why. Curtiss said, "Christ all mighty, we can forgive Germany, but we can't forgive Ike Turner?" Good point, Curtis. Welcome to the wacky world of artist relations.

I cobbled together the calendar that was handed to me, holes and all. My predecessor left nothing behind, not surprising, and I was left to track down phone numbers and addresses from blues cats who sometimes had neither. Joel Johnson, longstanding West Bank bluesman, DJ on the Lazy Bill Lucas Show on KFAI, an outstanding community radio station that featured blues, among dozens of other shows, stopped by my house and gave me a copy of his rolodex of blues musicians and said, "You will be needing this." He was right.

I put together an all-star show of local luminaries, including headliners Dave "Snaker" Ray (the best twelve-string guitar player this side of Lead Belly), Willie Murphy, and others. It was my coming-out party, and it was scheduled for the third week of September. And then, a lighting bolt of evil struck all Americans on 9/11, and things changed.

The obvious turn-on-a-dime decision was to turn my show into a benefit for the first responders. The place was packed, everyone gathered together with friends wondering what the hell this attack on our soil meant. I did my usual happy hour gig before the big show, and at the end, like leaves falling off an autumn tree from heaven itself, I started to play the "Star Spangled Banner." Those listening—even those who weren't—stood up and faced the stage, hands over heart. I finished the melody and song, and the throng assembled responded with an ovation, standing toe to toe, America resembling itself best when it remembers itself. All for one and one for all. I haven't seen that since. Firemen, in full regalia, passed the hat in the rubber boots that they use when on the job. Money overflowed, drinks were doubled up, money was starting to be collected, and for a moment we were all as one.

I was on a roll. I booked the tried-and-true blues acts, acts that had already played the club, and then reached out for the legendary names I had heard of but had yet to know: Son Seals, Hubert Sumlin, Jody Williams, Alberta Adams, W. C. Clark, Long John Hunter, Eddie Kirkland, Nappy Brown, Louisiana Red, Magic Slim, Jimmy Dawkins, Big Jack Johnson, Willie Kent and the Gents, and others. I also introduced nonblues acts like Commander Cody, Vini "Mad Dog" Lopez, and the Hacienda Brothers. I reunited legendary Minneapolis rock bands like the Litter, Pepper Fog, Crow, and the Unbelievable Uglies, bands I had heard as a teenager in the Virginia National Guard Armory. I also added some gumbo to the musical menu and featured zydeco and Cajun bands like Chubby Carrier and the Bayou Swamp Band, and BeauSoleil. I had a budget, a mission, and a sense that I could make a difference. My sense has always been to book honest and good music, and that honesty and goodness and truth will reward you in kind. And it did, time and time again.

And I have always maintained that the music business is the last *plantation*. I say this completely cognizant of the ramifications of that word and concept. What I mean is nothing in the biz has ever changed over the years. The aforementioned musicians, and then those and more, were on the end of a cat's ball of string, yanked around by managers, agents, record labels reps, and others who never had to live night to night in fleabag motels, cross the country in vans pushing three hundred thousand miles, or use amps that have bounced around in trailers like tennis balls. They never had to miss their wives, sons, and daughters, or doctors' appointments that could have diagnosed whatever ailments they didn't know they were suffering from. Yet to the person, these musicians would show up after many hours traveling on the thankless road, thankful for the gig and ready to jump the joint. I treated them with the respect and dignity they deserved.

I met Hubert Sumlin for the first time at the airport at 7 A.M., he in a well-pressed suit, blue eyes like they were plucked from a deep Icelandic sea, lapels covered with an American flag in gold, a music note that had to be a flatted seventh, and a tie that was given to him by Bob Dylan. He had his guitar in a gig bag slung over his shoulder and a smile that radiated beauty. We grabbed his suitcase, nothing more than a small saddlebag that held a rolled-up stage suit. He was wearing that suit when I picked him up at the hotel to bring him to the gig. It seemed fully pressed, and I was later to find out about the old bluesman's trick of straightening out a suit between the mattress and the bedspring. Life on the road.

This was the man, revered by Jimi Hendrix, Eric Clapton, and Stevie Ray Vaughn who fell into Howlin' Wolf's lap from a skylight in a juke joint in Greenwood, Mississippi, at thirteen years old and was called just four years later by Wolf himself to join him in Chicago. Hubert would put the signature sound on "Smokestack Lightnin,'" "How Many More Years," and "Red Rooster," among others. These were the songs that would midwife rock and roll. Brownie McGhee said it best: "The blues had a baby, and they called it rock and roll." These, my clients, really were my musical uncles and aunts, brothers and sisters, cousins, and mothers and fathers. One big happy musical family reuniting, and getting to know each other, one smokin' set and show at a time.

I did seven years of this and would like to think I treated all the musicians like kings and queens. I made sure they were fed well and treated them as if they were guests in my home. Most were easy to please. Occasionally, they had special needs and I tended to them. Whether it was tracking down an oxygen tank for Nappy Brown, a bowl of vanilla ice cream for Byther Smith, or a double shot of Cuervo for Magic Slim, I made sure they felt special, safe, and welcome. Give a musician 10 percent more than he is used to getting and get 150 percent back in return.

During my tenure, I had only three no-shows. One from unexpected illness, one from a booking misunderstanding, and one from inclement weather. Not bad, considering I was booking acts 365 nights a year for seven years.

I did have one nightmare gig early on. I booked a very well-known harmonica player who, though I did not know it at the time, was in the middle of a deadly crack and heroin addiction. It was a two-night stand, and due to his celebrity, all of the upper management and many Twin Cities celebrities, including former Viking and now Minnesota Supreme Court Judge Alan Page, were in the audience. The musician arrived at the club looking like he hadn't slept, bathed, or changed clothes in weeks. He was nodding off backstage, and I really didn't think the show would go on. The house was jammed to the gills. Sure enough, he gets on stage to a rousing applause and plays a devastatingly brilliant set. Unbelievable. The next night could have been problematic, as his manager and hotel staff had to call the fire department and get the Jaws of Life to open the steel door to his hotel room. He showed up, in the same clothes from the night before, and blew the roof off the joint. I never booked him again. He has since completed extensive treatment and is back on the road touring the world.

They were each unique, powerful, only occasionally a complete pain in the ass, and sometimes a reminder of why each child is born innocent and free of his father's sins. A cornucopia of American experience, and like the blues itself, a representative, for better and, rarely, for worse, of what this country is all about.

All told, it was a musician's dream job. I was a player-coach. I got paid to give money to great musicians, and I got paid to play a couple of times a week myself. I had a health and dental plan, got to witness a bunch of great shows every month, met many of my blues heroes up close and personal, and introduced dozens of up-and-coming musicians to new audiences. I was able to work the floor during those shows like Toots Shor, making hundreds of new friends and fans in the process. And I knew I was doing great work for the club. I got to produce several festivals and records on a budget that more than got the job done. And I was more than ready to let it last forever, blues falling down like rain.

SISU

Sisu is a Finnish word that simply means stubborn inner strength. Some define it as determination beyond all reason. When confronted with adversity, sickness, or a bad roll of the dice, the true Finn summons something within to rise above it. In the valley of the shadow of death, a Finn fears no evil.

My father, Elder, instilled *sisu* in my head before I was even old enough to say my prayers. He learned it from his father, Emil, who learned it from his father, John, who learned it from his father, Isaac, who learned it from his father whose grave lies somewhere near the river that divides Finland from Sweden in the Land of the Midnight Sun.

Great-grandpa John emigrated to Minnesota from Finland in 1888 with his wife, Selma, and two children. He started his new life in America as a miner, working a half-mile underground in the Soudan mine. After several years they accrued enough money to buy some land and, in 1904, moved their young family and John's parents, in horse-drawn wagons, along with three teams of horses, four cows, two chickens, and all the family belongings across twenty-two miles of trail from Soudan to Angora. There the Metsa homestead was established on 520 acres. By 1915, a seven-room, two-story farmhouse was completed. The children grew and helped run the farm, which during the most productive years yielded as much as fifteen hundred bushels of grain and thirty tons of hay. My father was born there, on New Year's Eve 1928, in one of the small rooms upstairs. The doctor from Virginia who delivered him made the twenty-mile trip in a blizzard, and while he was tending to the birth, the men carried hot bricks from their blacksmith shop across the road to place beneath the doctor's car engine to keep it from freezing. When he was finished, he charged the new parents $35, no small amount at a time when the going rate for the workingman was a dollar a day.

His parents, Emil and Elna, named the baby Elder, adding a link to the *E* chain of uncles and aunts named Erick, Eli, Edward, Eva, Eino (who married Elway), and Ellen. Curiously, when Elder later married my mother, her parents were Ernest and Evelyn. Eerie. Poetry played no small part in my family.

Dad grew up on that farm, an only child among his parents and older relatives. He was a favorite of his Grandpa John, and during their long saunas he'd be the water boy, pouring ladle after ladle on the hot rocks atop the stove, and whisking Grandpa's back with cedar bows. Back in the farmhouse in the dead of winter Grandpa let Elder sit on his lap and fire his BB gun across the room at the wooden staircase that led to the second floor, much to the consternation of Grandma and the rest of the family. After milking, it was young Elder's job to take pails of the skimmed milk to the pigs that would sometimes knock him down in their frenzy to eat. To this day he hates skim milk and confesses, "I can barely drink 2 percent, either."

Dad graduated from the University of Minnesota, Duluth, in June 1951, married in September, and moved to Bayfield, Wisconsin, where he had accepted a high school teaching position. Mom got a job as a delivery nurse in the local hospital. They returned to Virginia the following June, a time when the mines were on strike and there were virtually no jobs. Elder had already secured a teaching position in Mountain Iron for the fall but sought something to tide them over for the summer months. He approached his old boss at the city parks and recreation department, where he'd held a summer job in high school. "I'm sorry, Elder," he said. "I'm afraid the only job I have open is feeding the monkeys at the monkey house in Olcott Park, and being a college graduate, I'm sure you wouldn't be interested." "I'll take it," said Elder. "I'm not too proud to feed monkeys." His friends would come to the park and chide, "Hey, Monkey Man, throw us some peanuts!" He shrugged off the comments, and while friends were struggling to put food on their tables, Elder and Bess had a steady supply of leftover peanuts and bananas.

By 1957, with three children, they had purchased a small house on Thirteenth Street South. Mom worked full time at the hospital and Dad continued to teach school. On Monday nights he stood at a small podium in the basement of the Sears store on Chestnut Street selling Allstate Insurance. In 1959, they took on a new venture with Dad's parents, purchasing the Holland Hotel, which included a Chinese restaurant on the first floor and hotel rooms upstairs. Grandpa Emil bartended, Mom waited tables on her days off, and Dad worked the floor when he wasn't teaching. Too much work finally caught up with him. One evening Dad was rushed to the hospital bleeding from an ulcer. The doctor diagnosed stress, and the decision was made to sell the hotel and reorganize priorities. He ran for the school board and won, then obtained his real estate license, and resigned from teaching to devote his career to selling insurance and real estate.

In the summer of 1963 Grandma Elna came to ask my parents a favor. She had a friend who had three children and a very abusive husband. The woman had asked Elna if she could help find a place for her fourteen-year-old daughter to live. Mom and Dad welcomed her with open arms, and we gained a new big sister, Kathy.

Dad came home one day and surprised Mom with the news that he had just bought a house, much larger than the little modern bungalow that was now packed with four children. Mom was not particularly amused when she saw the house, once a two-story duplex, built in 1903, with the main floor kitchen in desperate need of remodeling, a dark and damp basement, another kitchen area in one of the four upstairs bedrooms, and a cavernous, drafty attic plastered with old newspapers on the sloped ceilings. But move we did.

My parents worked hard while we four kids were growing up. Mom worked nights at the hospital, leaving just before we'd go to bed and returning home in time to make us breakfast, send us off to school, and go to sleep herself. Dad always worked at least two jobs and was very active in civic affairs; he was the only person in Virginia to serve on the school board, the city council, and two terms as mayor. As such he didn't have as much time as he would have liked with the kids.

Not that we felt slighted. We had an extended family of grandparents, aunts, uncles, and close family friends who were always there to show love and support. Mom pretty much ran the show but would occasionally delegate the harder work of disciplining us boys. I stepped over the line many times, as boys will do, not intentionally setting out to defy him but just confident that I wouldn't get caught.

One day, while in tenth grade, my mother found my condoms (then called rubbers) in the pocket of my pants while doing laundry. She warned me, "Wait until your father gets home!" When he did, mom explained the situation, and he took me outside under the Chinese apple tree while my mother looked out the window. He looked at me, and while it looked to my mother that he was scolding me, he winked and said, "Paul, can't you hide these in the garage?"

One time, we got a brand new 17-foot Lund aluminum boat with a 40-hp motor to go alongside the smaller fishing boat we had used for years. Less than a week after we bought it, I cajoled my dad into letting me take my friends waterskiing. He was reluctant to let me drive it without him, but I promised I'd take good care of it. A half-hour later at 35 mph, I ran it aground over large rocks, more interested in watching my friend drop a ski and fall than looking where the hell I was going. He told me I had to pay for the damages. I worked all that summer after ninth grade, painting houses and mowing lawns, and finally made enough money to repair the damage. We drove down to New York Mills to get the boat, I gave him a big wad of money wrapped in a rubber band, and he went inside to pick it up. He came back out, and we hitched it to the trailer ready to head back up north. He got in the truck, looking at me as only a father can look at a son in these moments, gave me my money back, and said, "I had it insured, but I hope you learned your lesson." I had. We drove back home with the windows down, the radio on full blast.

Dad retired and sold his business in 1990. For a man who'd been a pillar of the community, civic servant, businessman, and breadwinner for a family of four, going full speed, it was a big adjustment. My mother passed away in 1994 after a battle with leukemia. Then in 1996, we tragically lost my brother's wife, Dianne, who was not just a daughter-in-law but also Dad's very good friend. For the first time in decades, he found himself adrift and lonely. A well-meaning friend of the family advised him to take a stiff glass of brandy and water to bed, and if he couldn't sleep at night, just sip it to get back to sleep. It wasn't long before he crawled right into the bottle.

It was the beginning of a six-year nightmare for our family. It was so completely out of character for the father we grew up with. Although he still dressed well, he looked like hell. I would get phone calls from my brother telling me how much Dad was drinking, how much time he spent at the bars, and how difficult he became when drunk. It was hard for me to tell exactly what was going on. I was really in no position to judge; I had spent more than my share of time walking on, and hanging off, the ledge of alcohol and drugs.

Toward the end of his trail of darkness, he would wake up at 6 A.M., have a shot of brandy, take a shower, have a couple of Bloody Marys while reading the paper, and then head to the bar for several hours of playing pull-tabs, drinking, and hanging out with his new barroom buddy, Misery—who loved company. On his way home, he'd stop by the liquor store for a bottle or two of vodka and Bloody Mary mix. I know from experience that it is damn near impossible to reach somebody when they are in that swirl of intoxication and denial. It sometimes takes an act of God, an arrest, or an accident before the person trapped within can escape and survive.

Just days before the weekend in 2002 when my brother John was getting remarried, my father took a fall on the stairs to his garage apartment. He felt a sharp pain in his side but managed to put away his groceries and drive forty miles north to the cabin, trying to ignore the pain. Once there, he called me, told me about the fall, and said he was taking care of himself with a little brandy, Bengay ointment, and a heating pad. I told him I was coming up to help prepare for the weekend wedding, and I would see him the next night.

By the time I arrived at the cabin, Dad was shuffling around. He was very pale, skinnier than I remembered him, and stubbornly proceeded to make dinner for John and me, dressed in his white V-necked T-shirt and pajama bottoms. He was quieter than usual. When we awoke Friday morning, I looked at him, now almost translucent, and we took him into the Cook Hospital. This was certainly not the agenda John or his beautiful fiancée, Carol, had envisioned as they were planning for wedding guests to arrive.

John and I walked with Dad down the hallway of the hospital while the doctor was reading the X-rays. He finally came out and asked, "When did this happen?" Dad answered, "Wednesday." The doctor asked incredulously, "And what day is today?" I answered, "Friday." The doctor said, "Elder, you have three broken ribs and a punctured lung!" Dad replied, "I'm a tough Finlander." "Apparently so," the doctor replied. They immediately admitted him into the hospital, the wedding took place without him, and on Sunday he was transported by ambulance to a hospital in Duluth while I was on my way back to my house gig at Famous Dave's in Minneapolis.

He was in a coma for the next two months. It was a heartbreaking and arduous situation. Here was our father, the man who had spent a lifetime instilling values and providing a dazzling example of hard work, honesty, the love of family, and the importance of friends and community, in a train badly run off the tracks, and now nearly slain by a devil's deal with bottled spirits. Had he died, I would have spent the rest of my life in anger, confused by what had brought him to this.

Fortunately, my sister Kathy, living outside of Duluth, and my brother John, living in northern Minnesota, could monitor him on an almost daily basis. I would drive up to Duluth at least three times a week to sit with him, hold his hand, comb his hair, clip his nails, wipe his brow. Occasionally, I could see his eyes tear up, and I so wanted to believe this was his way of letting us know he was there and loved us. We made friends with the chaplain named Dianne, in a sweet moment of synchronicity, and tried to make sense out of the reports from the doctors, who always seemed distant and on their way to somewhere else. I called my friend Dr. Jacob, whose family and three sons had adopted me like their wayward Ranger son when I moved to Minneapolis. He had gotten to know my father over the years. As best I could, I explained his situation, vital signs, and condition. He said, "For damn near anybody else, this is indeed a death sentence, but knowing your dad is one tough Ranger, I'd say he has a fighting chance."

I was able to spend four to five hours at a time with him while at the hospital. I was at a loss for answers and would occasionally have to ask the janitors for their opinion, since I was getting no real information from the team of anonymous doctors. My dad did not have a living will, and we had to take care of ownership issues of the cabin and his estate if he passed. Kathy, ever the realist, was always very blunt and matter-of-fact with us about his chances. As a nurse, she was our liaison to the doctors and medical staff. I, ever the optimist, hoped for the best and kept my fingers crossed.

Once I had to wheel him through the hospital to get a brain scan. He of course couldn't speak. We entered the testing room and the two nurses had the radio on. Creedence Clearwater Revival's "Who'll Stop the Rain" was playing at full blast. While they were applying the jelly and electrodes to his head, the lady said, "Does he have cirrhosis?" I thought he certainly might since he had been drinking like Foster Brooks for the past six years. I asked her how she could diagnose that. She replied, "Because his scalp is very flaky." I answered in disbelief, "I think you mean psoriasis." My good God, these people are taking care of my father? Indeed, who will stop the rain?

All I could do at the hospital was read, go outside for a smoke, conduct business, and stay in touch with my family and girlfriend on my cell phone. More than once, she'd answer the phone while I was balling my eyes out wondering if this was the last time I'd ever see my dad. I'd watch other families go in and out of the hospital, many in the same situation as ours. We were all troubled and, some of us, a long way from home.

After six weeks, my dad slowly showed signs of improvement. They moved him out of intensive care, and one day I was able to feed him some solid food. He still could not talk, and his head slanted slightly to the right. My dad was always rail thin and was proud of the fact that he could still fit into the tuxedo he wore to his high school prom. His pajamas loosely swaddled him and more than covered his skinny arms, chest, and legs. I fed him more than I should have and when I was driving back to Minneapolis heard that he was back in intensive care because the food got caught in his windpipe. I couldn't win.

There were calm and quiet days as well. A couple of times a week the Duluth *News Tribune* would feature animals, mostly dogs and cats, available for adoption at the various humane shelters throughout the northland. My goal now, if my dad made it, was to adopt a dog from one of them and give it a new life in Minneapolis at my house, which had a fenced-in backyard, grapevines, and a little vegetable garden.

I got the call that my dad was ready to be released from the hospital in Duluth, asking if I could rent a van to take him to the hospital and nursing home back up in Cook. I signed the release papers. Now weighing 103 pounds, skin draped over bones, Dad was equipped with an oxygen tank and tube to his nose. Halfway up the hill on our way out of Duluth I turned around to check on him. He was deathly grey and his head was tilting to the side. I yelled to the van driver to pull over. He checked the oxygen tank. The folks at the hospital had forgotten to turn it on! We turned the dial, and he slowly came to. Country roads, take us home.

Dad spent the next month in the Cook hospital, unable to speak, feed himself or walk. His Aunt Ellen, now ninety-eight years old, was in the adjacent nursing home at the time. She always offered him her sandwich or dessert. Love in action. She lived to be ninety-nine.

It was at this time I put my dog adoption plan into action. My girlfriend and I went to Contented Critters, a no-kill animal shelter north of Duluth in Makinen. Caretakers Walt and Faye operated one of the largest animal sanctuaries in the state, housing more than four hundred animals, including a three-legged horse, a nine-hundred-pound hog, a blind turtle, and dozens of cats and dogs, all of which needed a home. It was like some wayward fractured dream of Doctor Doolittle. My only criterion for the dog was that it not stand higher than my knees.

We looked at more than thirty dogs, a wide array of beat-up, abandoned, and somewhat wild mutts. I didn't really find what I was looking for and was walking back to the truck to get my checkbook so I could at least donate some money to the cause. Suddenly, a black dog in a distant corner of the property started to bark wildly. I asked Walt about him. "Oh, that's Blackie, but he has some issues." He told me Blackie had come there from a shelter in Crookston where he was too scared and anxious for them to control. A farm family adopted him, but two days after being leashed in their front yard Blackie had finally had enough. He chewed through his leash and spent the next four seasons in northern Minnesota roaming the woods. Tough little guy. There had been several Blackie sightings throughout the year, and finally, after putting out food in their barn, a family near where he had been seen found him skinny and shivering and was able to capture him.

He was in a little rusted cage, barking excitedly with ears tucked back, eyes bulging like he was rabid. My girlfriend asked Walt to take him out of his cage. She looked at him and said, "You don't look so tough." Blackie sat on his haunches as if recognizing a couple of like-minded souls, one ear up, one ear down like the Flying Nun. He quieted down. It was love at first sight. He was part border collie, black with a white chest, weighed less than thirty pounds, and came up to my knees. He was the one. I asked Walt how much he cost and said we couldn't pick him up for a couple of weeks. I loved Blackie's story, and in a way he reminded me a bit of myself—a true mutt, and even more of a survivor. I have always loved the underdog, and Blackie truly was one. We hadn't picked Blackie: he picked us. What a bargain for sixty-five dollars.

We went to pick him up a couple of weeks later. Oddly, he didn't bark (and wouldn't for several months) but paced the back of the car, probably wondering where the next part of his incredible journey would take him. We got him home, fed him (besides his dog food, a small rib eye steak), and took him outside, welcoming him to his new home. Of course, the first time he was in the fenced-in backyard he found the one small space in the fence, got out, and I had to chase him around the block. He made a full circle, ending up on my back porch. Okay, Blackie, I get it. He slowly got comfortable at my house and slept on a Mexican blanket and two pillows at the foot of my bed.

A few weeks after that, my dad had recovered enough to move out of the hospital. My brother, God bless him, got him into an assisted living apartment across the street from the hospital. I drove up to Cook to help him move into the place and had my girlfriend take Blackie to her apartment in the interim. Dad was now able to speak, had put on some weight, and his once-perfect Palmer Method penmanship was coming back, one postcard at a time.

We were watching the World Series, something I feared would never happen again, when the phone rang. My girlfriend was crying, as if maybe her mother had died. Blackie had made a swift dash out of her house when her brother came to visit and was now lost in the wilds of South Minneapolis. The poor guy, first lost in the north woods and now on his own in the big city. She put up posters in the lost-and-found sections of all the grocery stores and pharmacies and spent that night driving down Lake Street, a hotbed of illicit commerce after dark, windows open, shouting "Blackie, Blackie!" to the drug dealers and hookers who called that avenue their own.

I drove back the next day, and we spent six hours that night trying to track him down, to no avail. Fortunately, he had his collar and nametags with my phone number. I did my house gig at Famous Dave's and came back to two messages on my answering machine. The first from an unknown angel who called to tell us that he was with Blackie, who had been hit by a car, maybe two, at Forty-fourth and Chicago. He had called Animal Rescue and they were on their way. The second call was from the Golden Valley Emergency Vet, and Blackie was there under their care. I could never have lived with myself had we lost him. We were headed to Golden Valley, the town that John Steinbeck said in *Travels with Charley* is neither golden nor a valley. We arrived about 10 P.M., and they took Blackie out on a blanket, lips swollen, beat up, completely out of it, with a broken pelvis. The doctor wanted to keep him overnight to assess if it was worth trying to save him. He asked if I had a credit card. I had just received a new card in the mail with a $5,000 balance. I told the doctor, "Do what you have to do." Little did I know at the time that medical service for animals is as good, and as expensive, as it is for humans.

When we arrived the next morning, Blackie was in the intensive care section. Though scared and confused, unable to sit up, and highly medicated, when he saw us through the thick glass of the oxygen unit, one ear went up and one went down. He recognized who we were and knew Daddy had come to take him home.

Blackie still needed surgery at the University of Minnesota Veterinary School, and we admitted him immediately. Before surgery, they let us visit him, half-shaven, with as many tubes sticking out of him as my dad had in the hospital. He licked our faces and we looked into each other's eyes and I told him everything was going to work out fine. While I had adopted him to represent my dad's healing and recovery, he instead seemed to represent dad's accident, and we hoped for a small miracle for Blackie as well.

We took him home and covered my bedroom with plastic to deal with his accidents. The recovery took three months. One night while I was sleeping Blackie barked for the first time. I would take him out every day and carefully lay him on the porch in his diaper to enjoy the fresh air and sunshine. One day out of the blue, after several tries, he doggedly lifted himself onto all four legs, snout and eyes pointed toward the morning sun, and stood up! Shaky but standing, bruised but unbowed, he stood, like the canine Phoenix, ready to rise again. A water pail couldn't have held my tears.

Blackie's first paw-penned Christmas card described the whole story: price of adoption: $65. Price of emergency vet in Golden Valley: $1,400. Price of intensive care and surgery at the U of M vet hospital: $3,600. Price of having Minnesota's second-best folksinger take me out at 6 A.M. and hold me up while I poop: priceless! (Blackie's words, not mine.) He would be, and now remains, my $5,000 alarm clock wrapped in fur.

My father, like Blackie, made an amazing and complete recovery. Every day above ground for him is a gift from God to all of us. He rightfully credits Kathy, at one time a frightened young girl with blonde hair and glasses, whom he and Mom took into our house, no questions asked, almost fifty years prior, with helping to save his life. He has since been the president of the Lion's Club in Cook and, ever the salesman, sells Fuller Brush products on the side. (I know, I had no idea they were still around either.) When I was driving him to his first Christmas after the accident, I wondered if he would start drinking again. We now live in a world where almost every affliction has a self-help group like AA, NA, Al-Anon. I have attended a few myself. I asked him point-blank, "Dad, you think you are ever going to drink again?" Ask an honest man a question, you will get an honest answer quickly: "Nope, I filled the tank."

We get on our knees and pray for miracles. Some people don't pray at all, and yet miracles arrive out of nowhere, the benevolent hand of God meeting his children in their deepest hour of need. Yet time can sometimes dull the memory of the miracles and wonder of this world. For me, I try and always remember these gifts in spite of the chaotic minutiae of everyday life that often cloud the wonder and sometimes obscure the joy.

When my dad and I chat, I soak it up like a jellyfish, enjoying the sound of his soothing baritone voice, his simple words of wisdom, and envision his descriptions of the golden moments of our family's history, including his life as a boy on the farm, his struggle to raise our family, and his memories of family, friends, and teachers. He tells the occasional bawdy joke, talks about lunch with his buddies Bud and Carl, and how much he enjoys attending the little Lutheran church in Alango with the tall white steeple that has been welcoming people since before the family farmhouse was built, just a few miles through the woods where he was born eighty-two years ago. Dad always reminds me to pet Blackie for him, and with phone in my right hand I pet Blackie, who is always at my feet, with my left. It's as if an electrical current flows through me connecting these two survivors, who after knocking on death's door refused to enter. The mist of the day's concerns disappears, and I feel the purity of simplicity graced with a sense of wonder, what great poets describe as love. And then Dad ends the call as always: "Remember, Paul, that God loves you and so do I!" I sleep like a baby, with Blackie dreaming at the end of the bed, thankful for yet another day.

My dad and I became much closer after my mother died. While always my hero, in the subsequent years he became closer to me as a dad and just as close as a friend. About a year after his miraculous recovery I sent him a letter. I was more than a little surprised to see it on the front page of the *Mesabi Daily News* on Father's Day. After the letter appeared, Dad received numerous calls from friends, sons and daughters, and mothers and fathers who thanked him for sharing it. They told him it helped them reach out to estranged family members, once again proving the power of love.

Letter from a proud dad to his father

Father's Day gift to our readers

—Bill Hanna, *Mesabi Daily News*

He was mayor of Virginia for several years. I was editor for all of them.

So, it was only natural that we would bump heads at times. And, because of the very personal issues during part of his tenure, some of the bumps were a bit rough; the noggins and both egos a bit bruised.

But, so it goes with elected officials and newspaper editors.

Yet I always respected Elder Metsa as mayor, even though it was grudging respect at times. And I hoped he felt the same now and then toward me as editor.

I always had tremendous respect and really admiration for the mayor's son, Paul, a musician who plays the blues and folk songs with the best of them, and writes lyrics—with a probing perspective—that are so real they gently and easily but with great passion touch the soul.

The mayor's son and editor would talk a couple of times over the years and exchange compliments . . . and sometimes the mayor would pass on to the editor the complimentary words of his son.

The last few years I had seldom seen Elder and when we did meet only a nod or a "Hi" were exchanged.

But a few weeks ago up in Cook the meeting was a lot longer, more cordial and the greetings and words exchanged between a former mayor and an editor, who had been adversarial at times, were good for the heart. "Good to see you, my friend, take care of yourself," the mayor said.

A few days ago the former mayor called to offer condolences on my mother's death and to submit a letter to the editor praising the Virginia Marching Blues. A former mayor proud of his city's high school band.

The former mayor also brought in to the publisher a letter he had received from his son. It was shared with the editor. And the former mayor said he would have no problem if the editor shared it with readers in some fashion on Father's Day.

I do so here, in full. A letter written on March 7 of this year from a proud son to his father—a Father's Day gift to all:

Dear Dad,

I have been meaning to write this letter for some time now. I have a few minutes this afternoon and thought I would finally get around to it.

Basically, I have wanted to tell you what a wonderful gift your recovery and sobriety has been to me personally and to the family. I must admit I spent many years being angry with you when I would see and feel how your drinking affected the family. I tried my damnedest to talk to you about it but, as we all know, it sometimes takes an act of God to put things into perspective.

I used to sit up nights and wonder if something happened to you during that time if I would spend the rest of my life in anger and puzzlement. Angry because I knew you were a much better man than you were acting. Puzzlement because you were always one of the strong upstanding men of the community and many of us wondered how your behavior and self-control could change so radically. It sounds funny to say, but it is a damn good thing you fell down those stairs! Obviously, God had a better plan for you.

Throughout your ordeal and my trips to Duluth to visit you I had quite a bit of time to reflect on what a great life you and Mom have provided for all of us. There wasn't a day during your time in Duluth where you didn't have a family member visit or call to check on you, sometimes several times a day. Kathy was really your Duluth guardian angel. You have always said taking Kathy into our home was one of the things you were most proud of and it was really incredible to see how she paid you back. God does work in mysterious ways.

No matter how stressful or hard my life is at any one time I always manage to take a deep breath and know my Father is only a phone call away. It makes all of my problems seem so minuscule. Like you always said, "First you must have your health, then your family, then your friends." How true, how true!

Sister Jackie and I have great conversations about your progress and how you really do seem to be enjoying your life to the fullest. You have really become the living embodiment of your saying how adversity will always open another door to positive experiences.

I really feel blessed to have had such a strong and beautiful Mother, great-grandparents, great siblings, and such a wonderful Dad. We should always take a part of our day and thank God for this as there are millions of people that aren't as lucky as us.

I really appreciate you taking the lead to set up a situation at the cabin that will include all of us for years to come. It is an oasis in an increasingly troubled world. Believe me, that cabin is the glue and magic that has helped all of us lead strong, positive, and accomplished lives. There will never be a price that you could put on that piece of property in terms of its positive spiritual effects on the family.

I have gotten to a point in my life when I truly enjoy the little gifts that life affords us day by day. It can be as simple as taking Blackie for his morning walk and seeing him scoot out the door like he is doing it for the first time, his tail a-waggin'. It can be a cup of coffee with my carpenter as he works on my kitchen. It can be a simple thanks from Famous Dave's after a great weekend at the club. Or an e-mail from a fan saying how much my music means to them. Or a call (or e-mail) from the Thin Finn from Cook, MN. When I add them all up it signifies a very rich life indeed.

I am looking forward to many more years with you. You must feel truly blessed to look at your family and see all the great things they have accomplished and the good lives they are living. I know Mom and Dianne sometimes must be beaming from above.

There will be a time when each of us leaves this earthly plane to reunite with our loved ones and friends that have passed on before us. I want to make you a deal. Whoever gets there first, circle Mom, Dianne, and Grandpa and Grandma in a warm and loving circle, holding hands and crying tears of joy for being together again and welcome the other guy into the circle. We will all live in eternity forever always bounded by our love. Our short time apart will be eclipsed by that eternity and any tears at death will be those of thankfulness, hope and gratitude for a life on earth as father and son.

You gave me life and opportunity. And I remain forever in your debt for showing me in the twilight of your life that there is always an oppor-tunity to change behavior, thus changing fortune, and not only recover from the curve balls life throws you, but take a bad pitch and hit it out of the park. This may be your greatest gift to all of us.

You have always been, remain, and will always be my hero.
All the love in the world!
Your son whose middle name is your own.
Paul Elder Metsa
and Blackie
Minneapolis

TEXAS IN THE TWILIGHT ZONE

In 2007, I was down in Austin, Texas, one of my favorite cities in the country, attending the South by Southwest (SXSW) Music Festival. I have attended this festival several times since 1986. Austin is a lot like Minneapolis–St. Paul: a river town, state capital, and liberal. Both towns have great music scenes. Musicians from all over the world come to Austin in search of fame and fortune. After getting hooked up with three record deals at SXSW that went absolutely nowhere, I go down to Austin to hear music, eat Texas barbeque and fresh breakfast burritos with iced bottles of Coca-Cola, and fall in love with a variety of waitresses and bartenders who magically seduce me with their honey-laced Texas accents, sundresses, cowboy boots, and Spanish skin.

On the Saturday afternoon of the festival, I was picked up by my old buddy, a musician himself, in a '68 Chevy convertible, fire engine red with immaculate white leather interior. It was a beautiful Austin afternoon, seventy-five and sunny. My buddy is on strict orders from his wife—no drinking, ever. Of course, his buddy Paul was in town, and what's a couple of cold Shiner Bocks between friends? My friend is a dry drunk, and after two beers, was shit faced. I was anxious to get out, put the top down, and enjoy a ride into the hill country on this beautiful afternoon. An hour and a half later, rain clouds approaching, and most of the six-pack gone, I finally coaxed him into hitting the road. He lost his glasses (fifteen minutes) and then his keys (another fifteen minutes). We finally got in the car, and it immediately started to pour, the kind of rain that inspired the song "Texas Flood." We put the top up, and he was speeding and weaving from lane to lane. The last thing we needed was to be pulled over by the cops.

I was starting to remember all of his psychoses that I have witnessed and endured over our twenty-year relationship (no doubt, he had witnessed some of mine). They were all on full display, floored and over the limit on several levels. I talked him into pulling into Threadgill's Bar and Grill on the river. Henry Threadgill is considered to be the godfather of the Austin music scene, and the original Threadgill's Restaurant, still up and running, gave a young Port Arthur singer named Janis Joplin her start. Henry and Janis are gone, but the new Threadgill's was hosting a much-anticipated concert featuring the legendary Roky Erickson of 13 Floor Elevators' fame in its beer garden. In fact, some say Janis Joplin picked up a bit of her Bessie Smith wail from Roky's improvisational rock and roll screams. The 13th Floor Elevators was one of the first psychedelic bands in the country, country cousins to the West Coast psychedelic scene. In the mid-1960s LSD was legal and plentiful, and certain hippies took it like their parents took Bayer aspirin. Roky took enough to fry his cerebral cortex, spent years in and out of the psyche ward, homeless on the streets, and now properly medicated was making a much-welcome comeback. I was jacked to see this Texas legend in his own backyard.

I didn't have a SXSW wristband and was directed to buy a ticket at the bar for the show. I was waiting for a bartender when I hear a voice behind me say, "Hey, Kilo." I turn around, since it seemed to be directed toward me, and see a uniformed Texas cop. He asks me, "Are you Kilo?" I say, "No, my name is Paul, and I am from Minneapolis." The cop says, "Why did you answer to the name Kilo?" I tell him politely that I heard someone talking to me, over the din of a crowded bar, and when I saw it was a police officer, I thought the polite and proper thing to do was to address him. The cop asks me to move away from the bar. This is not going well. The spiked- and red-haired promoter comes up and tells Joe Friday, "Several people told me this guy was Kilo!" I am guessing perhaps, that Mr. Kilo, given his handle, may have had something to do with the drug trade and may now pose some threat to Roky's sobriety and safety. Roky is making a comeback, and I can understand this. I am all about the comeback, but this situation is becoming embarrassing.

The cop asks if he can pat me down. Now, mind you, I have been doing the twenty-four-hour crawl within a teenager's slingshot of South Austin for four days, and I have no idea what may be in my pockets. I ask him what he may be looking for, and he says, "Illegal recording equipment." I respond, "If it will get this nightmare over with, by all means, search away." My buddy stumbles forward to see if he can help. The cop says in no uncertain terms, "Stay on the perimeter." You have got to be kidding me. He searches me and finds one comb, several guitar picks, and a pocket full of change and dollar bills that have seen their better days. I realize it is hard enough to prove who you are, much less who you are not. The promoter, still not believing I am not Kilo, banishes me from the gig. The cop tells me I can stay at the bar as long as I don't start any trouble. I am fuming, and the bartender who has witnessed the whole thing slides me a shot of Tito's vodka on the rocks and on the house. Onward through the fog.

I rejoin my friend and a couple of his friends at a table and try to compose myself. One of his friends points out the owner of Threadgill's through the window, and I go outside to pitch my bitch. I tell him my tale and he says, "Was it that sombitch red-haired punk promoter? He has been a real burr in my saddle." Spoken like a true Texan, although he doesn't offer to get me into the gig. I have let out a little steam but am still pissed that I can't go and see Roky. I try and walk it off.

After several minutes I walk back into the bar, now empty since everyone is out in the beer garden to catch the show. I see a short balding white man, in a pale-blue button-down, white khakis, and wire-rim glasses at the host stand. I realize it is Karl Rove. I am now caught between the two furthest hitching posts of the Texas psychic, political, and pharmacological landscape. Roky to the left of me, Karl to the right. I am looking for Rod Serling in the shadows.

I ask him if he is in fact Karl Rove. He says yes. Great balls of fire. I say, "I must admit, I am a lifelong Democrat from northeastern Minnesota, but we have a friend in common." His blue eyes light up and he asks, "Who?" I say, "Norm Coleman. I played several benefits for him while he was running for mayor of St. Paul, as a Democrat, and in fact played at his inaugural ball before you guys got your hands on him."

The dark angel chuckles and asks me if I live near the BWCA, short for the Boundary Waters Canoe Area, more than a million acres of wilderness and more than a thousand lakes, rivers, and streams, and some of the most pristine wilderness anywhere in the world, located in northeastern Minnesota. I used to be a canoe guide there in the mid-1970s. I say yes, hoping to God he and his posse don't have eyes to make this into the next big industrial development of the new century. Remembering the precedent set by the iconic photo of Elvis and Nixon, I ask him if he doesn't mind, if I find a camera, having a photo taken. I will need this to prove to myself, at some point, that I wasn't hallucinating.

I walk back outside and find a man from Norway with a camera. I tap him on the shoulder and ask him if he can do me a favor. He turns around, looks at me, and asks in a clipped Norwegian accent, "Are you Kilo?" This is fucking unbelievable, the nightmare continues. I shudder and stutter and start walking backwards in a half-time Michael Jackson moonwalk. The next person I find with a camera is a Japanese man, and I ask him if he could take a picture for me. He smiles and tells me he would, but his camera is broken. Finally, I find a woman with a camera, explain the situation to her, and she says, "I am a Libertarian, I get it." We track down Karl and get the shot. As we are leaving, Karl says, "I will say hi to Coleman for you." Yeah, please do. The lady sent me the photo a couple of weeks later. Sure enough, it was Karl Rove and yours truly side by side. Only in America. Behind, in the background, was an old poster of Jerry Lee Lewis. If you look closely, you can make out the word "Killer" over Rove's left shoulder.

My buddy, now inside and chin on chest, comes to and starts bitching at me for taking so long. I carry him to the car, get his keys, and drive him home and sneak him past his wife, to the shower, and then to bed. I tell her the story—well, most of the story. She is amused that I bumped into Karl Rove but says, "That *is* weird, but what are the chances of running into a Japanese person with a broken camera?" She has a point.

I am running on fumes at this point, Santa Anna at the doors of the Alamo of my mind. I took out my wallet to check my cash supply. I saw that behind my driver's license I had remnants of a leaf I gently lifted from the Treaty Oak in Austin years before. Native Americans would gather under this legendary five-hundred-year-old tree before battles, and legend has it that Stephen Austin signed the first Texas boundary treaty there and Sam Houston napped under its boughs.

Later that evening at an outdoor café drinking double martinis with another friend of mine, a squad car pulls right in front of us and stops, lights blazing and sirens blaring. I look at my friend and say, "I hope they ain't looking for Kilo!"

Postcript: the *Austin American Statesman* reported the next day that Kilo was arrested at the Roky Erickson show and charged with assault.

SLINGS AND ARROWS

On a chilly afternoon in April 2001, Tony "Tilt" Rubin sat next to me on a plane bound for New York City. I was scheduled to play two gigs out there, one at the Mercury Lounge on the Lower East Side and the other at the Stone Pony, in Asbury Park, New Jersey. Tony was a Duluth native and a University of Minnesota student whom I had met at Nye's and was now renting my upstairs apartment. He had done some Web design for me, and I had told him that, in exchange, I would one day take him to investigate the Woody Guthrie Archives in New York, courtesy of my friend Nora Guthrie.

As the plane sat on the tarmac, I opened the metro section of the Minneapolis *Star Tribune* to see a headline announcing that the Walker Art Center was planning to demolish the historic Guthrie Theater. The theater company had outgrown the building and was aiming to create a new complex on the Mississippi River downtown. The Walker, which was designing an enlargement of its 1971 building, owned the theater and wanted to use the two acres on which it sat for an expansion of the eleven-acre Minneapolis Sculpture Garden. I could not believe my eyes. The iconic building was still completely functional and held great cultural and artistic significance. It also had the finest acoustics of any performance space I had ever been in. I told Tilt that we'd have to do something about this, though I had no idea what.

Both gigs went well, and then we drove out to the Woody Guthrie Archives. I introduced Tilt to Nora, who led us to the visitors' table. The archivists brought us the first of many scrapbooks and two pairs of white gloves. "Gentlemen, put on your gloves," one of them instructed us. The first page I turned to contained a drawing of a Madison Square Garden boxing match Woody had attended; it showed two boxers and a referee in the center of the ring with a caption written by Woody: "Gentlemen, put on your gloves." Holy Moly! Guthrie was in the air.

Whether it was the gloves, Guthrie's caption, or both, the experience gave us that little kick of motivation. Upon our return to Minneapolis, Tilt and I came up with an initiative to help save the Guthrie Theater from demolition. We fleshed out a plan in Tilt's apartment, created a Web site, and SavetheGuthrie.org was born. Over the next five years, I would learn much about the history of the theater, but more about the politics of how great buildings are created and, sometimes, destroyed.

Ralph Rapson, architect of the original Guthrie Theater, is in the pantheon of Minnesota artists and architects. His cutting-edge designs and progressive visions have prompted some to call him "the Bob Dylan of architecture," though he was in his prime while Dylan was still in knee pants. His designs for churches, embassies, theaters, and houses in the United States and Europe are thoroughly modern and, in some cases, downright futuristic. Born in Michigan in 1914, Rapson studied under the famed Finnish architect Eliel Saarinen at the Cranbook Academy of Art in the 1930s and became a dedicated modernist. In 1954, he moved to Minneapolis to head the University of Minnesota's school of architecture, remaining there until 1984—thirty years during which his students spread his concepts of modern design across the country and around the world. Rapson lived in Minneapolis's Prospect Park neighborhood, across the street from the old Witch's Hat water tower, a structure he sketched frequently over the years and even included in some of his holiday cards. Rapson went to his office on Cedar Avenue daily until his death, at age ninety-three, in March 2008. He was drawing up to the day before he died. Unfortunately, he lived long enough to see his masterpiece, the Guthrie Theater, torn down in December 2006.

The Englishman Sir Tyrone Guthrie was considered one of Europe's foremost theatrical directors. According to Jane King Hession in her 2002 report "An Assessment of the Significance of the Tyrone Guthrie Theatre," written for the Minnesota Historical Society's State Historic Preservation Office, two productions secured his reputation as the definitive director of classical plays on the open stage. The first was a "lucky accident" that occurred when a 1937 production of *Hamlet* at Kronborg Castle in Copenhagen was forced inside due to rain. The performance took place in the center of a large room, the audience surrounding the actors. "According to Guthrie," Hession wrote, "this was theater-in-the-round, although the phrase hadn't been invented yet." The second production was Guthrie's 1947 staging of the mid-1500s Scottish satire *The Three Estates,* performed in Edinburgh's Assembly Hall on a platform that projected out from a gallery wall, surrounded on three sides by audience. In his 1959 memoir, *A Life in the Theater,* Guthrie wrote, "One of the most pleasing effects of the performance was the physical relationship of the audience to the stage. . . . Seated around three sides of the stage, they focused upon the actors in the brightly lit acting area, but the background was the dimly lit rows of people focused on the actors." Rapson would soon translate this dream into bricks and mortar.

T. B. Walker made his fortune harvesting the great white pine in northern Minnesota and, by 1923, was considered one of the world's ten richest men. Like his fellow capitalist barons Henry Clay Frick and Andrew Carnegie, he had an appetite for acquiring artistic treasures, with a particular taste for Chinese jade and porcelain, Syrian glass, ancient Greek vases, Japanese ivory netsuke, and romantic nineteenth-century French and American landscape paintings. In 1927, on a four-acre parcel of land purchased from Thomas Lowry, godfather of the Minneapolis–St. Paul streetcar system, he built a substantial Moorish-style art gallery to house and display his collections. To fund the gallery, he created the T. B. Walker Foundation. In 1959, the gallery, known since 1939 as the Walker Art Center and now focusing almost exclusively on modern art and design, needed a new auditorium.

Concurrently, Sir Tyrone had an idea to create an American repertory theater somewhere far from the financial pressure and commercial noise of Broadway. In 1959, he and several of his colleagues considered cities for the theater's future home, finally narrowing their choices to three: Detroit, Milwaukee, and Minneapolis. Guthrie was then romanced by a contingent of Minneapolis civic leaders led by John Cowles Jr., publisher of both the *Minneapolis Star* and the *Minneapolis Tribune,* who offered $400,000 toward the project and a prime building site next to the Walker Art Center, courtesy of the T. B. Walker Foundation. Guthrie was impressed, and on May 31, 1960, he and his team flew to Minneapolis and confirmed it as the lucky winner. Ironically, it was Cowles who, four decades later, would lead the charge to demolish the theater and create a new Guthrie complex on the Mississippi River—much like the middle-aged man who leaves his faithful wife for a younger woman.

Rapson, who previously had been hired to explore designs for the Walker Art Center's new auditorium, was chosen by the museum's steering committee to plan the Guthrie Theater. But Sir Tyrone had his own ideas. He flew the Minneapolis team to Ontario to see the Stratford Festival Theater, which he had helped create. It featured a thrust stage—developed by Tanya Moiseiwitsch, a British set and costume designer and associate of Guthrie—the first of its kind for the production of Shakespearean plays.

From the beginning, the relationship between Guthrie and Rapson, who was not Guthrie's architect of choice, was strained and over the next few years would become a true battle of heavyweights—an English theatrical aristocrat in the ring with the Midwesterner who supposedly knew little about theater. Their first meeting, at the legendary Algonquin Hotel in New York City, did not go well. At six feet eight inches, Sir Tyrone towered over Rapson by almost a foot. His visage, with prominent chin, beaklike nose, and a hypnotist's eyes, was suitable for caricature, his commanding presence informed by a life in theater. Rapson, steeled by midwestern grit, was unwavering in his resolve. Early on, he yanked Guthrie's chain by sharing that besides having helped design three theaters he had once portrayed Gainsborough's Blue Boy in a high school play, a part that required him to sit covered in blue, center stage, throughout. Guthrie was not amused.

The two men agreed on nothing. Rapson referred to Guthrie as "Sir Tyrant" and occasionally skewered him in sketches in which he was depicted with devil's horns. And Guthrie treated Ralph like a bit player in one of his productions. Yet from their fractious relationship eventually emerged the first theater in the world with an asymmetrical auditorium and a thrust stage—a radically new prototype. As remarkable as the auditorium was, the magic of the theatrical experience began outside, where an abstract, plywood-stucco-and-glass screen of solids and voids, designed to allow passersby to peek in and theatergoers to see out, beckoned outsiders as if blowing a kiss.

Still, the heavyweight bout raged. A week before opening night, the fourteen hundred auditorium seats had not been delivered. Guthrie had insisted they be upholstered in earth tones of beige or brown so as to not create any visual distractions from the performances. Rapson fought for a colorful array of seats and kept the delivery time a secret. Three days before the theater debuted, as both men waited on the loading dock, the seats arrived—in ten vivid, confetti-like colors. Sir Tyrone exploded; Ralph had landed one last metaphoric left hook.

From the beginning, Minnesotans believed in the theater and enthusiastically donated funds to help bring the structure to life. As in the 1884 effort spearheaded by newspaper publisher Joseph Pulitzer to raise funds to build the pedestal for the Statue of Liberty, hundreds of volunteers canvassed the state to raise money. Individual donations large and small came in from more than three thousand sources, including $6.37 from a Sunday school in Mankato. This work of art—made of steel, wood, glass, stucco, and concrete—belonged, in small pieces, to all Minnesotans.

On opening night, May 7, 1963, an occasion fit for royalty and common Minnesota folk alike, the audience enjoyed a production of *Hamlet*, with George Grizzard in the title role and Jessica Tandy as Queen Gertrude. *Time* magazine said of the building's facade that it was "as if Henry Moore had been doodling on it with a jigsaw. Through the holes of the outer facade peeks a structure drawn with a Mondrian ruler in a rectilinear austerity of charcoal gray, white and glass. Suspended over the stairs and lobbies are globes of light, a child's army of upside-down lollipops." Minnesota had landed squarely on the nation's cultural map.

Subsequent theatrical performances thrilled adult audiences, and they also became a rite of passage for school kids, arriving in yellow school buses from around the state, who were mesmerized by the beauty and magic of the plays they saw there. I was one of those kids, bused all the way down from the Iron Range.

In the mid-1960s, the adjoining Walker Art Center started programming amazing shows at the Guthrie, including dance, string quartet, opera, jazz, folk, and blues performances. Avant-garde choreographer Merce Cunningham and his New York troupe might appear there one weekend, followed by artists such as Coleman Hawkins or Mississippi John Hurt or Doc Watson the next. The Guthrie was becoming a beloved concert venue and would remain one for four decades.

When I started the campaign to save the Guthrie, my focus was on preserving a building I considered to be a true temple of sound and one I knew could serve the community for years to come. I took this argument to a meeting of the Minneapolis City Council's Zoning and Planning Committee in the council chambers the first time the issue went on its agenda, in October 2001. As I sat near the second-floor elevator waiting for the meeting to start, wearing a suit jacket, black T-shirt, and cowboy boots and carrying a small gray Samsonite briefcase, the lawyers for the Guthrie and the Walker walked past me, two by two, wearing suits more expensive than the car I drove.

A moment later, the elevator doors opened and standing before me was eighty-seven-year-old Ralph Rapson himself, looking with his white hair and white mustache like a Minneapolis Mark Twain and holding the arm of his companion, Leslie Myers. Right then, I realized that the struggle was not just about saving the building. His presence gave me strength: Rapson, who more than forty years earlier had rejected prestigious job offers on the East Coast to make Minneapolis his home, represented the highest rung on the artistic ladder. As a fellow Minneapolitan and midwesterner, I felt it was my obligation, and honor, to help protect his legacy.

When it was Ralph's turn to speak, he stood his ground, much as he had many years earlier when up against the great Sir Tyrone Guthrie. Asked by a city councilman what the demolition would mean to him, he said simply, sadly, and strongly, "It would be like losing a child." It was a heartbreaking statement, and I knew it was time to start gathering the troops.

It was at that city council session that I met Aaron Rubenstein, an architecture buff and community activist; Phil Freshman, an editor; and Dore Mead, a city councilwoman. They would join me as founding members of a group that took the Web site's name, SavetheGuthrie.org (STG). Later that week, community politics reporter Todd Melby interviewed me about the issue on KFAI radio. Joining me on-air to discuss our opposition to the planned destruction of this cultural icon was Bob Roscoe, a preservation architect and former Rapson student. That was my first encounter with Roscoe, who would soon become STG's subversive agent, blogging weekly about our efforts and helping to spread our mantra, "Landmark, not landfill."

During the KFAI interview, I put out a call to arms, hoping to attract others to our cause. Soon I received a phone call from Joe Gioia, who was working at the Bryant-Lake Bowl, a beautiful old eight-lane alley on Lake Street. Gioia, a writer and New York City transplant, offered us meeting space in these quaint digs. At the first STG meeting, we were joined by an enthusiastic group of interested citizens. The group met weekly, sharing ideas and strategies about to how to move forward. We started gathering signatures on a public petition of support. We also created enough momentum to support a study by the State Historic Preservation Office that would deem the Guthrie eligible for nomination to the National Register of Historic Places due to its exceptional significance, despite not meeting the customary fifty-year threshold required for historic designation.

We also helped get the Guthrie included on the Preservation Alliance of Minnesota's annual Ten Most Endangered Historic Properties list.

The folks who attended the weekly STG meetings were an energetic and soulful bunch that included a musician, an architect, a writer, a friend of the Rapson family, a retired woman, a college student, a community activist, and others who would drop in from time to time. We reached out to other like-minded people and groups and formed an alliance, the Historic Guthrie Preservation Coalition, whose partners included the National Trust for Historic Preservation (NTHP), the Preservation Alliance of Minnesota, SavetheGuthrie.org, and the Minnesota Chapter of the Society of Architectural Historians. Altogether, it felt as if we were getting somewhere.

A few weeks after the October 2001 city council session, Kathy Halbreich, director of the Walker Art Center, invited Ralph and his son Toby to a meeting in her office. In condescending tones not unlike those of a son or daughter informing an elderly parent that it's time to surrender the car keys, she told them the building had outlived its usefulness. She also asked them not to support SavetheGuthrie.org's efforts. The meeting over, Ralph and Toby walked back out onto Vineland Place, in the shadow of the theater, to catch a breath of fresher air. Toby said to his father, "I think we have just met the devil."

In 2002, due to great work by Aaron Rubenstein, we convinced the NTHP to include the Guthrie Theater on its annual national list of Eleven Most Endangered Buildings. This helped garner wider attention and generate articles in the *New York Times* and the *Wall Street Journal*. We had now gathered more than six thousand signatures on our petition, including those of NTHP president Richard Moe (who, as a native Minnesotan, wrote an op-ed piece for the *Star Tribune* advocating saving the building) and three world-renowned architects: Cesar Pelli, Kevin Roche, and Steven Holl. Other designers, including some of Rapson's former students, also voiced their support. We organized protests (including one across the street from the Guthrie, featuring immense comedy and tragedy masks, to mark its fortieth birthday in May 2003), had booths at local festivals, marched in the popular annual May Day parade to Powderhorn Park, held house parties, and put on fund-raising concerts, including a four-day event in September 2005 that featured more than a hundred musicians. Also, we wrote op-ed pieces and letters to the editor whenever an apt opportunity arose; the Minneapolis *Star Tribune* even printed several of them.

Although we had gained a legion of supporters, including many Guthrie and Walker members who dropped their memberships and season subscriptions in protest, we couldn't hook everybody. For example, there were those who worked for the Guthrie and the Walker and supported our cause but couldn't get involved for fear of jeopardizing their jobs. There also were actors and artists who wanted someday to work with both institutions and didn't want to subvert their chances of doing so; as a longtime freelance musician, I well understood that. Two pillars of the arts community, Jack Reuler of Mixed Blood Theatre and Colleen Sheehy, director of education at the Weisman Art Museum, stood bravely with us, and we appreciated their support.

Larry Millett, a respected architectural historian and author of the great book *Lost Twin Cities,* backed the Walker's position that renovations over the years had seriously compromised the building's architectural integrity. In response, we held fast to Ralph's claim that "despite the reduction in some of the side seating, the interior is very much the original theater, and provides the almost exact experience that people felt on opening night in May of 1963." Although the marvelous screen of Mondrian-like solids and voids that originally wrapped the facade had been removed in 1974 due to faulty building materials (a consequence of cost cutting during construction), one aim of our mission was to see that part of the exterior eventually rebuilt.

Bob Roscoe eloquently defended the building's design in a fall 2001 piece for *Architecture Minnesota* magazine. "Some buildings possess an ineffable quality that makes them truly sublime," he wrote. "The quality by which a cathedral becomes ethereal, a library becomes gracefully cerebral, a theater becomes the imagination's vessel. Taking cues from such early 20th-century artists as French painter Robert Delaunay, who distorted circular forms on his canvases, Rapson combined the two archetypes to create a modernist expression in three dimensions that has become the Guthrie Theater."

For me, and for countless others who performed at and attended concerts there, the Guthrie had amazing acoustics that were due in large part to a canopy of floating "clouds," or panels, that both magnificently managed the sound and hid the mechanics of the system. I had played on that stage seven times, between 1982 and 1994, and likened the experience to being in the sound hole of the world's largest guitar. In addition, I had seen dozens of concerts there over the years, not least of which was a 1972 solo show by guitarist Leo Kottke that had a profoundly inspirational, career-sparking impact on me.

That stage had also featured some of the twentieth century's greatest musicians, including Julian Bream, Johnny Cash, Ofra Haza, Bob Marley, Bill Monroe, Gerry Mulligan, Buddy Rich, and the Who. And it was the stage where both Bruce Springsteen and Patti Smith made their Twin Cities debuts. Besides being one of the first theaters in town to present a play with an integrated cast, the Guthrie had been graced with appearances by some of the finest African American musical artists, including Count Basie, John Coltrane, Miles Davis, Duke Ellington, Ella Fitzgerald, Dizzy Gillespie, Coleman Hawkins, John Lee Hooker, Miriam Makeba, Thelonius Monk, Odetta, Muddy Waters, and Howlin' Wolf. We referred to the Guthrie as the Carnegie Hall of the Midwest because it was. For me, playing the Guthrie was like standing at the sacred altar, occupying the same spot where giants stood.

Due to our protests, the Walker Art Center was put in a defensive position regarding its demolition plans. To cover their tracks, the Walker's leaders commissioned the consulting firm of Sutton and Associates in July 2001 to study the cost of rehabilitating the building, interview potential new tenants, and explore possible philanthropic funding sources for such a venture. We suspected the Sutton study would be conducted in such a limited way as to justify a foregone conclusion. Instead of a broad search—throughout the state, if not beyond it—to find suitors for this internationally recognized landmark, the Sutton analysts restricted their survey to arts groups and philanthropists within the Twin Cities' borders. The scope of their hunt seemed akin to the Minnesota Twins limiting their search for a star pitcher to the fine town of Mankato. The formal study, issued in October 2001 as the "Guthrie Theater Reuse Analysis," had taken less than four months to complete.

Several years later, the Walker convinced the city of Minneapolis to build a $25 million parking ramp under the Guthrie as work on the museum's new expansion and remodeling, designed by the Swiss firm of Herzog and de Meuron, got under way. At the time, City Finance Director Patrick Born suggested that "the city has a better chance of recouping its money if the Guthrie Theater stays." The ramp's revenue over the past several years alone bears this out. It costs the city more than $1 million a year to operate the facility. In 2008, the ramp took in revenues of $221,000. In both 2009 and 2010, and after a large cash infusion by the Walker in a special assessment by the city, money that the institution could have used to fund new artistic endeavors was instead steered toward a state-of-the-art garage that bleeds upwards of $100,000 each year.

I have long believed that the Walker leadership did not fully appreciate the synergy it enjoyed by being right next door to the Guthrie, much less understood that if the theater were destroyed, it would lose a powerful marketing magnet as well as the powerful artistic pull inherent in having two substantial arts entities exist side by side. Nor did it comprehend the meaning of the costs associated with the Guthrie's reuse. The Sutton study estimated costs to rehab the original Guthrie fully would run between $9 million and $17.5 million. By comparison, the new Guthrie on the river, which opened in June 2006, cost $125 million to build; and the Walker Art Center expansion, debuting in April 2005, cost $130 million.

Then there's the case of the 1915 Beaux Arts–style Shubert Theater. Originally located at Seventh Street and First Avenue in downtown Minneapolis, it hosted touring Broadway plays, vaudeville shows, and burlesque revues and showed movies until being shuttered in 1982. It sat empty except for pigeons and bats, until a campaign to restore it began. In February 1999, the city of Minneapolis moved the Shubert, hoisting nearly three thousand tons of brick and steel onto dollies, a quarter of a mile to its new site on Hennepin Avenue—at a cost of $4 million. (It made the *Guinness Book of World Records* as the largest building ever moved.) At this writing, the building is being refitted and rechristened, at a cost of nearly $40 million, as the Cowles Center for Dance and the Performing Arts (named for John and Sage Cowles). In light of these various expenditures, it surely seems there was a potential for the historic Guthrie Theater to find the funding it would have needed to remain a strong and integral part of the community's artistic fabric.

Although our abiding goal was to save the Guthrie for future generations, our tactics and vision evolved over time. I talked to anyone who would listen and tried as hard as I could to enlist nationally recognized artists in the cause. For example, in April 2004, I was a panelist at the Future of Music Conference in Washington, D.C. During my four days there, I bumped into Patti Smith as well as Ira Glass, the host of National Public Radio's *This American Life*. They were also conference participants and I bent their ears about our efforts. Both were supportive. Also during the conference, I visited Minnesota's U.S. senators, Norm Coleman and Mark Dayton. The following year, when his Devils and Dust tour played Minneapolis, Bruce Springsteen was kind enough to give us room for a table in the lobby of Northrop Auditorium at the University of Minnesota to help spread our word. He also gave us a shout-out from the stage.

Throughout our campaign, I held out the hope that, like Ebenezer Scrooge, whose ghosts helped him see the errors of his ways, the Walker might still be swayed. In my vision, I saw this as a win-win situation times two—for Rapson's masterpiece, for the city, for the Walker Art Center, and for the new Guthrie complex on the river. I imagined that for its part in saving the Guthrie, the Walker could receive several acres on the river, next to the new Guthrie, for a satellite sculpture garden. This would give the museum a presence on the river and more real estate on which to display art. Meanwhile, the historic Guthrie Theater could be utilized to train actors on the thrust stage but also be a space where existing and emerging arts groups could introduce new audiences to a range of culturally diverse art, music, and theater—offerings complementary to those at the Guthrie on the river and the Walker Art Center. The urban fabric could be further strengthened if all three properties were linked by a two-mile-long sculpture trail (created under Walker and city auspices), winding from Vineland Place, across Loring Park, through downtown along Nicollet Mall, and on to the Mississippi. Minneapolis would then be able to boast and profit from two sculpture gardens and two thrust stages—a civic arrangement unique in the world. Sculptors, actors, and musicians would have opportunities to create new work, setting an example for how progressive art institutions can solve problems—by offering only solutions. In short, I believed that Minneapolis had an extraordinary chance to create a model that powerfully combined the synergistic forces of community, urban planning, culture, politics, technology, business, and art—all catalyzed by a dynamic reuse of the singular theater Ralph Rapson had designed four decades earlier.

As our fight wore on, the building served for me as a vibrant surviving remnant of the early 1960s, a time when anything seemed possible. But in the end, it became clear that the weight of money and influence was squarely on the side of wanting to tear down the theater and permanently close off any possibilities that saving and repurposing it might create. The combination of financial and legal heavy-hitters, a massive and well-funded public relations campaign, and the respect that both the

Guthrie and the Walker had garnered over the years comprised a powerful force that helped this poisonous idea become a reality.

Toward the end, when we were running on fumes, Lisa Goodman, the Minneapolis city councilwoman representing the area that included the Walker-Guthrie complex and constituents who sat on the boards of both institutions, went into bulldog mode in her opposition to our efforts. At one point, reminding the Walker leaders of their aim to replace the Guthrie with more sculpture garden space, she suggested that they "keep their eyes on the prize." This seemed a twisted use of the old civil rights–era rallying cry, in part because the theater had, from the 1960s forward, witnessed performances by some of America's greatest black artists. Later, after the building had been destroyed, Goodman became involved in a struggle to save an old mansion in the Walker's neighborhood, declaring herself an "avowed preservationist." If she's a preservationist, then I can call myself a vegetarian because I occasionally have a salad with my steak.

Our battle was hard fought and we rode out every wave, sometimes momentarily on top but ultimately swept under by more powerful forces. We also suffered from several strategic mistakes and reversals of opinion. For example, R. T. Rybak, who supported our cause during his first successful Minneapolis mayoral campaign, subsequently supported the Walker's death wish for Rapson's masterpiece, saying, "The train has left the station"—seemingly forgetting that a train can run in reverse.

On February 16, 2006, the Walker finally received an official demolition permit from the city. I was crushed but, to my everlasting regret, never had the heart to call or visit Ralph Rapson and offer my condolences. In a strange way, I felt personally responsible for this loss.

Like many, the first time I drove to Vineland Place and saw the chain-link fence and bands of bright yellow crime-scene tape encircling the Guthrie, in the fall of 2006, I was shattered. One frigid late afternoon in December, I visited the site with Phil Freshman and his teenage son, Noam. We watched the earthmovers and wrecking balls do their business, and as the wind, freezing rain, and snow whipped around us, stared through the chain link at the concrete outlines of the Guthrie's stage and seating areas. It had a dignified sadness, like the ruin of an ancient Greek or Roman amphitheater. I walked away, depressed, cold, and hurting because I couldn't do anything more. Minneapolis, my hometown for almost thirty years, had finally broken my heart. The demolition proceeded through the year-end holidays, when everyone was too busy to pay attention or do anything about it.

Today, six years after the Walker Art Center opened its $130 million addition, the museum has yet to break ground on the sculpture garden expansion for which the Guthrie Theater was sacrificed. Half the year, the two-acre site is alternately a brown hillside or a white sledding slope. The rest of the year, it's an unadorned grassy knoll, with makeshift seating and a food stand at street level, where art-related activities are sometimes offered. Late in 2010, the *Star Tribune*, which had been a cheerleader on the demolition bandwagon, ran an editorial supporting the Walker's request for $8 million in state funding to create the sculpture grounds at last, fatuously declaring that there is "perhaps more art being created there than ever."

As for the new Guthrie, it looks very impressive from the outside. I disagree with my friend Bob Roscoe, who calls it a giant blue IKEA clone. When I look at it at night from across the river at St. Anthony Main, I enjoy the inviting large, vertical flashing yellow sign that advertises current and upcoming productions. Something else happens, though, when you're inside the building itself. You enter near a small gift shop that hawks books and trinkets. Then you find yourself deposited into a vast, high-ceilinged lobby that has all the warmth of the intake desk at Riker's Island. Next, you step onto a vertigo-inducing four-story escalator that ascends slowly to a dark, low-ceilinged upstairs lobby area with plenty of bars and cushioned seating. From there, you step along seemingly undulating hallways that lead to the two main theaters; a third, experimental black-box space is several floors above. The hallways recall an airport concourse but with better carpeting. If you like, you can walk up a ramp, past another bar, and go outside onto the cantilevered "endless bridge" that showcases a stupendous view of the Mississippi River. This is by far my favorite part of the structure, and one wonders why the architect, Jean Nouvel, didn't take better advantage of this view in the rest of the building. The welcoming "pageantry" and playfulness of Ralph's original design are nowhere to be found.

When Nouvel met Rapson, while the new complex was in development, he told him he wanted to "replicate" the elder architect's historic design for the thrust-stage theater—one of the complex's two key performance spaces. With his characteristic disarming directness, Ralph replied, "Why don't you try to design something of your own?" Of course, Nouvel didn't, and to many of us who loved the original Guthrie, entering the new one feels like stepping into a mausoleum with a thrust stage.

I have seen two shows on the Wurtele Thrust Stage, as the Rapson-like space is named. During Leo Kottke's annual Thanksgiving concert in 2010, I watched and listened from several different vantage points. The room has average acoustics at best: you can hear sound emanating from the speakers but not from the room itself. Nouvel might have been able to mimic the form of the auditorium, but, unfortunately, he couldn't replicate the godlike acoustics.

There are people who applaud the design of both the new Guthrie and the expanded Walker Art Center. I am not one of them. Nevertheless, I wish both institutions well as they continue into the twenty-first century, and I hope they keep providing audiences with soulful, thought-provoking art; it is sorely needed. Art is made from the focal point of human wonder, a vessel of transcendence from our everyday lives, and we need more beauty in this world, not less. We at SavetheGuthrie.org enjoyed what both the Walker Art Center and the Guthrie Theater provided: world-class art with neighborhood accessibility. Our fight was not with the Walker as much as it was with the very notion that, as my friend Joe Gioia put it, "an art museum could consider itself better for destroying so carelessly a living work of art."

SavetheGuthrie.org started as two guys with a Web site, and it evolved into a five-year-long campaign in which many people participated. We dedicated ourselves to it because we believed, and believe now, that it was the right thing to do. We led a valiant fight, raised consciousness, and, most important, let Ralph Rapson know that thousands did indeed value him and his work. I received several of Ralph's holiday cards over the years, bearing his whimsical watercolors or drawings on the front and hand-penned notes. He always thanked me for our efforts, and I think he knew how hard we tried. I have a message from him on my answering machine that I will never erase.

After Ralph's death, a memorial service was held at the Wurtele Thrust Stage. The place was packed with admirers and with those who, just a couple of years earlier, had done their best to bury Caesar but now had come to praise him. I looked at the captains of industry and commerce, disguised as lords of art and poetry, as well as at individuals who had known better but had buried their heads in the sand, as they threw wilted rose petals on the path to Ralph's final resting place.

The friends I made through the crusade to save the Guthrie remain trusted and true. Often, we were accused of tilting at windmills. But in the end I know this, to quote Jimmy Stewart in *Mr. Smith Goes to Washington*: "Lost causes are the only ones worth fighting for."

BARBEQUE AND BLUES

In the fall of 2005 I had a meeting with the general manager at Famous Dave's. I had been working there since 2001. He told me that I would just be receiving one check instead of two. I was getting one check to play and one to book the club. The downside was that they were going to have to start taking taxes out of it, which turned out to be a blessing in disguise. (Instead of turning my couch upside down to try and find enough change to pay my taxes on April 15, I would start to get a refund instead.) It gave me less walking-around cash, but I was still taking home more than $1,100 a week. The upside was that I was going to get full health and dental benefits, and two weeks paid *vacation*, a term that in a musician's world is either an oxymoron or simply doesn't exist. I was also supposed to get thirty days' notice in case I was terminated. He wrote it on a napkin and handed it to me. Hell, over the years I've done most of my business over a handshake, so the scribbled napkin felt formal. (I still have it.)

The accounting department called me at the end of November and told me that if I didn't take my vacation by the end of the year I would lose it. I got online and found the best seven-day flight/hotel deal that I could find and would soon be bound for Florida, the state where Jack Kerouac died. It was my busy time of year and I wasn't able to use all fourteen vacation days, but I was happy nonetheless. Kelly, my best friend from the Range, lived in Tampa, so apart from a few days in Orlando, printed T-shirt capital of America, I would get a chance to see him and his wife, Mary. Life was good.

I chose a hotel that had a sauna, a Finnish tradition that I had grown up with and that over the years had flushed out enough toxins from my system to kill a team of lumberjacks. I bought the new Woody Guthrie biography, packed a suit and a killer pair of fake green alligator shoes I had bought on sale that had Florida shuffleboard written all over them, and was off. My goal was to read, sauna, sun, and hang with my best friend.

I arrived at the airport and took the tram to the shuttle bus. While I have been able to travel and do gigs in New York, Austin, Miami, and Boston, I have never had enough disposable cash, or the wherewithal to tour around the country in a way that I would have enjoyed. It was part of the price I paid for the life of a musician who lives gig to gig, paycheck to paycheck. I looked out and saw palm trees swaying in a humid breeze, standing beside people dressed for a July in Minnesota. I got to the hotel, checked in, and made friends with the older Jamaican fellow named Cartwright who ran the ground floor operations. He saw my guitar and told me that Johnny Cash had stayed here several times before. Cool. We bonded and I was home.

I was looking forward to filling the hotel room's refrigerator with fresh fruit and ran into two problems. There was no refrigerator in the room, and I was soon to find out you can't find fresh fruit in Orlando to save your life. The refrigerator would cost an extra $20 a night. I asked Cartwright about it, and he told me to tell the front desk that I needed it for my medications and they wouldn't charge me for it. I told them a little white lie and said I needed it for my "diabetes." The lady I spoke with had probably heard this song and dance before but sent one up anyway. Though I have always believed that you can lie to booking agents, bar owners, and occasionally your mother, I felt a little guilty about this charade. I should have. Two months later, utilizing my health benefits in my new contract arrangement, I took my first complete physical in years and found out I did indeed have diabetes. Damn!

It was the first week of December, between tourist seasons. For the most part I had the sauna and steam room to myself and would often be in the pool by myself or with a couple from Germany. I was in the steam room one day when a man entered. He said hello in an accent that had to be from New York City. I asked him, "And what borough are you from?" "Brooklyn," he replied. I could barely see him through the steam, but we started chatting and I came to find out he was a cop down to attend a wedding. One thing led to another, and we started to talk about the HBO series *The Sopranos.* I was a big fan, as was he. Every Sunday I would make myself a plate of pasta, get a bottle of Chianti, turn the phone off, and enjoy some of the best storytelling, characters, and sound track that television had ever seen. The next season was to begin in January, and the first episode was kept under wraps, tighter than Gene Krupa's snare drum. Only a handful of people were let on the set to film it, and the secret shared between the chosen few. It created an unbelievable tension for the audience, built huge ratings, and kept the fans like methadone addicts waiting in the alley for the street clinic to open. Brilliant.

He told me that he had been working an overnight in Brooklyn in November. At about four in the morning he pulled over a white guy in a BMW. He was suspicious that he would be driving in this part of town, much less so early in the morning. The driver told him that he had just got done filming the last episode of *The Sopranos* and was on his way home. The cop told him to be careful and, as a fan of the show asked, "So what happens?" The driver said, "I am sworn to secrecy." So the cop told him, "Okay, then pull out your license and registration." The driver started to do so and the cop said, "I am just bustin' your balls. Get home safe and sound." The driver started to pull away, stopped, and rolled down his window to say, "Tony gets shot!" You have got to be freakin' kidding me! I could have gone to my hotel room and posted that on the Internet, and then on to international infamy. Rather, I held the secret in part because James Gandolfini as Tony Soprano seemed so real, I didn't want to walk my dog in fear every morning waiting for him in the alley. Sure enough, that January, enjoying my workingman's plate of pasta and cheap wine, I enjoyed the first episode where Tony gets shot by Uncle Junior. I felt like some member of the Illuminati (had it been founded by Aaron Spelling).

Three years later, in August 2008, I had returned to the job after a splendid week vacationing at my family's cabin in northern Minnesota. My younger brother John has spent more than twenty years keeping the place up, and before that my dad and grandfather. My great-grandfather, also named John, bought it in 1928. He had gone with a real estate agent and an Indian guide in a canoe paddling three miles to survey properties on the lake. He found this beautiful point on a hill overlooking the biggest bay on that side of the lake. He got it for $500 and paid for it with five crisp $100 bills, in 19-freakin'-28. To me, this is where the soul of the family lies. There is no price you can put on this place. This is where my family broke bread, made love, argued, drank, and dreamed. I spent the week polishing logs, scrubbing floors, and cleaning windows. Those logs my grandfather laid (my great-grandfather had built a shack and fireplace that still stands), while he and my dad built the road that would lead to this island. The island we now share with cousins represents my great-granddad's landing in America from Helsinki, first as a miner, then as a lumberjack, and then as a bar owner, then farmer, who saved enough to secure this sacred ground where future generations have gone to rest, relax, and recharge against all that the modern world will hurl at you when you least expect it. I take nothing for granted up there. I dream of it in winters that no sane person should have to suffer through, and when skinny-dipping, after a sauna on the shores of the vermilion waters, bathed in the light of either northern lights or the milky way, and this week, in the arms of my new true love, knew I was luckier than most.

I came back on a Monday night. I had an e-mail message from a guy who was large and in charge and had been promoted once or twice since I got hired. He was calling for a meeting with me. As the world of handwritten letters evaporates along with the American history it has always represented, we are reduced to communicating through e-mail. Devoid of tone and nuance, all we are left with is whether or not the message was capitalized or not, what time it was sent, and how it is addressed. As a guy who learned early on, the hard way, that there should be a breathalyzer on the keyboard—no after-hours e-mails to ex-girlfriends, fellow employees, and letters to the editor if the writer is blowing a 0.20 blood alcohol content—I could tell something was up.

I sat at the bar waiting for the meeting to begin. One of the managers, Sean, dropped a chocolate chip cookie off in front of me to dunk with my coffee. I entered the Lava Lounge, the place where special guests went to enjoy a great night of blues, ribs, and friendship. Maybe two minutes into this meeting, where I went, calendar in hand, to brag about the wonderful fall lineup I'd secured at great prices (I'd cultivated good relationships with all the agents and acts who dug what I was doing), I was about to receive a massive blow to the gut. In no uncertain terms, my ring-wearing, ex-punk, rock-loving boss told me I was being laid off. No thirty days' notice written on a napkin. I was out the door faster than you could say, "Thanks for bringing us back from the dead, for helping us win five *City Pages* awards, and for putting Famous Dave's back on the musical map again." This is how quickly it happens in their world—never mine. Can I remind you that this was a corporation priding itself on "family values"? I felt like throwing up or passing out.

To top it off, he asks me if I have anything I want to take out from the club. Like my $1,500 Fender Pro Reverb amp? I would leave it there for when Magic Slim came in and his amp didn't work, or when Hubert Sumlin would arrive without one. It was there because the proverbial show must go on. "No," I said. "I'll get it later in the week." And he said,

"Well, when you do, don't take anything else." I should have decked the bald motherfucker right then and there, but I didn't. Instead I said, "Randy, you are talking to a gentleman." Then I turned around and walked out.

I got into my 1992 Ford Exploder and put my seat belt on, even though it was still legal to drive without it. I drove back to the house, down Lyndale Avenue, the street where I came into age in this city, and everything seemed to be in slow motion, stopped in time. I was gasping for breath. After the highway, I pulled up into the driveway, next to my Andy Griffith garage, in the back of my Mark Twain house, just a stone's throw away from the Mississippi River. I was buckling at the knees.

My girlfriend was in the kitchen, looking beautiful as usual. I sat down in one of my yellow Formica chairs, surrounding my 1950s *Father Knows Best* table, and broke down. Now I, like everybody, cry every now and then. Most of the time it's when I remember my mother, sometimes out of the blue, wishing she was still on this earthly plane, guiding me, wiping my brow as she did when I was a kid sick on the couch, watching *I Love Lucy*, and waiting for Grandpa to come over with the Popsicles and ice cream. A million bucks right now for that in this moment.

I told my girlfriend what had happened, and even though she acknowledged it, I don't think she really understood. It was my own cross to bear, and somehow I was reminded of the statue of Jesus that towers over Rio de Janiero, and he seemed that far away. The earth had shifted in an angel's moment of doubt, that quickly and abruptly. I took a deep breath and got ready to make some calls. I called my dad first. He got laid off from Allstate Insurance, out of the blue, at fifty-seven years old after working for them for thirty years, and had to figure his own way around the block, four kids in tow. He understood. I was my father's son. Then my harp player, my brother, and anyone else who'd listen. Although they had laid off fifteen people that day, most making more than I, I could not help but take it personally.

In retrospect, I now realize I was being hung up, beat down, and strung out on so many levels. I lost an income, an income that most middle-class white guys could only dream about. A job that was musically related, and one that I could use my thirty years of experience to do well. A job I could do out of my house, in my pajamas, and walk my dog anytime he shook his collar and said "Let's go." A job that I took extreme pride in, and this from a guy who never believed that pride was one of the deadly sins. A job that I would describe, without being facetious, as one that entailed "giving money to other musicians." I loved it and did it well, and it enabled me to help shape the artistic geography of this city, my hometown of thirty years.

I was on new and barren ground. I made not a deal with the devil but a gentleman's agreement, that I would not pursue my life as a songwriter and performer and would instead bow down before this corporate entity's dream and further their cause, because I did believe in it. Of course, a biweekly paycheck that most musicians would give both nuts for didn't hurt. But in the days and weeks to come, I had nothing to show for it. A divorce, the deepest and bluest of its kind.

Of course, life being what it is, the Republican National Convention was to be in town the next week. And oddly enough, I was hired by Famous Dave's at the Mall of America to play there during the convention. Thank God for small favors, a paycheck being a paycheck. Surrealism has played no small part in my life.

In fact, I had actually played the opening of this American nightmare in 1994, a place I have long since called the Fall of America. They had hired us as strolling musicians. My friend and I devised a plan to get us through this gig. We would walk around with our guitars, place ourselves next to a group of people, and play the opening chords of "Proud Mary," stand there for twenty-five seconds, and move on to the next group. Our paycheck minus the gram of blow meant we would clear about $200. We would occasionally run into the Ghermezian brothers from Canada who developed this monstrosity. We'd just smile and keep the big wheel a-turnin'. The headliner, Ray Charles, was on the same wavelength. He was hired for $60,000 to play for an hour set. He got out of his limo, came in, did a killer version of "America the Beautiful," and left. As the song says, people on the river are happy to give.

I had met Terry Carlson at Dylan Days in Hibbing in 2007. Like me, he was both an Iron Ranger and a lifelong Democrat. We had a shared fondness for progressive politics, Bob Dylan, and strong martinis. Though a high-powered corporate lawyer working in the medical field, he was extremely unassuming, friendly, and very connected in political circles. He was a few years older than me and had spent time as a teenager playing in a band called the Civilized Few and, I would find out, had followed my career over the years. He had scored passes to the party at the Landmark Center immediately after the Republican National Convention, which was being held at the St. Paul Convention Center. While we watched John McCain introduce his vice presidential candidate Sarah Palin on the television at a St. Paul watering hole, we doubled up on the martinis and braced ourselves for the GOP celebration that featured free top-shelf vodka, free Budweiser Light (courtesy of Mrs. McCain), and an 80's disco band. We were ready to party like it was 1984.

We walked into the Landmark Center in St. Paul. The place is the sterling jewel in the crown that is St. Paul. It had housed the city government in the '20s and '30s and also was the site of the municipal courthouse. St. Paul, during Prohibition, was the city where Dillinger, Capone, Pretty Boy Floyd, and the rest would go to take a little well-deserved R&R, from the Feds who spent all their time trying to track them down. All of the above made a little financial arrangement with the mayor, cops, and whoever else and would spend some well-earned money buying time until their next caper. But every now and then, they had to convict somebody, and this was the same place that sentenced the Karpis-Barker gang for kidnapping the heirs to the Hamm fortune, a local beer company.

Enter the two of us. We were a couple of Iron Rangers interested in politics, but mostly drawn in by the free Grey Goose vodka. A free drink is a free drink, no matter who's serving it, and we drank as if the ghost of Barry Goldwater owed this, all of this, to us. My attendance there, swinging hot Republican babes across the dance floor, was noted in a *Star Tribune* gossip column that Friday—next to an item about my layoff.

The buzz of that night, like all buzzes, wore off. A few days later, I was looking at no steady income, persistent bills, and a mortgage payment staring me right in the face.

It was going to be the coldest winter in years. I was scrambling for a way to pay the bills, my diabetes numbers had skyrocketed, and I was feeling woozy and weak. During the few gigs I had, I experienced episodes of anxiety that rendered my hands lifeless and unable to play. The recession had started and no one was hiring. Then the depression I used to have bouts with as a child kicked in, and I could barely get out of bed in the morning. Thank God, Blackie was by my side every day. I'd hold him tight and pray that I could put food on the table for both of us.

My live-in girlfriend, whom I'd fallen in love with the year before, was in no hurry to find work, and when she did, besides buying groceries, she shared none of the living expenses. I couldn't really hold it against her, as she was used to me as the sole breadwinner. To add to the madness, I had let an ex-girlfriend move into my upstairs rental unit with her one-year-old daughter. For some reason or another, she wasn't able to cover rent or utilities, so I ended up shouldering that burden for the coming year as well. I didn't have the heart to evict her, and her daughter was adorable. When her meth-head boyfriend moved in, under the cover of darkness, I had to deal with that, too. Hard times, all the way around.

I made it through until spring, spending much of my time looking for work and the rest with my head buried under the covers. One day a longtime fan named Todd Anderson called and booked me for a weekly gig playing on the deck of a local golf course. Though I thought I was beyond these types of gigs, I took it gladly. I adjusted my diabetes meds, and my strength and stability slowly came back. It turned out that many of the golfers were also old fans of mine, and they started to fill the deck at happy hour. They would request songs I hadn't played in years, buy CDs, and keep the tip jar full. It wasn't Carnegie Hall but I appreciated the work.

In a way, I was back now, full circle. I started to pick up a few other gigs as well. I was starting to remember who I was. My live-in girlfriend had a job offer and left for California over the Fourth of July weekend, never to return. I was finally able to replace my ex-girlfriend, her loser boyfriend, and her lovely young daughter (whom I would miss) in my upstairs rental apartment with a rent-paying, reliable tenant. Most important, I was starting to write songs again, and my confidence was coming back, one gig at a time. The sun was shining and the fog was lifting.

IKO-IKO

The summer of 2009 marked thirty years since my first gig in town at the infamous Skyway Lounge that would be followed by five thousand more gigs (and counting) on the highways and byways that led from there. It seemed only fitting to do an anniversary show. I booked the Parkway Theater at Forty-eighth and Chicago in Minneapolis, run by my old friend comedian Joe Minjares. As a play of words on AC/DC's famous 1979 rock album *Highway to Hell* and a shout-out to the Skyway Lounge (not to mention Minneapolis's largest urban skyway system in the world), I decided to call the show Skyway to Hell.

It was scheduled for the day after Thanksgiving. I invited my A-list of favorite musicians and friends to play: Sherwin Linton (the Midwest's answer to Johnny Cash), Tom Lieberman and Tim Sparks (two of my favorite guitarists), Gregg Inhofer (who can still sing "Whiter Shade of Pale" in the original key), Willie Murphy (piano-pounding godfather of the West Bank), Mari Harris (my favorite gospel singer), Sonny Earl (my blues partner), my old buddies the Cats Under the Stars, and my new friend, songwriter and guitarist Mary Cutrufello.

Photographer Howard Christopherson spent dozens of hours putting together a ten-minute photo collage that ran while hockey announcer Greg Harrington, in a hilarious impersonation of Howard Cosell, read a piece I wrote as a prologue to a book. In the lobby were 55-gallon drums to collect food for the local food shelves, and next to them a bar that stretched almost the length of the room.

By show time the place had sold out. Walking from the entrance to the stage, I opened with "Stranger Blues" on a wireless guitar, a tune I had played as an opener for almost every solo show over the years. At the end of the song I told the crowd: "This show tonight will be the story of how it took me thirty years to get from Seventh and Hennepin to Forty-eighth and Chicago." People howled, and we were off to the races, all the musicians taking the tunes we'd rehearsed, and some we hadn't, to new heights, surprising even ourselves at times. Originally scheduled to run from 9 to 11 P.M., the show went on until almost 2 A.M. Cats band member Tim O'Keefe remarked a few weeks later, "The lights came up, and I have never seen that many drunken sixty-year-old women in my life!" It was the biggest night the theater bar had ever had, thanks in no small part to the Iron Rangers who came down for the show.

I had started playing around town again, rebuilding my solo act, and pleased with the new iterations. Gone were the stage dives and climbing on tables like I did during my "Take no prisoners/swing from the vine" period, but on a good night I could plug in and jump the joint in a San Juan Hill state of mind, as long as it was preceded by a one-hour power nap before the gig. (I also never travel these days without my slippers.) The new style feels good. While all those thousands of gigs didn't make me the richest man on the mountain, they have made me one of the happiest guys on the hill.

I had met Big Jay McNeely—king of the tenor sax honkers—at a festival several years earlier. Big Jay is a direct link between rhythm and blues and early rock and roll. He's also a madman in a good way, one flip-city-gone cat. He calls himself "a jazz musician who plays for dancers." In 1952 he wore white gloves and highlighted his horn with a strobe light, two decades ahead of the fluorescent San Francisco light shows of the late '60s. He'd climb the tables, walk the bar, and lead his dancing disciples out the bar, around the block, and back to the stage, squeezing the face off every Lincoln penny that people paid to see the show. That, my friends, is rock and roll.

Big Jay was one of the headliners at that year's blues festival at Famous Dave's, where I was music director at the time. I had hooked him up with the Solid Senders, a local swinging blues and jump-swing band from town. They had played together before. It was late afternoon, several thousand people there waiting for this legend to take the stage, and Famous Dave himself was on his way to the stage to introduce Big Jay. Just as he was about to go on, Big Jay pulled me aside and said he needed the last $300 he was promised, in cash, or he won't play. I showed him the check in my pocket, but that wouldn't do. I made the lightning rounds backstage, borrowing tens and twenties from anybody with a wallet or a purse, getting just enough cash and just in time for Famous Dave to say, "And now ladies and gentlemen . . . from Watts, California, the legendary Big Jay McNeely!" He smiled, took the bills, and on he went. I had been pinned to the mat by a man who over the years had played many times and not gotten paid. I had to admire the move.

The next morning I was playing my regular brunch gig at the club. Big Jay showed up with his driver Julia who had located a Sunday morning service at a local Jehovah's Witnesses church. Jay was a devout member and had dropped out of the music business in the late '50s because he was missing too many services. He went on to work for the postal service for years. That morning he showed up after church with his horn and asked me if he could sit in. Is the Pope Catholic? We played a forty-five-minute set, replete with a cross-pollinated version of "Summertime" with overtones in his voice of Louis Armstrong, Cab Calloway, and Lead Belly. We bonded like blood brothers and never missed a note. Outside on the patio on the break, Big Jay suggested we do a record together. It was one of the rare moments I've been speechless. We exchanged numbers, and I rearranged my mental to-do list of projects that need to take place sooner not later. Neither of us is getting any younger.

In the summer of 2010 I got a call from Steve Barberio, the new owner of the Music Box Theater in Loring Park. Originally called the Loring Theater, it was built to show silent films and host vaudeville performances in the 1920s. It closed in the midfifties. Later, a Pentecostal church moved in and evangelist Jim Bakker preached his first sermon there in the early 1960s, marrying his wife Tammy Faye on that same stage. At the time of this writing the 440-seat theater building serves a variety of artistic groups. Steve wanted me to put together a series of Blue Thursday shows, featuring conversations and concerts with tried-and-true blues acts. Big Jay was my first call. I would also book Scarlet Rivera, who came to fame by way of Bob Dylan's record *Desire,* then touring with the subsequent *Rolling Thunder Revue,* and Willie Walker and Willie West, two rhythm and blues singers both living in the Twin Cities, neither of whom had gotten their due but were well known in the international R&B circles.

I had met Scarlet Rivera in the mid-1980s at a Mississippi River Festival organized by Larry Long, a well-known folkie who helped organize the Local P-9 strike against Hormel in Austin, Minnesota. Larry had gathered a group of musicians to put out a compilation cassette, the proceeds of which benefited the striking workers. I wrote "Slow Justice" for that, one of my most enduring songs, of which the *Star Tribune* wrote "the most powerful all-purpose protest tune since 'Blowin' in the Wind.'" Larry also single-handedly led the charge to get Okemah, Oklahoma, to recognize Woody Guthrie as their favorite son.

The show was on the first night of Rosh Hashanah and the Minnesota Vikings home opener. The crowd was slight, but the gig was sublime. The first set was just conversation, and she explained how she met Dylan. It was in New York City. He was driving a station wagon and saw her walking across the street with her violin at the corner of Thirteenth Street and First Avenue in the East Village. They exchanged numbers, and Dylan called her a few days later. He invited her to his studio to hear his new tunes, most of which would end up on the *Desire* record. After that he took her to the Bottom Line to hear his friend Muddy Waters. Muddy invited Dylan up to play harmonica, and Dylan then introduced his "new band member," and Scarlet came up and ripped it up on violin. After the show, Bob took Scarlet up to Victoria Spivey's apartment in Harlem where they listened to records until the sun came up. Years earlier, Victoria had invited a young Dylan to play on one of her records after he had just moved to New York. Perhaps Bob was returning the favor. For the second set Scarlet was backed up by Geno LaFond's band. Geno was Larry Kegan's best friend and backed him up for years on guitar.

Afterward, I booked a recording session at IPR, the recording school in downtown Minneapolis where my buddy Kevin Bowe taught. To kick-start my next record, I invited Scarlet to play on my tune "Six Roses" while she was in town. She showed up with her violin, plugged in, and started to warm up with riffs dripping with tonal authority, with a reckless gypsy freedom. She told me the song reminded her of an Oscar Wilde poem. I was duly honored, and the session remains in my drawer while I wait for the rest of the songs and project to meet in a midnight clearing and find their way home.

Big Jay came to town a couple of weeks later. The day after our Blue Thursday show, Jay moved into my house and we prepared for two days of recording that I had booked. He made me smoke on the porch, and I ended up having a couple of glasses of wine in the garage, as he didn't approve of that either. He chained me to my kitchen table on Saturday, and we rehearsed for six straight hours, the longest I have ever rehearsed in my life. We were more than ready to go the next day to record. We cut eight songs in two days, including a fifteen-minute version of "Big Jay's

Blues," his life story that wasn't rehearsed and appeared completely off the top of his head, while I played a twelve-bar blues underneath it. The tape remains in the drawer next to Scarlet Rivera's, awaiting its divine release.

My sister Jackie called me seven or eight years ago and asked if I had ever heard of Willie West. I hadn't. She said Willie had married Patty Gambucci, a girl who grew up two doors down from us on Thirteenth Street in Virginia, and they were now living in New Orleans. I went on-line, and it did not take long for me to realize that Willie was somebody I should know and would love to meet. He had impeccable credentials and had recorded a few minor hits in the late 1960s, then recorded and was produced by Allen Toussaint. He had also been the lead singer for the Meters, a band as good as the Rolling Stones, whom they had opened for. After Hurricane Katrina hit in 2005, they decided to sell their house (which fortunately had not suffered major damage) and moved to St. Cloud, Minnesota, ninety miles from Minneapolis. I booked a few shows for him at Famous Dave's and saw him in action. His band could not keep a candle lit next to his flame. He held the crowd in the palm of his hand

We got to be fast friends. I booked several shows around town for us. Willie sent me his set list, most tunes I already knew, and when we played we developed a hand-in-glove rhythmic rapport that was seamless. We'd drive to the gig, and Willie would get on his high horse and we'd argue about Aaron Neville, one of my favorite singers, and Willie would say he could kick his ass. Willie was an old-school cat, a guy whose job, back in the day, was to blow any other act off the stage. In contrast, when opening for headliners, I believed it was my job to heat up the stage and audience. We'd argue like two old aunts bantering about who loved their favorite nephew more.

We got a call to open for the Aaron Neville Quartet two nights run-ning at the Dakota Jazz Club. Aaron and Willie had done dozens of gigs together back in New Orleans. After the first night, Aaron invited Willie up to sing with him on the second. Now you can compare batting aver-ages, goals scored, or the number of Super Bowl rings, but not music. I never compare great musicians. But sure enough, Willie, now side by side with the guy I consider to be the greatest ballad singer of our time, gave Aaron a serious run for his money, a meeting of two old friends that delighted them both and truly raised the roof on the club. I was honored to share that night with the two of them. *Jack-a-mo-feen-nah-nay*, the chorus from the New Orleans staple "Iko-Iko," loosely translates as "If you don't like what the big chief says, you can kiss my ass."

Willie Walker had similar credentials to Willie West. A native of Mississippi, land where the blues were born, moved to St. Paul as a kid. He played in a number of bands and had a few minor hits on the Goldwax Label. Among his label mates were James Carr and O. V. Wright. Walker played the R&B circuit in St. Paul for years before retiring and taking a job at a metal factory, where in a fluke accident, he lost a finger on his left hand. He had been resurrected by Curt Obeda and the Butanes, the best blues band in the Twin Cities that also backed up New Orleans favorite son Earl King. I met Willie through them.

The two Willies had only met once. I booked the two of them for a Blue Thursday show in the middle of October. My goal was to get them to sing together, something that had never been done. Proud bulls that they were, I knew neither of them would have suggested it but knew what had to be done. I bought them each a half-pint of their favorite brown liquor: · Jack Daniels for West and E&J Brandy for Walker. We met at the sound check; I reintroduced them and gave them each a hip-pocket taste of their favorite mash. Sure enough, after a couple of pulls, they warmed up like long-lost cousins. We started the show, and when one sang, the other would harmonize—two good guys hooked on doo-wop and seasoned in street-corner harmonies. It is all on tape, heavenly stuff. I hope to call the album *Paul Metsa Gives You the Willies*.

My tenure at Famous Dave's also afforded me the opportunity to meet two other fine musicians. Both had shyly introduced themselves to me on Sunday brunch breaks. One was Alabama-born Reverend Gary Timbs, who was bandleader for gospel great Sonny James for years, and who had passed up a chance to sing backup for Elvis Presley in the early 1970s. He had recently married and relocated to Minneapolis from Arkansas. The other was Ron Hacker, the same age as Gary (about sixty-five), a bluesman who had moved to Minneapolis from San Francisco. Timbs sings gospel in a heavenly tenor and plays piano like Jerry Lee Lewis. Hacker sings the blues and plays slide guitar, as good as I've ever heard. I treasure the times I've worked with these men, as comrades and friends.

Cats Under the Stars did our Thirty-fifth Anniversary show on August 7, 2010, at Bunker's Bar in downtown Minneapolis. We had my buddy Kenny Wilson on pedal steel, a new guy on piano, gospel singers Joyce Williams and Mari Harris, and brought Willie West up to sing the New

Orleans material. Our old bass player Skip Nelimark sat in as well. The band was totally smokin', and as everyone had kept playing over the years, we sounded as good as we ever had. The bond of thirty-five years of friendship among the original members highlighted this amazing night. Willie told us afterwards, "It reminded me of the Meters," a high compliment indeed. We ended the night with my song "Stars Over the Prairie." The crowd, as they did so many years ago at the Union and Cabooze bars, sang along, and it felt like no time had passed at all.

The older I get, the more I am drawn to these kinds of men and women, tried-and-true American musicians, artists each and every one. From the heartbeat in their mothers' wombs, into a world that bounces us all around like pinballs, they became musicians because it was in their blood. They survived and prospered, not necessarily in terms of money but as beacons to guide the rest of us in troubled waters to that shore that we all call home.

I started out as a guitarist, became a songwriter, and I will end as both. Playing the guitar is like enjoying the companionship of a dog that will never die. It sits patiently in a corner until you pick it up and play, or as my buddy Rodney Jackson used to say, "Hit a hot note and watch it bounce." I've enjoyed the pleasure of its company for more than forty-five years and still can't say I've mastered it and not sure if I ever will. I envision on my deathbed my beloved Martin D-28 keeping a silent vigil in a corner, and in my last mortal breath whispering, "You won." And then I will pass it on in my will, probably to someone in my family, who I hope will love it like I did, in sickness and in health, for better or for worse, faithful companions as long as they both shall live.

SLOW JUSTICE

I have always enjoyed playing for any group of people needing a musician to help aid, advance, or artistically support their cause. While in the beginning it was not a bad way to get my name around as well as meet like-minded people, in the end, no matter what your walk of life, it's all about who you serve. I have played hundreds of benefits, fundraisers, and events of all shapes and sizes. I consider it one of music's highest callings.

Recently, I played at a VFW in a first-ring suburb of Minneapolis and, along with my friend actor-songwriter Chris Mulkey and dozens of volunteers, helped raise ten grand for a six-month-old baby boy who had just had heart surgery. His grandfather was a friend of a friend. At the end of our set, they brought out young Riley, in a Vikings jersey the size of a lumberjack's sock, with a glorious head of raven hair and sleeping, his stitches still red from heart surgery beneath the jersey. The room smelled of homemade spaghetti and was full of items from the silent auction. The little guy opened his eyes for a moment and caught a glimpse of the couple hundred people in the room who were there to help, many of whom, like me, didn't really know the family. On a certain level, it doesn't get better than that, and it gives you hope that underneath the divisiveness of modern life, we are all in this together, building a more perfect union, one benefit at a time.

Rock and Wrestling for the Homeless ran for several years starting in the mid-1980s. I played all of them. Started by boxing/wrestling promoter and rock fan Ray Whebbe, it featured semipro wrestlers, rock bands, and free food. At one of those gigs, at the St. Paul Armory, I met a homeless gentleman who was selling leatherwork. He offered to make me a guitar strap at a great price but said he would need my lucky red strap from which to design the new one. I was hesitant to give it up, but I did, for what was supposed to be a few days and $30 down. I didn't hear from him, and he vanished into thin air, lucky red strap in tow. I called the Dorothy Day homeless shelter in St. Paul, which he was calling home, to find out he had high-tailed it to Arizona. I loved that strap, my good luck charm that held my trusty red Takamine close to my heart. Cursed thief! I had to let it go and move on. A year later I got a call from the pay phone at Mickey's Diner in St. Paul. It was the homeless guy. He asked me to meet him, and when I did, there he was with not only my lucky red strap but a lovely new black-and-red strap with large rust-colored buckles. I gave him another $30, bought him a steak breakfast with O'Brien potatoes, coffee, milk, and fresh apple pie for dessert. I still use the strap he made, a reminder to never judge too quickly. My faith in humanity was restored once again through this homeless pilgrim who I can only hope now has a home.

Not all benefits are successful. Some are very disorganized, some are for candidates with no chance of winning, and sometimes you play to help someone pay for hospital expenses who dies within the next spinning of the moon. It is all about intent. Many of these shows, I am joined by other musicians as eager as I am to help. Say what you want about musicians, and it has all been said, they are the first-call responders for those in need. They *always* come through, and to them I raise a glass.

The beauty of being a working musician is that you get a chance to rub shoulders with the entire panorama of American experience. Sure, I have run into my share of knuckleheads, but for the most part I wouldn't change how I've led my life. I take pleasure in other hard-working Americans, some faceless and anonymous, who appeared at just the time I needed to hear their point of view or share a laugh in passing. I've also met and befriended some powerful characters, like Clyde Bellecourt, at one time a real badass who spent time in prison, found the American Indian movement, turned his life around, and now is a guiding light for both his tribe and others like me. At the YWCA where I work out, I run into Jim Beattie, once ninth-ranked heavyweight boxer in the world, and revel in his wisdom and strength. Walking around Lake of the Isles, I sometimes bump into poet Robert Bly and former vice president Walter Mondale, and once I met Meridel Le Sueur, one of the finest writers Minnesota has produced, at a benefit on the shores of the Mississippi. Simply put, I am a very proud Minnesotan—proud as punch, as Hubert Humphrey used to say—and I applaud everyone who has made the North Star State one of the finest in the country.

Paul Wellstone ran for Senate in 1990 against Rudy Boschwitz, an independent Republican. Paul came out of nowhere, a short and stocky former wrestler, now a professor at Carleton College in Northfield, Minnesota. He was a true progressive fire-and-brimstone Democrat, the likes of which we hadn't seen in years. He was a community organizer and in his early years championed help for single mothers on welfare, public housing assistance, affordable health care, the Jeffersonian concept of public education, day care, and free school lunches for poor kids. On the Iron Range, we were well aware of our own political history, whether it was the unionization of early miners or the rise of the co-op movement. We were also proud of progressive politicians like former U.S. Senator and Vice President Hubert Humphrey, who came to national prominence after his 1948 speech at the Democratic National Convention, condemning Jim Crow laws, saying, "The time has arrived in America for the Democratic Party to get out of the shadow of states' rights and to walk forthrightly into the bright sunshine of human rights." I consider myself a prairie populist, informed and influenced by progressive political ideals. The rest I learned in Sunday school.

In the summer of 1990, Tom Rukavina's wife called me and asked if I would like to play at her husband Tom's fortieth birthday party. Tom was the state representative from my home district in St. Louis County, had served on the school board with my dad, and graduated with my older sister Kathy. I was to play at the party with my friend Dave Morton ("Mort"). I met Dave on my first day working construction in 1976. He was easy to spot, with a handlebar mustache and carrying a Munsters lunch bucket. Dave "Snaker" Ray called him the Godfather of the West Bank. He had an influence on a young Bob Dylan and is featured in the chapter in Robert Shelton's *No Direction Home*, an early Dylan biography, in which it says, "When the student is ready, the teacher will appear." Dave moved to California in the early '60s, had a jug band called the Juke Savages, who when Frank Zappa saw them at one of Ken Kesey's L.A. Acid Tests, said, "They made the Mothers of Invention look like the Beach Boys." Dave had a farm a mile from the original Metsa homestead and still played music when he wasn't working as a cement layer.

Mort and I spent the birthday party afternoon trading songs, and Rukavina joined us at the end for his version of "Brown Eyed Girl," a tune that he and I would play several times over the years at various DFL fund-raisers. We chatted about the upcoming election, and Rukavina rhetorically asked, "How the hell does Wellstone stand a chance against the incumbent's $7 million campaign chest?" I replied, "The power of ideas Tom." Though being outspent seven to one, Wellstone was elected U.S. Senator in 1990.

I shared dozens of gigs with Wellstone: picket lines, strikes, political dinners, homeless shelter openings, environmental gigs, and more. Paul was one of the only politicians who knew not only the chorus but several verses to "This Land Is Your Land" and sang loud and a bit out of tune, like he meant it, like Roger Daltry when he described the best rock and roll singing as a "bum note and a bead of sweat." His Iron Range office was across the street from my father's, and my dad, an independent voter, was honored to receive his call of condolence when my mother passed.

Bill Clinton and Al Gore were scheduled to hold their last rally on their bus trip campaign swing up the Mississippi valley in Minneapolis on August 7, 1992. My friend Norm Coleman, then still a Democrat, had gotten me the gig to play before Clinton and company arrived. The organizer booked me with implicit instructions that "I was not to do any of my political tunes or bullshit of the like" (I quote his exact words). I had my quintet ready to rock the street that ran between the government center and city hall. We started at 5:30 P.M., and Clinton's entourage was to arrive at 6 P.M. The streets were packed; a syndicate of Pro Lifers with signs of bloody fetuses on the raised hill behind us to the south, Democrats right in front of us, and a cavalcade of media just to the north in front of city hall, ready to broadcast the rally nationwide for the six o'clock news. There were more than thirty thousand people there, representing the disorganized madness that is democracy.

I realized about a halfway into it, and after hearing that Clinton was still an hour out, that I could play whatever the hell I wanted. Chaos, after all, had its upside. For whatever reason, as if I didn't have enough on my mind, my guitarist whom we'll call "E-Man," threw some bitch fit and left the stage several turns into the set, never to play with me again. It was the least professional move I have ever seen. I had invited Larry Kegan up, a quadriplegic rabbi and a great friend, to sing a couple of tunes. Somehow through the manic crowd he showed. We lifted him up to the stage, several hundred pounds of wheelchair and man. We sang like the Everly Brothers, did a Dylan song, and one of his, and I was reminded who my friends were. Larry nailed it, and the crowd responded in kind. Bill Clinton finally arrived around 7 P.M., gave a great speech, and had on the platform with him Muriel Humphrey, widow of Hubert, and Walter Mondale.

I went on to Eli's Bar to have a couple of cocktails and shake the ley down. On the way I dropped off my guitar and amp at my house a checked my messages. Several were from friends around the countr, who had seen the Paul Metsa Group on the six o'clock news. We had gone viral before there was such a thing.

It was Friday night and the place was packed, but I spotted an empty seat at the end of the bar. I ordered my regular, a Stoli's martini. The guy next to me looked at me and asked me who I was. I told him, and he said, "Yeah, I saw your band on CNN, and they had a picture of the astronauts in the Space Station watching the rally and your band in outer space!" Jimmy the bartender, without skipping a beat and pouring my martini, keeping his eyes on the business at hand, eyes toward his shoes, said, "Outer space, not really virgin territory for Paul."

Though I usually vote straight DFL, I voted for Arne Carlson—a moderate Republican—for governor of Minnesota when he advocated the legalization of marijuana. I voted for Jesse Ventura after I heard him say, almost Zen-like, "I believe the government should be invisible." I couldn't agree more: plow the streets, levy taxes as you must to keep things in order, field an army when attacked, and stay the hell out of my bloodstream and bedroom. I consider myself a conservative: conserve the environment, conserve civil rights, conserve the constitution, conserve my pocketbook, and overall, conserve my freedoms, all of them. At the end of the day, I think Democrats and conservatives have many of these things in common, and I wish both sides would take more time to explore what they do have in common. As Ben Franklin said at the signing of the Declaration of Independence, "We must hang together, or we shall most assuredly all hang separately."

Senator Wellstone was always on the side of the working class and had a conscience, sense of honor and fairness, and never backed down from the core ideology he ran on. He was the only senator to vote against both Iraq war resolutions, and yet he was an outspoken champion of veterans' rights. He was a guy you could trust and had the JFK-like ability to do what I feel is the most important thing any politician can do (and for that matter musician, artist, or writer)—and that is to inspire. He never compromised his integrity while working with those on the other side of the political spectrum.

A little more than a week before the 2002 election, Wellstone and his wife, Sheila, his daughter Marcia, and three staffers were on their way to

in "Benny" Rukavina's funeral, Tom Rukavina's dad, in my home-
wn of Virginia, Minnesota. Paul was to debate now-Republican senate
candidate Norm Coleman later that evening in Duluth. They never made
it. The plane went down and crashed in a swamp a mile from the airport,
extinguishing the light that was the liberal conscience of the Senate, kill-
ing him, his wife and daughter, the three staffers, and both pilots. Most
Minnesota progressives, and others, remember exactly where they were
when they heard the news.

A week before the 2010 election I was hired to play a DFL rally and fund-
raiser at the Miners Memorial Building in Virginia. My nephews Jason
and Jordan were both working on Mark Dayton's gubernatorial campaign. It housed the hockey rink where I used to play peewee hockey, and
where I would see the Carlson brothers, Steve, Jack, and Jeff, practicing
early before everybody else under the watchful eyes of their mom and
dad. Jack went on to play six seasons in the NHL, one of the most feared
enforcers in the game. Steve and Jeff starred in the cult classic hockey
film *Slap Shot* with Paul Newman. I had gone to dozens of high school
dances in that building and would eventually play several there as well. I
felt like I was walking back in time.

While I was driving up Highway 53 into Virginia, the sun had started
to set. It was covering the landscape in a hue of incandescent orange,
bleeding fire bolts of red, with splashes of tawny yellow like fading dan-
delions. It cast a fiery shadow over Rouchleau Pit, an abandoned open-
pit mine on the east end of town, whose mother lode of iron ore ended
up in battleships, bullets, and the Empire State Building. I drove slowly
to admire it and stopped at Southside Park, where I used to hold hands
and walk with my first girlfriend, some forty years ago. It was one of the
most commanding sunsets I had ever seen.

I pulled up to the front door of Miners Memorial and started carrying
my gear in. Not much had changed, although it seemed smaller than I remembered it. I set up on a makeshift stage across from the kitchen where
I had eaten so many spaghetti dinners over the years. Tonight's menu was
beans and brats, an old staple of Iron Range DFL gatherings. The crowd,
which would eventually wrap around the brick and glass block structure,
started to arrive.

I started to float back in time. I saw many people I remembered, whom
I hadn't seen in thirty or forty years, a bit grayer, some balder, and seemed

to recollect their younger selves. The older folks looked a lot like I membered the older folks looking, way back when. It was reassuring in a way and refuted Thomas Wolfe's claim that you can't go "back home to the escapes of time and memory." I saw old friends of the family, a former art teacher, an old girlfriend, townsfolk whom I never knew personally at the time and still didn't, and others, including my dad and nephews, who reminded me of the bedrock spirit of this small American town, one I have always been proud of being from.

The room filled quickly and I did an hour set, which was very well received given the noise and cacophonous acoustics of the room. The politicians lined up to speak, and I went, as I had done so many times before at these events, from featured performer to the thankless job of soundman. I did my best to keep the unruly ghosts of feedback from drowning out the speeches, and I had a front-row seat to what might have been one of the last great Iron Range DFL rallies in my lifetime.

Tom Rukavina, who had long since inherited Paul Wellstone's ability to rabble-rouse the faithful, kicked it off in grand style. A few other local politicians followed him and paled by comparison, until Jim Oberstar, the U.S. representative from the eighth district, took to the stage. Oberstar was elected to the seat in 1975, an assistant to his predecessor, John Blatnik, who had held the seat since 1946. I had never heard Oberstar speak. He was in front of a roomful of staunch Democrats, a handful of independents (and a few that my dad would remark just came for the beans and brats), whose sons and daughters had gone on to successful lives, most beyond the working class of those assembled. They were living proof of the power of the unions that helped create the middle class, gave us the weekend as we know it, and fulfilled the promise of what I hope is still known as the American Dream.

Oberstar started his speech remembering when Harry Truman spoke at the Hibbing Armory in 1948. A woman in front, almost ninety years old, shouted out, "I was there!" He went on to say how he became aware of class struggle when as a teenager he would bring sandwiches to his father and other miners on strike. The speech crescendoed and eventually brought all of us to our feet. He not only encapsulated the history of all in attendance but offered a vision for the future. The average age of the audience was around sixty, and I could only wonder where the hell the younger generation was, who should have been to hear this, to be reminded of where the hell they came from. When it ended, I came back another half-hour of song. A few days later Oberstar lost, the state senate and house went over to the GOP, but Dayton became the first DFLer elected governor since Iron Ranger Rudy Perpich way back in 1986.

I awoke the next morning, a warm, late October day. I picked up my gear from the venue and stopped by campaign headquarters, which was in a state of organized pandemonium. I said thank-you for having me, hugged Jason, and headed back to the Twin Cities. I grabbed a long john from Pepelnjak's Bake Shop in Virginia, a pastry filled with whipped cream, a sprinkle of walnuts on top, and headed south.

I saw the sign for the Wellstone Memorial south of Eveleth and decided to swing in. Earlier that day, I had stopped by the Virginia cemetery, and with a bottle of water, and a cloth, had cleaned all the graves: my mother's, my sister-in-law Dianne's, my grandpa's and grandma's, my aunt Eva's, and my roommate Tony's. I left a purple guitar pick at Mom's and Tony's.

I pulled up to the Wellstone Memorial by myself, on this late October day, when the wind was sleeping, the sun still kissing the meadow. I had been there before. I went to the silver metal signpost with a picture of Paul and Sheila, and the description of the crash. I saw it needed cleaning. I grabbed the bottle of water and white cloth out of my truck. I went to the ancient purple rock with the engraved poem and cleaned that as well. The poem, written by a Native American poet named Littlewolf, had a caption next to it that said, "When the rescue teams arrived, eagles were circling the site." I walked to the observation site, two thousand feet from the crash, and was silent for a moment. I walked back to my truck, ready to go, and reconsidered. I grabbed my guitar, unleashed it from its case, and walked back. I took out another purple pick and sang "This Land Is Your Land," a little louder than usual and for a brief moment felt some sort of invisible harmony. It could have been the two gunshots off in the distance, the hawks flying between the birch and twisted pine, who the hell really knew? I felt several souls a-sleeping, and for them I sang that song. I put my guitar in its tattered black bag, broke a small twig from a battered balsam tree that looked after I put it on my dashboard like a perfect cross, and headed home.

STARS OVER THE PRAIRIE

I formed my first band, the Positive Reaction, when I was twelve years old. While the name of the band seemed to roll off the tongue, it may have also come subliminally from the whispers of wisdom and encouragement from my dad, a businessman and acolyte of writer and self-improvement guru Dale Carnegie, the Deepak Chopra of his time with a '50s suit and tie. Carnegie died on the day I was born, November 1, 1955, and I'd spend a lifetime trying to win friends and influence people one show at a time.

When it came to bands, the Byrds were my favorite. Their magical mix of an electric twelve-string guitar, heavenly harmonies, and Mulligan stew of old folk songs, Dylan numbers, and originals blasted first from transistor radios, soon after on a turntable. They lifted me off the ground and shot me eight miles high into outer space. In preteenage ecstasy I felt imbued with some southside superhero strength when I'd listen. I wanted nothing more than to play like that. I wanted the Positive Reaction to be the next Byrds.

An article in the *Duluth News Tribune* told of a Duluth native who had relocated to Canoga Park, California, and started a record label. He had released a 45-rpm single of a band from Duluth, which I ran out and bought at Range Music on Chestnut Street. I wrote him a letter and mailed it to the address on the kelly-green record label. In no uncertain terms, and with the deep conviction of a young boy soon to be thirteen, I told him I thought we could be the next Byrds and asked him for advice. He was kind enough to write back and said that as good as the Byrds were, he thought we were better off searching for our own sound. I'm hoping (thinking positively) the letter will one day resurface from a dusty file.

Fast forward. The Blood on the Tracks Band was booked to play their Tenth Anniversary show at an amphitheater in St. Louis Park, a southern suburb of Minneapolis. I had organized the Million Dollar Bash at First Avenue in 2001 celebrating Bob Dylan's sixtieth birthday, including forty different acts on two stages and the original members of the Minneapolis ɔn musicians who played on that classic Dylan album. They had not ⸍yed together since those sessions and were reuniting again tonight. ⸌omedian Al Franken, *New York Times* columnist Thomas Friedman, and the moviemaking duo the Coen brothers had all grown up in St. Louis Park. Other notable residents included television star Hugh O'Brien who starred as Wyatt Earp, and Guy Bannister, an FBI agent who some believed may have been involved in the shadowy ring of the JFK assassination. I was invited to play at the show by Kevin Odegard, now the leader of the band for tonight's show. He asked what song I would like to play. I chose the Byrds' version of Dylan's "My Back Pages," as both the song and the sound set my ship a-sailin' back in 1967 using "ideas as my maps."

I love playing music outside in the summertime. Minnesotans are gifted with three months of summer, and Mother Nature rewards us latitude-wise, after months of frost, snow, and bitter cold, with long days in June, July, and August with which to enjoy all that our ten thousand lakes (and almost as many treatment centers) have to offer. There is something about music on a cool breeze that mingles with butterflies and birds straight toward Heaven, electrically charged by rays of sunshine during the day, then at night under a canopy of the moon and stars.

The amphitheater for that gig was built behind a faux town square. I parked my truck and went to find it. After walking past coffee shops, chichi clothing stores, and restaurants, it appeared innocently and invitingly, a small prairie down a rolling hill, just far enough away from the suburban sprawl, an oasis of solitude with lots of green grass and trees. It featured a humble stage with wooden benches for the audience, which swept gently back up the hill in front, in a semicircle around it—a glorious place to end the summer. August was slipping quietly away, yielding to the falling leaves and colder winds of September.

It has been said that the earth has music for all who listen. From the loud thunderclaps that follow lightning, from dark clouds that give birth to the rain that bounces off rocks and trees, when waves kiss the shore, when dusk raises its baton to call a million croaking, singing creatures to their evening summer symphonies on sidewalks and in swamps, music summons our spirits. Musicians do what they do because of a force within that seeks outward expression. There is grace in that, beauty, and truth. Add a backbeat and an electric guitar, and Elvis Presley is in the air.

I was dressed in straight-fit black Levi jeans over black boots like the Beatles wore. My new black cowboy shirt had fancy embroidered green

stitches and white mother-of-pearl buttons, handsome beneath m
Grandpa Paul's bolo tie, a polished oval jasper surrounded by gold leaves
that my mother had given me. With my trusty, weathered red Takamine
acoustic guitar, and red leather strap with Hi-ho-Silver conch buckles
twice the size of Susan B. Anthony dollars, I was ready to rock.

Backstage were the musicians—performers and listeners—who were
there to enjoy the evening along with the crowd that was now arriving
from all directions. Wherever lifer musicians gather the bonds are felt—
those who know the decades of blasts of glory, music itself a life-lasting
love. Followed by rejection, broken-down cars, the times in sickness and
in health, other band members, friends at first, only in it for the money
(like there ever was any) who will jump ship for a few dollars more. The
slow suicide of drugs and booze that lurks in the guise of midnight angels
and whiskey queens, sirens who call from corners with the dove-like eyes
of your first true love, but the intent of prostitutes who follow the feet of
their victims in the quicksand of slow and meaningless death. Bar owners, booking agents, and record labels that could give a good goddamn.
Audiences more interested in pinball or pool tables or television screens,
the band on the stage nothing but a bother. Death and destruction, love
many times lost, and the occasional one-night stand hotter than the skil-
let of a New Orleans short-order cook, lighting up the skies like Times
Square on New Year's Eve. Or real love with a human touch, made to
last with lovers sometimes drawn from opposite magnetic poles that
proved marriage was possible and strong like David's slingshot against
the Goliath that was the music business, sweeter than honey from the
bee. Building families that stand the test of time and kids that are now
musicians themselves. Or the kids who never knew Daddy's name, and
some only remembering it as long as child support was paid on time, the
waiting for that to come around, as music is nothing if not the discipline
of hope. And all of the rest—the poison gigs and the majestic ones that
vanish as quickly as they came, all the things you could only wish would
happen but would never bet on—that reminded us why we were here in
the first place, like black-robed priests who take an oath of poverty and
service to the lords of music, whose faces we never saw but whose presence we always felt. It was warm summer evenings like this that brought
out the best in everybody, including us musicians who have always lived
for the moment. For the next several hours there would be peace in the
valley. So I mingled.

I saw Slim Dunlap first. One of the finest electric guitar slingers in town, he walked slowly and surely, in a white T-shirt, loose jeans, cheap sunglasses, a guy who wouldn't have been out of place playing chess with the old men in Washington Square Park. Curtiss A, for whom Slim was wing man for dozens of years, walked alongside, in yellow T-shirt, red shoes, and white sunglasses, his ever-present holy pipe sending intoxicating smoke signals throughout the crowd. Curt, the greatest rock singer in the world, a Minneapolis boy who never left town and, though nearing sixty, could still channel Eddie Cochran, Elvis, or John Lennon on any given night. He then laid in the grass, gently petting a brown Chihuahua puppy leashed to a little girl and her mother and wearing a small fake diamond collar. Geno LaFond, in his ever-untucked shirt, a longtime partner of my old friend Larry Kegan, showed up and began to unpack his guitar. I hoped for a minute that Larry might show up next, back from the grave, in his wheelchair, and as always, ready to sing. The sun was setting lazily behind us sending blades of light through the oak trees.

The show was about to start. The hill was now full of people and a crescent moon appeared with the two stars of Jupiter and Mercury in alignment, which also bounced off of all of Minnesota's lakes, rivers, and streams, beyond this place, and reflected back into the sky.

Tuning my guitar I took stock of my fellow performing musicians, all now friends, a flesh-and-blood scrapbook of my time in Minneapolis. There was bassist Billy Peterson whom I first heard in town with his jazz fusion group, Natural Life, upstairs above the Longhorn Bar and whose three bandmates in that group included guitarist and my teacher Mike Elliot, the best chordal jazz player this side of Johnny Smith; his cousin, keyboard player Bobby Peterson; and drummer Paul Lagos, now all dead and gone to a place where great musicians go. Drummer Joe Luoma whom I had played with since 1978 and could lay down a train beat as good as any drummer in the country and swung like Buddy Rich. My old friend Stanley Kipper, a master percussionist who played on "Thunder Island" by Jay Ferguson, my favorite guilty-pleasure song from the 1970s, along with his musical partner of forty years, Chico Perez, both of whom had been beating the tubs together since LBJ was in office, bringing back dead ghosts from forgotten cemeteries one at a time. And master musician Peter Ostroushko, who once said, "My solos are a conversation with God." Rounding out this rogues' gallery was none other than Dr. Matt Fink, subbing for original Blood on the Tracks member Gregg

Inhofer, who had another gig, an original member of Prince's band Revolution. It was time to party like it was 1999. Let the revolution beg...

There were several performers before me, and I paced back and forth backstage smoking cigarettes, drinking bottled water, and playing my guitar. I looked at the crowd, those in front caught in the glow of the stage lights. Magic Marc Percansky, our hometown Houdini, was there with his mother, Marilyn, dressed as flamboyantly as ever with a wide-brimmed black hat and a leopard skin pillbox dress, and in her arms, a granddaughter as well. Phil Freshman and son Noam, whom I had gotten to know when trying to save the historic Guthrie Theater, and whose hair a Jew-fro helmet passed down from father to son. And six hundred more, including other friends and longtime fans celebrating this divine night in honor of Minnesota's favorite son Bob Dylan, and his record *Blood on the Tracks*, released during my last year of high school. Each song seemed stronger than the last, each performer reaching for the stars hanging above us as mystic twilight. The assembled, who had arrived as individuals, were now becoming an audience and responded after each tune as they had just received a loud love letter from home, reminding them, and us, from whence we came. The old man in the moon was winking and blinking from tip to tip, and the sky now a golden blur of stars, all of us on this floating electric Carter Family Gospel Ship, on a voyage to the Milky Way.

I was called up and introduced as the man who had started this all some ten years before. There is nothing like an ovation before you have even played a note. The drummer counted off the tune and the band started to swell and groove behind me. I blew a bit of the first verse, but in a moment "the crimson flames tied through my ears," as Dylan's lyric goes. We were on a charging silver horse and ready to ride it home. The sound was perfect, the band a loud, well-oiled machine, gloriously loud. Like a dog sticking its head out the window at sixty miles an hour, it felt like the wind was blowing us both forward and backward into time. The band hit the first chorus with harmonies that brought 1967 to this golden evening, the crowd was standing and dancing, swaying back and forth and singing along, almost now louder than the band itself, the reverie backlit by the moon. The muses slipped down from the heavens and were swaying in time as well.

In an instant we became one with the audience, one big breathing heartbeat. During the third verse, out of the corner of my eye, I noticed

Kevin Odegard's electric Rickenbacker twelve-string had become ąplugged, and I thought I might have to take his solo. Not to fear, Odegard got it together and seconds later played that solo forever seared in my head, note for note that sprang forth out of his amplifier like lightning bolts from the head of Zeus himself. We ended the tune with original harmonies, some doubled and all sung by the audience, that timeless refrain, "We were so much older then, we're younger than that now."

The crowd exploded. We were all eight miles high. Me? I sounded like the Byrds. After forty-five years, I finally sounded like the fucking Byrds.

FIREWORKS ON THE FOURTH OF JULY

It was the Fourth of July on the Iron Range, 2010. This most American of holidays is celebrated on the Range like a second New Year's Eve. Starting at sun up and going deep into the evening, it is fueled by some sort of psychic/spiritual nitroglycerin that runs through the working-class veins of this special part of Minnesota, rust red, white, and blue hearts beating as one.

Since the turn of the twentieth century we have gathered on bandstands, by the lakeshore, in union halls, backyards, town squares, on soap boxes, and down on Main Street where high school marching bands in formation proudly display school colors and play their school songs. Masons in their fez hats drive and weave their little cars in figure-eight patterns up the street. Calithumpian clown bands with makeshift horns and drums (stopping at every bar along the way), flags and penny candy, mayors, merchants, high school kings and queens riding in the back of classic convertibles or Cub Scouts and Brownies in the backs of pickup trucks with their troop numbers taped to the doors, Elvis look-a-likes, majorettes either leading the charge or following close behind, little kids, moms and dads, grandmas and grandpas, aunts and uncles, waving back to their loved ones who walk proudly in the center of the street, and aging color guard veterans marching upright and in time, reminding us this Fourth of July that we are the Land of the Free because of the Brave, and then a street dance at sundown before sending us home.

Back home, the whistle whetted by beer, home brew, and occasionally whiskey from a homemade still, then downtown to bars and saloons, now loud and boisterous, that dotted these streets like checkers on a board. Walnut potica with a honey twist, stick-to-your-ribs beef, and rutabaga pasties with thick edges of crust that hungry miners of old could hold without getting ore in their mouths, hot dishes, Italian pastas, kalamojakka (Finnish fish stew, with the head and eyes still intact, floating to the top, scaring young children one bowl at a time), fry bread and dishes of native wild rice harvested by the Ojibwe, generous slices of juicy watermelon, and then blueberry pie, hot out of the oven, bluer than

~ue, with a light-brown crust topped by sprinkles of sugar. Gathering in large groups, all ethnicities represented, sharing the bounty and recipes from the old countries from which all our forbearers came, now as one, on this most American of holidays.

I was booked to play a solo show on Saturday, July 3, in northern Minnesota at an old resort, now refurbished and owned by a couple young enough to be my kids. It was on the east end of Lake Vermilion, considered by some to be one of the seven greatest freshwater lakes in the world. It stretches for 40 miles, has 40,000 acres of sky-blue water, 365 islands, and 1,200 miles of shoreline. The Ojibwe called it *Onamuni*, "land of the sunset glow." It is located in the beating heart of the Arrowhead region of Minnesota (the area looks like an arrowhead on a map). It is bordered by Cook on the west where my great-grandfather purchased three acres on the lake in 1928 for $500. Tower-Soudan lies on its eastern shore, where he started his working life in America, a Finnish immigrant, working nearly a half-mile in an underground mine in the early 1900s. Last year, a University of Minnesota–sponsored Cryogenic Dark Matter Research Team discovered in that same mine what they say may be the key to the universe, "dark matter," pre–Big Bang stuff that holds the stars and galaxies together and accounts for most of the universe's matter. It is characterized by the simultaneous release of electrical energy and heat. My great-grandfather John is buried within the shadow of that mine, along with his wife, both parents, and two sons.

The gig worked out perfectly as I was going to be up there anyway for the Fourth of July weekend. It paid well, came with a room and dinner, and the hours were from 7–10 P.M. There was a time, when I was a young buck full of piss and vinegar, that I could do a gig in the afternoon, sometimes two, and another at night, no worse for the wear. These days, I limit myself to one gig per day, and if it is at night, it has to be proceeded by a nap. I also do transcendental meditation at least once a day, something I started in 1976. I read awhile back that you should never do that type of meditation while high on marijuana because it will cause brain damage. I wish I would have known that earlier. I take my solo performances seriously, and I put a lot of energy into them. I want to jump the joint as if I were playing with a band. I beat the hell out of the guitar when I get going, improvising to an imaginary drummer and bass player, and hope to see people dancing by the end. It is energizing and exhausting at the same time.

I packed lightly and was looking forward to the gig and see family. In the middle of the winter I always start dreaming about me in the sauna at the lake, and then skinny-dipping under the Milky V and, if I'm lucky, the northern lights. The dreams are without fear, and when I awake relatives who have passed on and have visited me in my sleep leave slowly, their voices the last to disappear.

I had forgotten to take my insulin pen along (I had been diagnosed with diabetes in 2005) and was starting to get a little shaky from my unstable blood sugar levels. While I was planning on having a nice dinner before the gig, I arrived in just enough time to set up and start to play. The place was packed, and most of the folks there had started to party much earlier in the afternoon, some that morning. It was kind of a homecoming for me, as I hadn't played up north for a couple of years. It was like walking back into my high school yearbook. I saw one old girlfriend—she and I used to light up the backseat of the '59 baby blue Cadillac—now here with her husband. An old next-door neighbor with her mother and daughter, and an old little league teammate. The entire French family including Gregg French who had bought Dylan's boyhood home in Hibbing where I had house-sat when they were away, sleeping in the basement on the linoleum floor with four aces from a deck of cards in the middle of the room, hearing the wind or ghosts swirling through the upstairs. A band member, my fifth grade teacher, and a schoolmate who went on to become a director of slasher films in Hollywood, old and new fans, my best new friends, Terry and Jeanette and family, who showed up on their houseboat, and a couple of hundred others who were just along for the holiday ride. I set up outside on the middle deck, next to the beer cooler like a coffin for a very large man with ice, and next to the stairway where a half-dozen waitresses took full trays of adult beverages to thirsty customers. There was also a bar inside, and one on the lower deck with three bartenders, all of them full and busy.

I started to feed off the energy in the crowd, cranked my PA system to be louder than them, and blasted out "Stranger Blues" like I had done thousands of times before: "I'm a stranger here, just blowed in your town." It was still ninety degrees, but enough of a wind off the lake to make it seem cooler. Then the brandy started to flow: first in shot glasses, then in soup bowls, and finally in minnow buckets. Drinks were appearing from out of nowhere, and others were handed to me by folks passing by. At around 9 P.M., the sun started to set in a rust-colored amber

...nd I should have tried to hold on to that sunset and never let it .elcome home.

By the third set my old friends the Hotchkiss brothers, Kevin and Kyle, showed up. Kyle pulled out his harp, and we traded blues songs and licks when the brandy, now mixed with fatigue, hot weather, no insulin, and no food started to play tricks with me, in a way that only brown booze can do. It starts like an innocent kiss, passing your lips gently, and sliding down your throat, a bitter soothing for your tired throat. A few more, and even the people in the crowd you were avoiding become your best friends. And they are now buying you drinks, too. The gig ended a bit of a ramshackle, but like all good rock and roll shows, with a bang and a resounding round of applause from the crowd, now almost all as lit up as I was. It was now time to go to the upstairs bar and start drinking with my friends.

People on the Iron Range take their drinking seriously, especially on a day like the Fourth of July. Growing up, it becomes a badge of honor to handle shot after shot and still stay standing. It was in that spirit I continued to drink, celebrating a great evening, a great gig, and the company of friends. At around eleven, in a moment of clarity, I asked Gregg French if he would help me pack up my gear. By now, the deejay outside had started pumping out the hits, had turned the lights off on the deck, and had turned his laser strobes lights on instead, covering the entire area in a swash of psychedelic and fast-moving colors. My gear was at the bottom of the second deck, seven steps down, now right next to the deejay. I missed the first step, and the rest, as they say, is history.

The first thing I remembered in the ambulance ride to the Virginia hospital was the sound of two people talking in hushed voices, and something that sounded like a faraway siren. I was floating above somewhere, everything in slow motion, suspended in time. I remember being wheeled out of the back of the ambulance, on my back, my head strapped to a gurney, and for a brief moment I thought I was being waterboarded. The next thing I remember, after an hour of complete darkness, the kind of darkness you expect at death, was someone shining a small flashlight in my eyes. I opened them long enough to see a doctor, and I asked him his name. "I am Dr. Jameson." I answered, " Dr. Jameson . . . of course you are," and passed out again.

Gregg had watched me fall like a Gumby doll down the stairs. He thought I had broken my neck, or maybe even worse. Fortunately, there was an off-duty EMT at the party, and he immediately called 911. Th party continued around me, the lights of the ambulance now adding to the ambience of the laser light show. People probably thought it was part of the act, dancing not far from where I lay. He followed the ambulance to the hospital and stayed with me until my brother and nephew Jason arrived. The doctor wanted to keep me in overnight, but all I wanted to do was get back to Blackie at the cabin. I unstrapped my head from the gurney that was perched atop the bed and to the doctor's dismay made my way to Jason's car, my arm around him holding on for balance, and we headed straight for the cabin.

I woke up early in the morning very sick. The ceiling of the "honeymoon cabin," the little log cabin where I stayed (a dozen couples had honeymooned there), was whirling. I was too dizzy to get off the bed, though I tried. My dad came out to check on me and brought me back a pail, which I threw up into several times. Blackie lay at the foot of my bed, a bit spooked by what he was sensing. My dad brought me some toast, which I was able to keep down, and a jug of water. I was thirsty as hell, and through the fog of a steel-driving headache, knew I had fucked up royally.

I was finally able to go outside and get some fresh air around noon. Blackie had been waiting patiently by my side and was delighted to get out, but we didn't go far. I sat on the bench outside the old cabin and tried to gather my wits. It wasn't long before I had to lie down again, the room still spinning as I tried to lie on the bed. I'd drift in and out of sleep, and when I awoke and would try to stand, I was gripped by vertigo and very unsteady. So I lay there.

For the next several hours in the haze of dizziness, and feeling like homemade shit, I tried to put the pieces of the puzzle back together. I couldn't remember much of the evening before, but for some reason the past thirty or forty years of my life came back to me, in fractured glimpses, voices from the past swinging by to say hello, and some just pointing wary fingers at me. Family members would come to the screen door appearing like the Tin Man, the Lion, and the Wizard now as their regular selves visiting Dorothy while she was waking up from her fall.

One incident came back in a most vivid way. It was my friend Dudley and his fatal car accident. Dudley was the guy who introduced me to Leo Kottke and who took me down to Leo's show at the Guthrie Theater the night I decided to become a professional musician. We never hung out much after that but would see each other at parties and enjoy each other's company. One night after a party on this very same road that leads to our cabin, he left with two others to drive back to Virginia a little after midnight. The party was breaking up, and my friends and I left about ten minutes after them. Twenty minutes later, and about ten miles from Virginia, we came upon a head-on crash. There were two cars, completely totaled, and one was on fire. The sheriffs hadn't arrived, and before I realized who was in the car, I ran to the nearest farmhouse, woke the family up that lived there, and had them call the ambulance. I ran back to where the cars were, and in one was Dudley on the passenger side, the driver, and another guy I knew in the backseat, who was so drunk he didn't realize his leg was broken. The sheriffs arrived a few minutes later, and I asked one of them to check on Dudley, who was lying back in his seat, not a hair out of place, looking angelic amid this carnage. The sheriff put his hand on Dudley's neck, checking for a pulse, looked at me, and said, "Your friend is dead." I was the first one to know.

That afternoon in the honeymoon cabin I didn't remember his funeral, where they had played tapes of him playing guitar, or the time a few months later when I was playing Leo Kottke on my morning shift on WHLB, and a lady called to say that Leo's playing reminded her of her son's. It was Dudley's mother, and I told her the story. I hoped it comforted her, but I am not sure it did. All I could remember was seeing him in that car, looking peaceful, now somewhere beyond this mortal coil.

By early evening I had talked my brother-in-law Al and his daughter Heather into driving me back to the resort to get my equipment, car keys, and truck. Al Lakoskey, the drummer for the Small Society, had been there and was kind enough to pack up my stuff and put it in a corner of the bar, although the full tip jar that I was collecting for Contented Critters was gone. Oh well, worse things can happen. The owner of the place came up and was happy to see me, as he had heard I was airlifted to Duluth and was on life support. See how rumors start? He also told me he loved the show, and to let him know the next time I wanted to play there. Really? When I called my best friend Kelly to tell him what had happened, he said he heard it from his brother Kyle, who played with me and described it as a scene out of the movie *Crazy Heart*, and then Kelly suggested I missed a perfect chance to fake my own death and start anew. For the first time all day, I was able to laugh.

As we were packing up my stuff, I turned around and saw a classmate

who I hadn't seen since high school graduation. She hadn't changed ⦁
And after saying hello, I remembered she was the sister of the man w
was driving the car in the head-on collision. For the first time in years, .
didn't know what to say. Dudley, are you there?

American rock and roll started around a campfire in a dark and howling
wind. It was blues, country, and hillbilly music then. Once it was moved
inside four walls—juke joint or gin joint, rent party apartment, greased
alley garage, or some full-moon Ozark barn dance—it became rock
and roll. First, gut-bucket whiskey passed around in coffee cans, then
ordered over the bar, smoke from hand-rolled cigarettes misting blue
windows, both inviting the night and keeping it at bay, beautiful women
writhing with imaginary lovers on sawdust dance floors, young men on
a weekend pass from some hell-forbidden job doing the Hucklebuck and
the Chicken Strut, these sons and daughters then joining in this Church
of Saturday night together, while the band in the corner jacks it up, like
drill hammers toward heaven, until the sweaty crowd stumbles out sanc-
tified and satisfied.

Somebody once asked Dylan if he ever considered getting out of the
music business. He replied, "Every day." Of course he wouldn't, some
boys are just born to rock and roll, enjoying that hollered-out loud glory
shout, a teenager's hallelujah when first starting out that reappears over
the years, sometimes unexpectedly. This is what sustains the men and
women who have dedicated their lives to it and, while plying their trade,
have become artists in the process. For most of us, it's too late to stop
now. Manifest musical destiny.

I bumped into Bob Mould at the Dakota Jazz Club in October 2010. I
had left my gear, from a show I did there a few days before, in the dressing room, and Bob was there getting ready for his show. We have known
each other for almost thirty years and have the utmost respect for each
other's work. He told me he was writing a book, and I told him I had just
signed a book deal recently as well. We both got a kick out of that, jokingly saying, "So this is what the publishing world has come to?" I asked him
if he remembered the night of the 1986 Minnesota Music Awards at the
Carleton Celebrity Room, where Prince was headlining (and Hüsker Dü
and I had both won awards), when he, Minnesota wrestling icon Verne
Gagne, comedian Tom Arnold, and I were at the bar. Arnold looked at
Gagne and said, "You don't look so tough!" In land-speed record time,

ormer WWF champ had Arnold in a full nelson, face-down on the ɛ, begging for mercy. Bob replied, "How could I forget?" As I wandered ɔut onto Nicollet Avenue, in the warm glow one gets when enjoying the success of friends and family, I remembered my favorite Van Morrison quote: "It doesn't matter what you've done; all that matters is that you are still around."

As I have gotten older, my commitment to the ramble on the blue guitar highway has strengthened, in part in honor of great musicians— friends of mine—who passed before their time. I feel duly obligated to continue playing music because if these men could still be here, they would be doing it, too. They can't, but I can.

Doug Maynard was one of the best and most soulful blues and R&B singers I have ever heard. His voice could create tritones, sounding as if he were harmonizing with himself. Always on the run from personal demons, those demons caught up with him, and he left us Thanksgiving weekend, 1991, the day before his old band was to reunite.

Percy Strother was known by his fellow musicians as the Mississippi Mound of Sound. He led the harshest of bluesmen's lives, leading his family away from Vicksburg, Mississippi, as a teenager after his father was hung by the Ku Klux Klan. His music was always about the positive and redemptive power of love. Percy was also a flashy dresser and devout fisherman, and he could often be seen on the shores of the rivers of St. Paul fishing in a three-piece suit and cape before a gig at Wilebski's Blues Saloon. Sonny Earl and I joined him for his last public performance, backing him on the blues classic "Key to the Highway" just days before he passed. He was billed up and bound to go.

Dave "Snaker" Ray was both the most cantankerous and sweetest man I have ever met, and one of the purest musicians. I was honored to have him and Percy both play my forty-sixth birthday party at Mayslack's in 2002. I saw him a week later, with a brand-new Gibson B-25 guitar he had just purchased, playing at a small Irish bar in my neighborhood. I watched in awe as he ripped blues riffs out of it sending them into the spheres. Mortality be damned. I talked to him after the show while he sat at the bar eating a late-night snack of pancakes, and when I walked into the darkness of the Northeast Minneapolis night, I knew I would never see him again. He died three weeks later, after a few more shows, on Thanksgiving weekend, 2002, at home, his lovely wife, Mary Jane, by his side.

Larry Kegan was a steel-wheeled hipster: a saint who shook, rattled, and rolled up to the very end. His world stopped spinning twice. A diving accident stole the use of his legs at the age of fifteen. Then on a Mexican road at midnight, he was in a car accident at the age of twenty-five that would lay claim to all movement below the neck. Besides being one of my best friends, he was a blues shouter, rebel Jew, songwriter, poet, author, speaker, student, scholar, son, brother, lover, father, and friend to many. He had a sixth sense born through the blood drops of struggle, never felt sorry for himself, and lived in a high-octane world infused with spirit. He died of cardiac arrest at the age of fifty-nine on 9/11. At his funeral the rabbi supposed Larry was called to heaven to help the other disabled people find their way home on that darkest of days. I do not doubt that. After forty-five years, he was out of that chair and dancing.

Bill Hinkley was considered the Godfather of the West Bank music scene. He was an air force veteran who spoke five languages, a self-taught multi-instrumentalist, a human jukebox of thousands of songs, a philosopher-king who held sway in saloons, concert halls, radio shows, campfires, kitchen tables, and festivals, and on speed dial for any benefit or cause, lost or otherwise. He was a teacher and mentor to hundreds of students. Bill's greatest lessons to me were "End every story with a smile or a laugh" and "The best music is played without pretension." He left this world with no enemies and no detractors. We will never see the likes of him again.

There is not a week that goes by when I don't think of all of them, and others. I always remember a postcard I got from Dave Ray, after I booked a gig for him. He sent a thank-you note after every one. This one said, "It was a bit of a thrash, but we'll train them."

And so in that spirit, I continue what I do, on the musician's path, doing a musician's work. Each day after my accident, I became stronger. The days seemed brighter, the sky a deeper kind of blue. I remember my brothers, breathe deeply, and head onward toward the light.

ACKNOWLEDGMENTS

I was fortunate to grow up in the independent school district of Virginia, Minnesota, from first grade with Mrs. Grace Norsted through my senior English class with Tom Moeller, who imbued in me a love of the English language. Writing seemed to come as naturally as learning to tie my shoes, swing a baseball bat, or bait a hook. Like playing the guitar or writing songs, the more I practiced, the more fluent I became.

In 1977, the University of Minnesota rejected my application for entrance into its music program, so I moved to Minneapolis to take night classes instead. I dropped out the night before my first exams. Music became my focus, my life's work, and I continued writing. In 2009, I sent samples of pieces I wrote to Kevin Avery at Mere Words and Media in Brooklyn; he suggested I had a great start on a book. An unlikely circle was connected in 2010 when the same university that rejected me thirty-two years earlier offered me a contract for a book about my thirty-five-year career in the music business.

There was a sweetness to the timeline of events. On what would have been my mother's eighty-first birthday the university approached me about the book deal. On what would have been my Grandma Metsa's 104th birthday, I met my editor, Todd Orjala. We came to an agreement on September 29, the day that would have been my parents' fifty-ninth anniversary. I was invited to a book signing for another book published by the University of Minnesota Press, *The Opposite of Cold: The Northwoods Finnish Sauna Tradition*, at the American Swedish Institute, the same place where I performed my first Minneapolis gig as Paul and Christian in 1968. I signed the book contract on October 30, 2010, and you'll have to ask me why that number is important.

In 2007, I was booked to play Dylan Days in Hibbing. Tom Moeller informed me then that he was one of B. J. Rolfzen's students and that Rolfzen had inspired him to switch his degree from coaching to English. Moeller was one of hundreds of Rolfzen's students, the most famous of whom was Bobby Zimmerman, whom B. J. called Robert. My favorite ᴧine from that student is "Take what you have gathered from coincidence." So I do, and here it is. And remember to tip your bartenders and waitresses.

And now, my thanks:

Kelly Hotchkiss—my best friend and, like me, a double Scorpio, who kept the home lights burning and me on track, through thick and thin, for thirty-five years. Mary Hotchkiss (Kelly's wife): thanks for putting up with us. Jackie Cheves, the sweetest sister in the world and great editor. Mom would be proud.

The Cheves family, John and Carol Metsa, the Metsa boys, Jason, Jacob, John-Paul, and Jordan, Kathy and Al Axtell and family, the Grey Wolf Lodge, Laura Bonicelli, Gladys Tuuri, Floyd "Flitch" Jaros, Jeanne Cornell and family, the Pagliaccetti family, the Vitali family, the Kishel family, Colleen Sheehy, Kevin Avery, Mere Words and Media, Todd Orjala, the University of Minnesota Press, Nora Guthrie, Jerry "Jake" Disrud, Scotty and Jerry Fishman, Harvey Van Horn, Chuck Christianson, Tim and Laura O'Keefe, Jack and Laura Pasternacki, Kevin Hotchkiss, Steven Baker and the Baker clan, Harry and Lila Jacob and family, Kenneth Jacob, Dr. Helen Enright, Professor Katherine Sedo, Dr. Craig Hergert, Mary Morin, Tom Moeller, Wayne Slater, Tony Perpich, Norm and Laurie Coleman, Jeff and Molly Cierniak, Robert and Lesa Wilson, Mick Spence, Dennis and Sara Pelowski, Randy Kouri, Donna Wright, Cray McCally, John McCally Sr., John McCally Jr., Booka and Edythe Michel and family, Loudhouse Records, Larry Monroe, Jimmy LaFave, Mari Harris, Willie West and Patty Gambucci West, Big Jay McNeely, Willie Walker, Monty Lee Wilkes, Max Kittel, Kevin Bowe, Chopper Black, Kevin Odegard, Patrick Courtemanche, Jon Bream, Jon Tevlin, Bill Ferguson, Bobby Vandell, Sherwin and Pam Linton, John and Barb Sullivan and family, Paul Mandell, Tom Korstad, Jason Korstad, Bucky Baxter, Dave Morton, Sue McLean, Gail Parenteau, Steve Martin and the Agency Group, Charlie Feldman, Tony Rubin, Billy and Tara Alcorn, Tom Arnold, David and Jill Carr, Ed Nagle and Laurie Farley, Eric Shogren, Tony and Mike Musial, Deborah Burke, Nye's Polonaise Room, Steve "Andy" Anderle, Dan Bell, Jeff Moritko, Tony and Frances Tieberg, Jimmy Moehlenbrock, Doug Ellis, Terry Monroe, William Rodgers and Christina Bucksbaum, the Egg and I Restaurant, Terry Katzman, Bob Mould, Mary Beth Mueller,

George Travis, Joe D'Urso, John Hall, Josh Horowitz and the Stop Handgun Violence Coalition, Famous Dave Anderson, Mike Wright, James Wrayge, John Nermyr, SavetheGuthrie.org (Aaron Rubenstein, Bob Roscoe, Joe Gioia, Dore Mead, Ann Berget, and Stephanie Klein), Phil Freshman, Rich Lind, *Cook News Herald, Rochester Post Bulletin,* Bill Hanna and *Mesabi Daily News,* Tom Rukavina, Gregg French and family, Nelson French, Jim Cope, David and Ank Kure, Curt and Lolly Obeda, Julia Schroeder, Hubert Sumlin, Scarlet Rivera, Terry Carlson and Jeanette Leehr, Joe Luoma and Melanie Banta, Gary and Laura Brekke and family, Peter Ostroushko, "Blueberry" Bill Hood, Judy Larson, Tom and Amy Lieberman, Icebox Gallery, KUMD, KFAI, KAXE, Knight Cap Bar, Grumpy's Bar, Jackie and James at Bunker's Bar, Tracy Burlow, Creation Studio, Bruce Wilson, Shelley Leeson, Skipper and Cheri Nelimark, Dr. Jeff Balke, Pamela Espeland, Jane Hession, Toby Rapson, the Parkway Theater, Todd and Leslie Anderson, Arne Brogger, John and Greg Rebeau, Contented Critters, Amy and Piper Donlin, Brad Begley, Al's Center City Saloon, Bill Wanner, 5 Corners Saloon, Anna Canoni, Woody Guthrie Publications, I-Ware, Terry Lundberg, Mary Ellen Smith, and Blackie "Sisu" Metsa—I couldn't have done it without you. Woof!

For more information on *Blue Guitar Highway,* including music, photographs, videos, and downloads, go to http://www.blueguitarhighway.com.

Might you be so kind to consider a tax-deductible donation to your local humane shelter or to Contented Critters, a no-kill animal rescue operation on the Iron Range? Tell them Blackie sent you. Thanks!

Contented Critters
4986 Town Line Road
Makinen, MN 55763
http://contentedcritters.org

You can learn more and keep up to date on my music and adventures by checking in at www.paulmetsa.com, www.maximumfolk.com, and www.paulandsonny.com.

And to musicians everywhere: never let the bastards get you down!

DISCOGRAPHY

1982 "Louie, Louie" b/w "Blues Ghosts," 45 rpm, by Cats Under the Stars, Monkey Business Records

1985 *Paper Tigers* LP, Raven Records

1985 *P-9 Strike* compilation cassette (Metsa contributed "Slow Justice")

1986 "59 Coal Mines" and "Stars Over the Prairie," 45 rpm, Raven Records

1987 "Ferris Wheels on the Farm" and "Party to a Crime," 45 rpm, Raven Records

1989 *Slow Justice* live and studio cassette, Raven Records

1990 *Live at the Guthrie* live cassette, Raven Records

1992 *Radio Motel* CD, Raven Records

1992 *Legacy II* CD (songwriter compilation), Windham Hill–High Street Records

1993 *Whistling Past the Graveyard* CD, Raven Records

1994 *Mississippi Farewell* CD, Raven Records

1998 *Lincoln's Bedroom* EP/CD, Raven Records

2000 *Brew House Sampler I* CD (compilation, live on KUMD), Spinout Records

2002 *Brew House Sampler II* CD (compilation, live on KUMD), Spinout Records

2005 *Texas in the Twilight* CD, Loudhouse Records (Austin, Texas)

2006 Producer and performer, Famous Dave's Barbeque and Blues Festival CD, volume 1

2007 Producer and performer, Famous Dave's Barbeque and Blues Festival CD, volume 2

2007 Paul Metsa and Sonny Earl, *White Boys Lost in the Blues* CD, MaximumFolk.com

2007 Produced *Mr. Bad Boy,* by Ron Hacker, MaximumFolk.com

2008 Producer and performer, Famous Dave's Barbeque and Blues CD, volume 3

2009 Paul Metsa and Sonny Earl, *No Money Down* EP/CD with bonus DVD, MaximumFolk.com

CONCERT APPEARANCES

Over the years I have had the great opportunity to appear in concert with the following musicians and performers:

Alberta Adams
Billy Alcorn
Rashied Ali
Mose Allison
Bucky Baxter
BeauSoleil
Carey Bell
The Big Wu
Mary Black
Bobby "Blue" Bland
Blind Boys of Alabama
Blood on the Tracks Band
Billy Bragg
Doyle Bramhall Sr.
Billy Branch
Lonnie Brooks
Nappy Brown
Savoy Brown
Michael Burks
J. J. Cale
Chubby Carrier
Roseanne Cash
Bruce Cockburn
Commander Cody
Joanna Connor
Ry Cooder
Robert Cray
Debbie Davies
The Dead Milkmen

The Detroit Rhythm and
　Blues Kings
Ani DiFranco
Dr. John
Steve Earle
David "Honeyboy" Edwards
Joe Ely
Ramblin' Jack Elliott
Alejandro Escovedo
Terry Evans
Jimmie Dale Gilmore
Greg Ginn
Tony Glover
Nanci Griffith
Guitar Shorty
Arlo Guthrie
Buddy Guy
Phil Guy
Hacienda Brothers with
　Chris Gaffney
Ron Hacker
John Hammond
John Wesley Harding
Cornbread Harris
Grant Hart
John Hartford
John Hiatt
Sara Hickman
Peter Himmelman

Bill Hinckley and Judy Larson
Peter Holsapple
Hot Tuna
Dakota Dave Hull and
    Sean Blackburn
Long John Hunter
Robert Hunter
Indigo Girls
Ipso Facto
David Johansen
Evan Johns
Jorma Kaukonen
Garrison Keillor
Willie Kent
Steve Kilbride
Kingfish
Eddie Kirkland
"Spider" John Koerner
Papa John Kolstad
Leo Kottke
Bill Kreutzman
Jimmy LaFave
Jonny Lang
Peter Lang
Bettye LaVette
Adrian Legg
Tom Lieberman
Gordon Lightfoot
Lil' Charlie and the Nightcats
Lil' Ed and the Blues Imperials
Sherwin Linton
Vini "Mad Dog" Lopez
Los Lobos
Louisiana Red
Lyle Lovett
Magic Slim and the Teardrops
Doug Maynard
Country Joe McDonald

Ellen McIlwaine
Big Jay McNeely
Big Bill Morganfield
Dave Morton
Maria Muldaur
Willie Murphy
Charlie Musselwhite
Willie Nelson
The Aaron Neville Quintet
The Neville Brothers
The Nighthawks
Willie Nile
Mojo Nixon
Pinetop Perkins
Dave Pirner
Ana Popovic
John Primer
Flora Purim and Airto Moreira
The Radiators
Dave "Snaker" Ray
Sir Mack Rice
Riders in the Sky
Rio Nido
Steve Raitt
Scarlet Rivera
Jimmie Lee Robinson
Peter Rowan
Dan Rumsey
Leon Russell
Doug Sahm and the
    Texas Tornadoes
Merle Saunders
The Saw Doctors
Melvin Seals
Son Seals
Pete Seeger
Dave Sharp
Jane Siberry

Soul Asylum
Bruce Springsteen
Percy Strother
The Subdudes
Hubert Sumlin
Taj Mahal
.38 Special
Tex Thomas
Richard Thompson
Ron Thompson

Timbuk 3
John Trudell
Willie Walker
Eric Weisberg
Willie West
White Iron Band
Jody Williams
Edgar Winter
Johnny Winter
Warren Zevon

Paul Metsa is a legendary musician and songwriter from Minnesota. Born on the Iron Range, he has been based in Minneapolis since 1978. He has received seven Minnesota Music Awards and has played more than five thousand gigs, including forays to Iceland and Siberia. He lives in Northeast Minneapolis with his faithful dog, Blackie; a dozen or so guitars; twenty-five orange crates of LPs; hundreds of books, compact discs, magazines, and vintage postcards; and several kitchen cupboards full of old cassettes.

David Carr grew up in Hopkins, Minnesota, and is a former writer and editor for the *Twin Cities Reader*. He now lives in New Jersey and writes a business column and is a culture reporter for the *New York Times*. He is author of *The Night of the Gun*.